GROUP COUNSELING FOR SCHOOL COUNSELORS: A Practical Guide

Second Edition

Greg Brigman
and
Barbara Earley Goodman

J. WESTON
WALCH
PUBLISHER

Portland, Maine

User's Guide
to
Walch Reproducible Books

As part of our general effort to provide educational materials that are as practical and economical as possible, we have designated this publication a "reproducible book." The designation means that purchase of the book includes purchase of the right to limited reproduction of all pages on which this symbol appears:

Here is the basic Walch policy: We grant to individual purchasers of this book the right to make sufficient copies of reproducible pages for use by all students of a single teacher. This permission is limited to a single teacher and does not apply to entire schools or school systems, so institutions purchasing the book should pass the permission on to a single teacher. Copying of the book or its parts for resale is prohibited.

Any questions regarding this policy or requests to purchase further reproduction rights should be addressed to:

Permissions Editor
J. Weston Walch, Publisher
321 Valley Street • P.O. Box 658
Portland, Maine 04104-0658

1   2   3   4   5   6   7   8   9   10

ISBN 0-8251-4276-8

Copyright © 1991, 2001
J. Weston Walch, Publisher
P.O. Box 658 • Portland, Maine 04104-0658
www.walch.com

Printed in the United States of America

Contents

About the Authors v
Contributing Authors v
Introduction vi
Group Counseling with Children and Adolescents:
  Why, What, and How vii
Getting Started x

Reproducibles
Sample Forms for Groups 1

Part 1: High School Group Plans
1.1 Academic and Social Support: Student Success Skills (Greg Brigman) 12

1.2 Refusal Skills (John P. Huerta) 24

1.3 Anger Management/Taking Control (Anya F. Koszas) 36

1.4 Loss/Bereavement (Doreen Cammarata) 56

1.5 Divorce/Changing Families (Mary Mills) 66

1.6 Pregnancy Education (Maryanne Brannigan Grimes) 78

1.7 Transition—The Buddy System (Gayle Kelley) 90

Part 2: Middle School Group Plans
2.1 Academic and Social Support: Student Success Skills
    (Greg Brigman and Barbara Earley Goodman) 106

2.2 Coping with Stress and Anger (Wes Hawkins and Greg Brigman) 132

2.3 Loss/Bereavement (Barbara Earley Goodman and Greg Brigman) 147

2.4 Divorce/Changing Families (Barbara Earley Goodman) 156

2.5 Handling Conflicts (Greg Brigman) 176

Part 3: Elementary School Group Plans
3.1 Academic and Social Support: Student Success Skills (Greg Brigman) 194

3.2 Building Math Confidence (Chari Campbell) 213

3.3 Social Problem Solving, K–2 (Donna Steinberg) 227

3.4 Social Problem Solving, 3–5 (Donna Steinberg) 241

3.5 Social and Academic Skills Through Storytelling (Lori Bednarek) 254

3.6 Loss/Bereavement (Michelle Feldman) 271

3.7 Divorce/Changing Families (Michelle Feldman) 280

Part 4: Group Plans for All Levels

4.1 New Student Programs (Greg Brigman and Barbara Earley Goodman) 290

4.2 Personal Growth for Teachers
(Barbara Earley Goodman and Greg Brigman) 298

Bibliography 315

About the Authors

Barbara Earley Goodman, Ed.S., LPC, NCC, is a two-time national award-winning middle school counselor in Hall County, Georgia. Mrs. Goodman is an adjunct professor at Georgia State University in Atlanta, Georgia, and an education staff development trainer.

Greg Brigman, Ph.D., LPC, is a professor in the Department of Counselor Education at Florida Atlantic University in Boca Raton, Florida. Dr. Brigman is also a two-time national award-winning school counselor.

Contributing Authors

We want to thank the following authors who contributed chapters. We are very proud of the group plans these professionals designed for this book. It was a great learning experience to collaborate with this talented group of counselors. We know that school counselors will appreciate the practical and easy-to-use style of each group plan.

Lori Bednarek, M.Ed., is an elementary school counselor and teacher in Palm Beach County, Florida.

Doreen Cammarata, M.S., L.M.H.C., is an adjunct instructor at Florida Atlantic University for a graduate course focusing on educating professionals on grief counseling issues. She is also a school counselor for at-risk youth and is a grief and bereavement specialist working with adults and children at a local hospice program. She

is the author of a book for children survivors of suicide, *When Someone You Love Commits Suicide.*

Chari Campbell, Ph.D., is an assistant professor in the Department of Counselor Education at Florida Atlantic University. Dr. Campbell is a former school counselor at all three levels and is the co-author of the *National Standards for School Counseling Programs.*

Michelle Feldman, M.Ed., is an elementary school counselor in Palm Beach County, Florida.

Maryanne Brannigan Grimes, Ed.S., is a high school counselor in Gwinnett County, Georgia.

Wes Hawkins, Ph.D., is a professor in the department of social work at Florida Atlantic University. Dr. Hawkins has developed curricula for group work with adolescents and has conducted numerous related research studies.

John Patrick Huerta, Ed.S., is a middle school counselor in Gwinnett County, Georgia.

Anya F. Koszas, M.Ed., is a high school counselor and director of guidance in Volusia County, Florida.

Mary Mills, M.Ed., is a high school counselor in Volusia County, Florida.

Donna Steinberg, M.Ed., is an elementary school counselor in Palm Beach County, Florida.

Introduction

The second edition of *Group Counseling for School Counselors* incorporates the growth in our understanding of how to effectively help children and adolescents deal with the most common issues they face. Since the first edition, there have been extensive reviews of research on successful youth, at-risk youth, resiliency, developing competence, social skills, learning skills interventions, and the efficacy of group counseling with children and adolescents.

Our goal has been to translate the research into practical, easy-to-use tools. Readers will find, in this edition, fourteen new groups with over 100 new group session plans. Based on the current research literature, the authors believe that the types of groups described in this second edition are the most effective interventions counselors have in helping youth with a wide variety of issues.

Group Counseling for School Counselors is a practical, step-by-step guide to leading effective groups for children and adolescents. It is designed for counselors, psychologists, and social workers interested in helping young people develop the skills, attitudes, and beliefs needed for success in school and in life.

The research-based topics, group format, and activities are field-tested, easy to use, and well received by young people. Some of the keys that have emerged from the research literature, which are embedded into the group plans, include:

- a structured, focused approach
- weekly goal setting
- progress monitoring
- modeling and coaching
- interactive application learning
- critical life skills

The group plans are divided into four sections: High School, Middle School, Elementary School, and All Levels. Each section has group plan categories that were carefully selected to address the issues most frequently encountered by students at this level. The group topics focus on the most critical learning, social, and self-management skills needed at the different levels for academic and social success. Also included at all three levels are group plans on dealing with loss/bereavement and parent divorce, two issues faced by a significant number of children and adolescents.

Group Counseling with Children and Adolescents: Why, What, and How

Group Counseling: Why?

There are many compelling reasons for school counselors to provide a solid group counseling program, including:

STRONG RESEARCH BASE—IT WORKS

Group counseling with children and adolescents works. Prout and Prout (1999) reviewed the research literature on counseling interventions with children and adolescents in schools over the last decade and found a distinct positive effect for group counseling. In well-controlled research studies, students receiving group counseling in schools were better off than 97 percent of comparison students. Borders and Drury (1992) reviewed 30 years of research on the effect of school counselors on student achievement, behavior, and attitudes. Group counseling was found to be effective in each of these three areas. In other reviews of the efficacy of counseling with children and adolescents, group counseling was as effective as, if not more effective than, individual counseling (Casey and Berman, 1985; Prout and DeMartino, 1986; Weisz et al., 1987; and Weisz et al., 1995).

NATURAL MEDIUM FOR LEARNING AND SUPPORT

Humans are social beings who live and work in groups. Groups provide a microcosm of a student's world in which students can practice new behaviors that are more constructive and adaptive.

ROLE MODELS FOR POSITIVE BEHAVIORS AND ATTITUDES

Modeling is one of the most effective learning tools. Groups provide multiple models. In groups there is more access to insights, confirming, and corrective messages than in individual counseling.

In addition, group counseling is considered a primary role of school counselors by the American School Counselor Association. Groups allow counselors to help more students. Without a solid group counseling program school counselors quickly become overwhelmed with individual counseling needs. School counselors are interested in providing the most effective and efficient services to help students. Therefore groups are a must for schools.

Group Counseling: What?

TYPES

Most school counselors offer groups on topics that represent the most frequent presenting problems or needs of children and adolescents. Group topics in schools also reflect the mission of the school: to help students learn the academic and social skills needed for success in living, working, and learning.

The most common types of groups offered by experienced school counselors include groups that focus on:

- social skills
- learning skills
- self-control/anger management
- divorce
- loss
- school adjustment/transition

The first three of these topics are in line with a recent review of research by Masten and Coatsworth (1998). They reviewed 25 years of research on developing competence and on successful and resilient children and adolescents and found three groups of skills that separated successful students from those who were not successful: Cognitive/learning skills, social skills, and self-regulation skills.

Another extensive review of research, covering 50 years, by Wang, Haertel, and Walberg (1994), focused on what helps students learn. They found similar skill areas, especially cognitive/learning skills and social skills, to be the most associated with school success. Group counseling involving these three skill areas are a must for any comprehensive school counseling program.

The encouraging news from these research reviews is that the skills students need to succeed academically and socially—and the model for teaching them these skills—are clear. The teaching model is based on Bandura's social learning model and involves a "tell, show, do, coach" approach. The group plans in this book follow this model, and many of the plans mirror the most critical skills found in these research reviews.

The last three group topics listed above—divorce, loss, and transition—represent areas of high need in most schools. Providing group counseling to address these needs is an effective and efficient way to help support students who are new to a school or school level or who have had a family change or loss.

Group Counseling: How?

Successful school counselors use both formal and informal needs assessments to determine which and how many groups to offer at what times. School counselors should be aware of the skills and information students need in order to be successful in the areas of learning, living, and working (see previous page under Types of Groups), and should base at least some counseling groups on these topics.

School counselors also make sure students, teachers, and parents are aware of the types of groups that are offered and know how to sign up to participate. School counselors provide information on group topics to students and teachers during classroom presentations and by posting flyers around the school. For parents, counselors make presentations during parent meetings and provide information through newsletters.

BUILD SUPPORT FOR GROUPS

- Tie group topics to the mission of the school and school improvement plan.
- Tie group topics to the most critical skills needed for student success.
- Tie group topics to providing the support students need to continue to learn.
- Tie group topics to increased achievement and prosocial behavior.
- Tie group topics to decreased antisocial behavior.
- Tie group topics to needs identified by teachers, parents, administrators, and students.

PLAN SESSIONS BASED ON RESEARCH AND SOUND THEORY

- 1–3 objectives for each session
- Strategies/activities for each objective
- Process questions and goal setting

Focused, structured, and goal-oriented group sessions have a better success rate and fit better with the mission of schools than those that are not. Effective counselors know the purpose of each group and have carefully developed group plans to facilitate teaching skills to children and adolescents. They are also careful to base each group on the research base rather than on activities that may be appealing but do not lead to positive student behavior change.

WHEN PLANNING GROUP LOGISTICS, "BEGIN WITH THE END IN MIND"

Remember that the purpose of group counseling is to help students improve in measurable ways. Set yourself and the group up for success by following the following logistical guidelines:

Length of group

- 8–12 sessions
- 30–60 minutes
- monthly follow-ups—booster sessions

Most effective groups have a minimum of eight sessions. Depending on age, the time per session varies from 30 minutes for primary students to 60 minutes for adolescents. Because the focus of most groups is on skill building and skill transfer, booster sessions have become prevalent. Wilson (1982) found the following success rates for various length groups for students at risk of academic failure:

- 8 or fewer sessions: success rate 1 of 5
- 9–12 sessions: success rate 5 of 9
- over 12 sessions: success rate 6 of 8

Based on experience and research such as Wilson's, many experienced school counselors provide booster sessions, usually spaced one month apart, after the regular eight-session group in order to achieve a high rate of success.

GROUP SIZE AND COMPOSITION

Group size is determined by the age of the students and the purpose of the group. Generally, the younger the students, the smaller the group. Most groups include 4–8 students. One or more "role models" (model students who are respected by their peers) are included in most groups. According to Myrick (1998), "experienced school counselors prefer to work with 5–6 and no more than 7–8. Having fewer members allows more participation by each person in the group."

Once you have developed a system for providing group counseling, it is important that you maintain its structure. Canceling or postponing sessions will impair the integrity of the program. If group counseling is to become one of the educational objectives of your school, students, teachers, parents, and administrators must understand what it is and know what to expect from it.

PRE-GROUP SCREENING

- Select only those students you feel reasonably certain can be helped in your group and who want to participate.

- Explain the purpose, benefits, logistics, expectations, and limits of the group.
- Use heterogeneous grouping. Select models when appropriate. Avoid loading a group with behavior problems.

Pre-group screening is essential. It is required by the code of ethics of the Association of Specialists in Group Work, the American School Counseling Association, and the American Counseling Association. Pre-group screening allows the student to understand the nature of the group and decide if he or she wants to participate. It also allows the counselor time to assess whether or not this particular group is appropriate at this time for this student.

Assuming that the counselor and student agree that the group is a good fit, a parent information letter describing the group should be given to the student to take home, have signed, and return. With older students some counselors prefer to send the letter home but not require that it be returned. This type of letter asks the parents to call the counselor if they have questions or concerns about the group. Each school district and school has a policy on informing parents about group participation. It is important for the counselor to know the prevailing policy.

FORMAT FOR SMALL GROUP COUNSELING PLANS

The following format is used for all plans in this book. It provides a simple and practical structure around which to build effective group plans. The format stresses self-monitoring, skill building through role-play and other active learning strategies, and transfer of skills to students' regular life.

Beginning

- Review last session.
- Check on student goals—applying lessons to their life.
- Check temperature of group, check on overall functioning—i.e., ask students to rate on a 1–10 scale how things are going on topics such as grades, homes, peers, teachers, fun, rest, exercise, diet.
- Preview today.

Middle

- Involve students in pair and whole group discussions.
- Ask before telling—related to today's topic.
- Provide some new information and ask students to personalize—which ideas would be most helpful/useful to you?
- Apply ideas in role-play and/or storytelling with multiple endings, provide feedback and coaching.
- Use a variety of mediums, e.g., art, music, games, bibliotherapy.

End

- Discuss what thoughts and feelings students had during the role-play/activity.
- Ask students to reflect on what the group did today, and what they learned or relearned.
- Ask them to commit to trying/applying some idea/skill from today's group meeting.

BUILDING SUCCESS INTO YOUR GROUPS

The last step in making your groups successful is to continuously monitor the impact on students.

What did you hope would happen when you designed the group? What are the goals for students who participate? How can you determine if the groups are working? Different groups require different measures of success.

Collecting simple data to show the positive impact of the group is essential to maintaining support for the group counseling program. This information will also tell the counselor when a group needs updating or changing.

Evaluate impact of group on stated objectives

- Pre/post student survey
- Pre/post teacher/parent survey
- Pre/post scores on grades or standardized achievement test already being administered by school

SUMMARY

- Conduct needs assessment.
- Develop written structured plan.
- Gain support/advertise group.
- Conduct pre-group screening.
- Implement research-based group plan.
- Evaluate impact of group and report findings.

Getting Started

1. Explain the group offerings to the students during the first two or three weeks of class when you are informing them of the different counseling services available. Leave sign-up forms in each class and have a box or basket at your office door where students can pick up or turn in their forms.

2. Develop or review lesson plans for groups you will offer. The groups offered should meet the needs of your school. The lesson plans in this book were developed based on: 1) needs assessments from teachers, students, parents, and administrators; 2) developmental theory; 3) counseling research; and 4) accepted practices endorsed by the American Association of School Counselors.

3. Around the end of September, send a referral sheet out to teachers. Let parents know about the groups through PTA presentations and newsletters.

4. By the time you get teacher referral forms and student and parent requests back, you will probably realize you have more students than you can handle. Keep a list of students who are not included in the first round of groups. Send them a note explaining that the group is filled and they will be placed on a list for the next group. It is important to plan several cycles of groups each year so that there are always groups available. Many experienced counselors offer the first series of groups in October, a second cycle in January, and a final cycle in March.

5. Conduct pre-group interviews or screening.

6. Send invitations/reminders on the morning of the first meeting.

Before the First Meeting: Pre-Group Screening

There are several reasons to meet individually with students who have been recommended by teachers and parents for group counseling:

1. To determine the appropriateness of the particular group for this student. It is your decision to determine who will be in the group. Certain students might be detrimental to the progress of the group. When teachers ask why a certain student isn't in your group, you can say, "It is not appropriate for him/her to be in this group. I am seeing him/her individually and I am working with his/her parents."

2. To give information about the nature of the group and your expectations regarding attendance, confidentiality, and so forth.

3. To gain commitment from the student regarding attendance, participation, and confidentiality. (Participation should be voluntary. If the student decides not to participate, advise the referring parent or teacher that when or if the student decides to voluntarily join the group, this service will be available, as soon as the next group begins.)

4. To help the student identify a goal(s) to work on in the group.

5. To clarify the student's expectations about the nature of the group.

6. To comply with ethical standards of the counseling profession (ACA, ASCA, AGSW).

This screening meeting usually takes approximately 10–15 minutes. Set aside a two-hour block per group for these interviews. If the student agrees to participate, the student is asked to take a group information or consent form home.

Here is an outline for a screening meeting:

Pre-Group Interview Outline

1. Introduction
   (a) General description of group (number of meetings, topics, and so forth)
   (b) Why the student is being asked to participate
   (c) Participation is voluntary.

2. What the student can gain from participating
    (a) Meet new people.
    (b) Work on goals.
    (c) Learn new skills.
3. Goal(s)
    (a) Help student select a general goal (goal more defined during group meetings).
    (b) Goals may change and are the business of the student.
4. Expectations
    (a) Attendance, participation, and confidentiality
    (b) Check student expectations.
5. Explain the parent and teacher forms and when they must be returned to the counselor.
6. Brief summary and emphasis on positive aspects of group

The screening process puts you in a better position to decide who is appropriate for the kind of groups you are offering. No one else can make this decision as skillfully as you. You know best your skills, the nature of the students participating, the content of the group, and the readiness of each individual screened.

What to Expect at Different Stages

It is helpful to be aware of the stages of group development as you prepare to lead your groups. We offer the following summary of three group stages to help you in your planning.

Stage 1: Trust—Orientation

In this stage, students get to know each other, establish trust, and decide how they fit into the group and how involved they will be. It usually takes 2–3 sessions for students to learn each others' names and to feel comfortable about being in the group. The leader provides more structured activities at this stage, and helps students identify goals.

Stage 2: Work—Productivity

The working stage is when the most insights and behavior changes occur. In an eight-session group, sessions 3–7 will contain most of the "work" of the group. This is the time when goals are acted on outside of the group and experimenting with behavior occurs inside the group. If the necessary conditions of trust, empathy, and hope have developed, students will gain from feedback, confrontation, and increased self-awareness and self-disclosure.

Stage 3: Closure—Consolidation

The consolidation stage begins by session 7 of an eight-session group. There is usually a feeling of community—sharing and caring—if sessions 1–6 have been successful. The need to summarize, solidify changes, carry learning over to the world outside the group, and attain closure characterize this stage. Session 8 might elicit responses like "I wish it wasn't over" and "Can we do this again?" It seems that just when you get a group going in the right direction, it's time to stop. Many experienced counselors decide to continue the group through booster sessions spaced a month apart to maintain gains. The benefits for some students will be wonderfully evident, and for others you will never know.

Process Questions for Each Stage

Here are some process questions for the different stages of group development.

STAGE 1: TRUST—ORIENTATION

Note: Most of the process questions for the Trust stage are used during pre-group screening and the first two sessions.

- What do you want to achieve by participating in this group?
- What are some concerns, doubts, and fears you have about being in this group?
- What would you most like to say you have learned at the end of this group?
- What do you need to give in order to get what you want from this group?
- What rules do we need to work out together in order to feel safe and enjoy ourselves?

STAGE 2: WORK—PRODUCTIVITY

Note: The process questions below for the Work stage should be used starting with the first session.

- How did you feel during this activity?
- What did you learn from this experience?
- How can you apply what you have learned today?

- What can you do this week to practice what you have learned?

STAGE 3: CLOSURE—CONSOLIDATION

- What are some of the most important things you have learned about yourself?
- How can you continue to practice what you have learned?

- What is one way you have changed during this group?
- What has been the most helpful part of this group for you?
- What is a goal you have set for yourself?
- How do you feel about the group ending?

Group Leadership Skills: Keys to Success

One of the most important ingredients for successful group counseling is the skill of the group leader. Take time to honestly evaluate your skill level, experience, and course-work background. There is no substitute for supervised practice. Developing your skills is an ongoing process. Jim Gumaer, in an article in *Journal for Specialists in Group Work* (1986), stated that "at a minimum level, graduating counselors should have passed successfully a group theory course, a group counseling practicum, and a supervised internship involving several counseling groups. . . ." If you do not have this background, we strongly recommend that you obtain it. In addition, it is very helpful to co-lead groups. If you are the only counselor in your school, try co-leading a group with another counselor or therapist in your area.

The group leadership skills that follow are basic and very effective. Listening to or watching a tape of your group session and identifying which skills you used or did not use can be a powerful way to recognize your strengths and weaknesses. Sharing your tape with a small group of trusted counselors in a peer coaching context or having a qualified counselor give you feedback can also be extremely beneficial.

Group Leadership Skills

PERSONALIZING

There are two important parts to this skill. The first is making sure that the group is sitting in a circle so that everyone can see everyone else's face without having to move. The second is making sure that you know the names of all group members and using their names frequently when responding to their comments. Encourage group members to use names when they respond to one another.

STRUCTURING

This skill is used to **explain the topic and time limit.** An important part of structuring is providing a rationale for an activity. The rationale needs to be framed from a student's point of view. The rationale clarifies the benefits to students and creates interest and motivation. Structuring occurs at the beginning of a group session and whenever a new activity or topic is introduced.

This skill is also used to **redirect** or get the discussion back on the topic when it digresses.

Example: "For the next few minutes we'll be discussing friendship." When Maria starts getting off the topic, you might say, "I'd like to hear about that, Maria, but I'm concerned that we won't finish if we don't move on."

MODELING AND COACHING

In the most simple form modeling is going first and showing the group how you want them to respond.

Example: "This is what I want you to do. . . . (then demonstrate) Is everyone ready? Good, I'll go first."

Modeling is central to role-play and role-play is central to skills building. Students are able to learn faster and at a deeper level when they can see multiple models performing specific target behavior. Whether the topic is managing conflicts, refusal skills, or learning skills, using the "tell, show, do, coach" model is a powerful group skill. Effective group leaders not only provide a powerful model themselves but look for opportunities for students to become models.

Providing **supportive and corrective feedback** (coaching) is a very important part of skill teaching. Teaching group members to give coaching feedback is very useful. Before giving feedback we recommend asking the student doing the role-play to comment on what he or she liked and if there is anything that might be changed next time. After the role-player finishes, the leader and other group members give feedback.

The model we use is the **sandwich approach.** First, supportive feedback: strengths, positive, helpful behavior are pointed out: "I liked the way you . . .", "I thought the way you . . . was very helpful." This is the first slice of bread of the sandwich. Next, corrective feedback: non-helpful behaviors are pointed out in a respectful way and alternatives are suggested: "You may want to consider changing . . .", "Instead you may want to try . . .", "What are some other ideas the group has?" This is the sandwich filling.

Last is the second piece of bread—more supportive feedback. To finish the feedback process give a summary of the supportive feedback offered and some comment about your faith in the student using the feedback to continue to improve.

CONNECTING

Connecting helps to build a sense of belonging and acceptance by helping the participants to see that others share their ideas and concerns.

Examples:

"Who else has had that experience?"

"How many of you have ever felt that way?"

Another way to connect is to link the comments of the participants. "Juan, that sounds a lot like what Venetta was saying earlier." "Carl, I've noticed that you and Jim enjoy doing a lot of the same things. Can anyone else remember an idea some of us had in common?"

EMPATHIC RESPONDING

To encourage participants to discuss freely, it is important to reinforce their comments through empathic responses. The leader paraphrases the participant's comment and tries to reflect the underlying feeling. This is an important skill to teach all group members.

Examples:

"OK, Maria, thank you for sharing that. I could tell you were very angry about your friend setting you up."

"So, Carl, you like to be with people who share some of your interests and feel bored and on edge when you are around people who don't."

"Jenny, you seem to feel pretty excited about that."

This skill is especially important at the beginning of a group. It sets the tone. Making it safe to respond is critical.

INVOLVING EVERYONE

Several simple techniques can be used to get everyone involved.

The **go-round** lets everyone know you expect a response from each group member. When using the go-round, give some time before beginning. The leader usu-ally goes first: "I'd like you to think of some qualities you look for in a friend. I'll give you a moment to think of two or three, then we will go around and hear the ideas from each of you." Or: "For the next few minutes I'd like us to think of things we enjoy doing for fun. I will give you a minute to think of three or four things, then we will go around the circle and hear from everyone."

If a group member does not have a response when the time comes, ask; "Would you like me to come back to you?" or "I'll check back with you in a minute." In addition, good eye contact and looking interested in each comment, nodding your head, and asking follow-up questions are important ways to keep participants involved.

The **hand-raise technique** simply involves asking participants to raise their hands if the statement applies. Often the request to raise your hand is given nonverbally when the leader models raising a hand. "How many of you have ever been in a group where one person tried to dominate?" (leader raises a hand).

Using **pair share** is a low threat way of getting high involvement. Ask students to share their ideas on a topic with a partner. Then ask pairs to report back to the group what they discussed.

In addition to the go-round, the "How many of you" hand-raise questions, and the pair share, remember to model the nonverbal behaviors of eye contact, leaning forward, and looking interested, and to ask follow-up, clarifying questions. Teach these important skills to the group and remind them to use them. Regularly provide feedback on your observations of their use of these skills.

SUMMARIZING AND GOAL SETTING

This skill can be used during the discussion or at the end. The leader can summarize or ask participants to summarize. The summary brings the focus back to the purpose of the discussion. An open-ended and personalized summary is often effective.

Example:

"We are almost out of time, and I would like for us to think about what we have talked about and have been doing. What can you remember?"

The leader fills in any gaps: "To end, I would like you to complete these two sentences: 'One thing I learned or relearned today was . . .' and 'One way I can use what I learned this week is . . .' I'll give you a minute to think, then ask you to share with a partner, and finally I'll ask for volunteers to share with the group."

In order for these skills to be effective, the group leader must communicate certain attitudes/qualities:

- acceptance
- caring
- being nonjudgmental
- warmth
- friendliness
- enthusiasm

Your caring and support, your leadership skills, the topics you choose to focus on, and the way you structure sessions will have a powerful impact on your groups. We believe that the group format is the most effective tool in a counselor's bag of interventions. We wish you the best in your work with student groups.

Reproducible
Sample Forms
for Groups

The following sample forms provide tools for the counselor, which may be modified to fit any of the group plans contained in this book and most of the types of groups offered by experienced counselors. The counselor leading each group should decide what changes (if any) need to be made to fit the sample form to the particular group.

Forms included in this section are:

- Referral for Group Counseling
- Group Membership Agreement
- Parent Permission Form
- Parent Permission Form for Participation in Anger Management Group
- Letter to Parents
- Group Attendance
- Feeling Faces
- Group Evaluation

Teacher _____ Date _____

Referral for Group Counseling

Please select, from the list below, the group that best fits each student you are referring.

Group counseling topics

- Student success skills (academic and social skills)
- Handling conflicts
- Self-control and anger management
- Bereavement
- Divorce

Student Name	Group Counseling Program	Reason for Referral (Be as specific as possible)

Group Membership Agreement

_____ has my permission to be in
(Student's name)

_____, which meets for _____ weeks

on _____ from _____ to _____ beginning _____.
    (Day)   (Time)   (Time)   (Date)

_____

Teacher's Signature

_____

I _____ agree that it is my
(Student's name)

responsibility to get any assignments I miss while in the group.

    I also agree to let the counselor know if I am unable to attend any of the meetings due to tests, reports, and so forth.

_____

Student's Signature

*Teachers: After signing, please return to counselors.

Parent Permission Form

Dear _____ .

      (Parent's name)

_____ has been recommended for our _____ group by

      (Student's name)

_____ . I have met with your son/daughter and explained the

      (Teacher's name)

content and nature of the group. The group consists of eight sessions, meeting once a week for 45 minutes. During these sessions we will be working on:

1. _____

2. _____

3. _____

4. _____

5. _____

6. _____

    If you have any questions or comments, please feel free to contact me. We want you to be informed of your child's activities. Thank you for your support in our mutual goals of raising competent, healthy, and successful children,

Sincerely,

Counselor

Return to counselor (check one).

_____ My child may participate in these counseling sessions.

_____ My child may not participate in these counseling sessions.

Parent's signature _____

Parent Permission Form
for Participation in Anger Management Group

Dear _____:

_____ has been recommended to participate in an anger management counseling group that I will facilitate this year. I have met with your son/daughter and explained the content and nature of the group. This group will meet once a week. Your child is aware that he/she will miss a different class every week and he/she is responsible for obtaining make-up work from teachers. The group will be working on achieving these goals:

- Recognize the feeling of anger
- Understand the student's own anger style
- Identify what triggers the student's anger
- Learn to use constructive ways to deal with anger
- Prevent inappropriate ways of dealing with anger
- Practice effective ways to manage angry feelings

Since counseling is based on a trusting relationship between counselor and client, all information shared by group members is kept confidential except in certain situations in which there is an ethical responsibility to limit confidentiality. If a student reveals information about hurting himself/herself or another person, the parent will be notified.

Sincerely,

School Counselor

_____

By signing this form, I give my informed consent for my child to participate in small group counseling. I understand that:

1. The group will provide an opportunity for members to learn and practice interpersonal skills, discuss feelings, share ideas, practice new behaviors, and make new friends.

2. Anything group members share in group will be kept confidential by the group leader except in the above mentioned cases.

Parent's signature _____ Date: _____

Student's signature _____ Date: _____

Letter to Parents

Dear Parents:

The counseling program at _____ is designed to
(Name of school)

be preventive and developmental. In addition to seeing students individually and in classroom guidance, we teach skills and information in small-group settings.

    Your child, _____, has expressed an interest in participating in the _____ group. We emphasize to students that groups are for everyone, and participating does not indicate a problem. Groups are structured and goal focused. Students learn important life skills that enhance their ability to succeed academically and socially as well as cope with stressful situations.

Listed below are the types of groups we routinely offer.
- Student success skills: academic and social skills needed for school success
- Communication and conflict management
- You in control: self-control and anger management
- Changing family: dealing with divorce
- Loss: bereavement

Please check one of the two statements below, then return this letter to the counselor. If you have any questions about your child's participation in the group, please feel free to call at _____.

Sincerely,

School Counselor

Check one and return this letter to the counselor.
_____ My child may participate in this counseling group.
_____ My child may not participate in this counseling group.

Parent/guardian signature _____

Group _____ Date _____

Group Attendance

Student	Teacher	1	2	3	4	5	6	7	8

Session Topics
1.
2.
3.
4.
5.
6.
7.
8.

Name of group _____ Date _____

Feeling Faces

Group Counseling for School Counselors: A Practical Guide

Name of group _____ Date _____

Group Evaluation

Overall, being in this group was:

_____ very helpful

_____ helpful

_____ OK

_____ not helpful

In this group I felt _____

_____

because _____

_____

Some important things I learned were _____

_____

_____

The most helpful part of this group was _____

_____

_____

Something I have improved in is _____

_____

_____

A goal I have set for myself is _____

_____

_____

Some changes that would make this group better are _____

_____

_____

I would/would not recommend this group to my friends because _____

_____

_____

Other comments: _____

_____

_____

Part 1:
High School Group Plans

1.1
Academic and Social Support: Student Success Skills

Grade Level: High School	Time Required: 8 Sessions	Author: Greg Brigman

Purpose

The purpose of this group is to help students strengthen the academic, social, and self-management skills needed to succeed in school.

Background Information

A review of the research literature involving school counselor interventions with low-achieving and under-achieving high school students by Wilson (1982), confirmed by Prout and Prout (1998), included the following:

1. Group counseling seems to be more effective than individual counseling.

2. Structured group programs are more effective than unstructured programs.

3. Group programs lasting eight weeks or less had positive results in only one of five programs evaluated. Of nine programs lasting between nine and twelve weeks, five were effective; however, six of eight interventions lasting more than twelve weeks were successful.

4. Programs in which students volunteered for treatment were more successful than programs with nonvoluntary participants.

5. Programs that combined counseling and study skills were most effective.

Logistics

GROUP COMPOSITION

Students grades 9–12 mixed with regard to activity level and behavior control. Avoid loading group with only overactive behavior problem students. Students need multiple models of appropriate behavior. Groups with only behavior problem students usually do not show significant gains in prosocial behavior. Mixed groups are generally very effective.

GROUP SIZE

6–8 students

GROUP TIME PER SESSION

45–60 minutes

NUMBER OF SESSIONS

Eight, with booster sessions spaced approximately one month apart after regular group ends

Recommended Resources

Full bibliographic details for these publications are included in the Bibliography at the end of this book.

Brigman and Earley, 1991: *Group Counseling for School Counselors.*

Brown, 1999a: "Improving academic achievement."

Brown, 1999b: *Proven Strategies for Improving Learning and Academic Achievement.*

Goldstein and McGinnis, 1997: *Skillstreaming the Adolescent.*

Hattie, Biggs, and Purdie, 1996: "Effects of learning skills interventions on student learning."

Lee, Winfield, and Wilson, 1991: "Academic behaviors among high-achieving African-American students."

Masten and Coatsworth, 1998: "The development of competence in favorable and unfavorable environments."

McWhirter et al., 1998: *At Risk Youth.*

Moote, Smythe, and Wodarsky, 1999: *Social Skills Training with Youth in School Settings.*

O'Rourke and Worzybt, 1996: *Support Groups for Children.*

Wang, Haertel, and Walberg, 1994: *Educational Resilience in Inner City America.*

Session 1
Topic: Get acquainted, self-evaluation

Resources
- Student Success Skills Self-Evaluation handout

Beginning

INTRODUCTION

Review the purpose of the group (this has been covered individually during the screening): To identify existing strengths and develop new strengths related to the skills most needed to be successful in school and with people. Emphasize that the group is very active with a lot of role-play and should be fun and very helpful. It will give each person a chance to understand how to use his/her strengths to be successful in school, with friends, and handling stress. Go over number of meetings, time, and place.

GROUP RULES

Ask: "What rules do we need to work together, feel safe, and enjoy ourselves?" Be sure to include: Confidentiality (you own what you say and can share that with anyone, but what others say stays in the group), respect others' opinions (no put-downs); right to pass.

Secure group consensus on each group rule.

Middle

INTRODUCTIONS

Students break into pairs. Partners interview one another and then each student introduces his/her partner to the group.

Some interview questions:

- Do you have siblings? If so, what age?
- What do you like to do for fun?
- What is your favorite or best academic subject?
- What is the one subject in which you would most like to improve?

DISCUSSION OF SIMILARITIES AND DIFFERENCES

Get the students involved in looking for what group members have in common.

STUDENT SUCCESS SKILLS SELF-EVALUATION

1. Introduce the Student Success Skills Self-Evaluation handout. Let the group know that they will frequently go over these items and learn how to use problem solving to improve in any area where they are not doing as well as they would like.

2. As you go over the form, use each item as a discussion starter. These are the behaviors that successful students are able to do well and that struggling students have not yet mastered. Repeated exposure to concrete examples of how to perform these essential skills is the core of this group. If deficits in reading and/or math are present it is advisable to also involve the student with tutoring.

End

Ask students the purpose of the group, how many meetings, and so forth.

Ask them to share one thing they are looking forward to about the group.

Preview the second meeting.

Name_____ Date _____

Student Success Skills Self-Evaluation

Directions: Rate yourself on the following skills that are important for doing well in school. Rate each item on a 1–5 scale, where 5 is the highest/best and 1 is the lowest/worst.

Skill	Not so good————Great!				
I go to class and arrive on time with the materials I need.	1	2	3	4	5
I read and understand all assignments.	1	2	3	4	5
I have a folder or notebook for each class to help me stay organized.	1	2	3	4	5
I turn in all assignments on time—no zeros.	1	2	3	4	5
I keep track of my grades and know how my teacher determines the final grade.	1	2	3	4	5
I listen and focus during class and usually understand what is being taught.	1	2	3	4	5
I ask questions when I do not understand what is being taught. I know when and how to ask questions.	1	2	3	4	5
I know what to study for tests and what is expected for reports and I plan ahead for both to avoid last-minute cramming.	1	2	3	4	5
I have at least one dependable study buddy in each class.	1	2	3	4	5
I work well in pairs or small groups with others in class.	1	2	3	4	5

My top three strengths from the list above are:

1. _____

2. _____

3. _____

The areas I most want to improve in are:

1. _____

2. _____

Group Counseling for School Counselors: A Practical Guide

Session 2
Topic: Life management scale, role-play

Resources
- Life Management Scale handout
- Progress Monitoring handout
- Folder for each student
- Index card with role-play questions

Beginning
1. Ask students to tell you some things they remember from last meeting. Get their summary of group rules and purpose of group.
2. Distribute the Life Management Scale handout, and ask students to rate themselves from 1–5 on the scale. Have a folder for each student with a blank rating form inside each folder.
3. Discuss the connection between performance in school and friends and the other seven items on the list. Discuss how energy and mood are affected by exercise, sleep, diet, social support, and doing well in school. Discuss the connection between stress and the same items.
4. Introduce the notion of monitoring these items as a way to see connections and gain knowledge about how students' bodies and minds interact to affect how they feel and act.

Middle
1. Ask the group members to pick one situation, either about school this past week or peers/social life this past week, to explore through role-play.
2. After a go-round of hearing a brief description of a situation from each member, have the group vote on a topic to role-play that has the most common ground among group members.
3. Ask the person with the chosen situation to become the director and choose 1–3 group members to help act out the story. The director plays herself or himself and shows/tells the other actors what to do/say. General guidelines for setting the scene and directing the story include answering the following questions. Give the director an index card with the following questions:

ROLE-PLAY QUESTIONS
- What is the setting (where and when)?
- Who are the main characters and how are they feeling at the beginning of the story?
- What is the problem?
- What happens first?
- What are the feelings and reactions of the other characters?
- What do the characters do to try and solve the problem?
- How does the story end and how are the characters feeling?

Limit role-play prep to 2–3 minutes and role-play to 2–3 minutes.

4. After the role-play, have group discuss the pros and cons of how the director handled the situation and explore alternative ways to handle the situation. Have group members act out alternative ways of handling the situation, and get group feedback as to strengths and things that may need changing.

Note: Discuss giving feedback/coaching. Both supportive and corrective feedback/coaching are needed to help people improve. Model the sandwich approach: Give supportive feedback (bread), then corrective feedback (the meat), then finish with supportive feedback (the bread).

Example: "John, I liked the way you stood up for yourself and did not get pushed around. One thing you may want to consider changing is saying what you have to say in a calmer voice, without yelling, but still getting your message across. With your self-confidence I think you will develop the assertiveness skills very quickly."

5. Ask students to use a go-round to share positives about the role-play—"I liked the way you . . .". Then have another go-round for coaching feedback—"You may want to consider . . .".

End
Distribute the Progress Monitoring handout. Ask the students to complete the handout for one subject and provide sheets for other subjects. Keep the completed sheet in each student's folder. Discuss the importance of knowing how you are doing at any given time in the grading period.

Ask group participants to share something they learned or relearned today and something about how they can use it this week.

Preview the next meeting.

Name_____ Date_____

Life Management Scale

Directions: Rate yourself on the nine items below on a scale from 1–5, where 5 is the highest or best rating and 1 is the lowest or worst rating.

	Not so good————————Great!				
How school was for me this past week	1	2	3	4	5
How my social life was this past week	1	2	3	4	5
How I got along with teachers this past week	1	2	3	4	5
Amount of stress I felt this past week	1	2	3	4	5
Amount of exercise I got this past week	1	2	3	4	5
Amount of sleep I averaged this past week	# of hours: _____				
Quality of my diet this past week	1	2	3	4	5
Amount of energy I had on average this past week	1	2	3	4	5
My mood on average this past week	1	2	3	4	5

1. What do you think is the connection between performance in school and with friends and the other seven items on the list?

   _____

   _____

2. How much are your energy level and mood affected by exercise, sleep, diet, social support, and doing well in school?

   _____

   _____

3. What is the connection between stress and exercise, sleep, diet, social support, and doing well in school?

   _____

   _____

Name_____ Date_____

Progress Monitoring

Subject: _____

Last report period grade	Goal for this report period	Midterm grade for this report period	Final grade

Date	Homework	Quiz	Test	Project/Report

Strategies to help reach goal:

1. Study for tests ahead of time.
2. Get high grades on homework.
3. Have a study buddy.
4. Turn in extra credit.
5. Use note cards/outline/concept map for key concepts.

Session 3
Topic: Progress monitoring

Resources

- Student folders
- Progress Monitoring handouts
- Student Success Skills Self-Evaluation handout
- Index card with role-play questions

Beginning

1. Ask students to tell you some things they remember from last meeting. Ask, "Who used something we talked about last week during the week? How did it go?"

2. Have students rate themselves on the Student Success Skills Self-Evaluation scale. Go through each item one at a time with the group. Ask, "How many had a 4–5 on item one? How about a 2–3? A 1?" Ask for events tied to ratings. "What happened that led to your rating?" This process usually takes 10–15 minutes and can take longer if some events are highly charged with emotion and need more time. You and the group are scanning these mini stories for 1–3 events to role-play for the next part, the group session.

Middle

1. Ask group members to help decide on 1–3 events for the group to role-play. Look for events with the most common ground among group members.

2. Ask the person with the chosen situation to become the director and choose 1–3 group members to help act out the story. The director plays herself/himself and shows/tells the other actors what to do/say. General guidelines for setting the scene and directing the story include answering the following questions. Give these questions on a card to the person who is acting as director.

ROLE-PLAY QUESTIONS

- What is the setting (where and when)?
- Who are the main characters and how do they feel at the beginning of the story?
- What is the problem?
- What happens first?
- What are the feelings and reactions of the other characters?
- What do the characters do to try and solve the problem?
- How does the story end and how are the characters feeling?

Limit role-play prep to 2–3 minutes and role-play to 2–3 minutes.

3. After the role-play, have the group discuss the pros and cons of how the director handled the situation and explore alternative ways to handle the situation.

4. Both supportive and corrective feedback/coaching are needed to help people improve. Model the sandwich approach: give supportive feedback (bread), then corrective feedback (the meat), then finish with supportive feedback (the bread).

5. Ask students to use a go-round to share positives about the role-play—"I liked the way you . . .". Then do another go-round for coaching feedback—"You may want to consider . . .".

6. Have group members act out alternative ways of handling the situation, and get group feedback as to strengths and things that may need changing.

End

Ask students to complete the Progress Monitoring sheet for math and English/language arts. Keep the completed sheets in each student's folder.

Ask group participants to share something they learned or relearned today and something about how they can use it this week.

Preview the next meeting.

Session 4
Topic: Handling conflicts

Resources

- Student folders
- Progress Monitoring handouts
- Flip chart
- Life Management Scale handout

Beginning

1. Ask students to tell you some things they remember from last meeting. Ask, "Who used something we talked about last week during the week? How did it go?"

2. Ask students to rate themselves from 1–5 on the Life Management Scale. Have a folder for each student with a blank rating form and their last rating. After completing the scale for this week ask them to compare it with their rating from Session 2. What differences and similarities do they notice?

3. Discuss the connection between performance in school and with friends and the other seven items on the list. Discuss how energy and mood are affected by exercise, sleep, diet, social support, and doing well in school. Discuss the connection between stress and the same items.

4. Introduce the notion of monitoring these items as a way to see connections and to gain knowledge about how their bodies and minds interact to affect how they feel and act. Plan to use these items each week or every other week for rating and reflection.

Middle

HANDLING CONFLICTS

1. Ask students to write down typical problems either that they have had with other students at school or that they notice lots of other students have with each other at school. Ask them not to put their names on the list. Tell them you will collect everyone's ideas in a moment and the group will discuss:

(a) if they agree that the problem is typical and (b) some possible solutions.

2. Collect list of problems. Read each one and ask if it is a typical problem for this age group. List on a flip chart all the agreed-upon typical problems. Ask the group members to rank the top three problems in terms of how interested they would be in having the group discuss possible solutions.

3. Lead a discussion on possible solutions for the top three problems selected. Use a brainstorming technique. List all offered solutions first. Then go back and have the group code each one as "H" helpful or "HA" harmful to self or others. *Note:* Some will be rated as both. Have the group decide if the helpful side outweighs the harmful side.

4. Ask group to divide into pairs and plan a role-play for one of the three problems. The role-play should include one of the helpful solutions. Allow approximately five minutes for planning.

5. Ask each pair to present their role-play. Ask the rest of the group to discuss how realistically the problem and solution were portrayed, and to demonstrate additional suggestions for handling the problem. The leader can also demonstrate various positive alternative ways to handle the situation or coach students in different ways to act. *Note:* It is the role-play and coaching that make this a powerful learning activity.

End

1. Ask students to complete the Progress Monitoring sheet for math and English/language arts. Keep the completed sheet in each student's folder. Ask students to share with a partner how they are doing in these two classes and share a goal for continued improvement.

2. Ask group participants to share something they learned or relearned today and something about how they can use it this week.

3. Preview the next meeting.

Session 5
Topic: Rating, monitoring, role-play

Resources

- Student folders
- Progress Monitoring handouts
- Student Success Skills Self-Evaluation handout
- Index card with role-play questions

Beginning

1. Ask students to tell you some things they remember from last meeting.

2. Ask, "Who used something we talked about last week during the week? How did it go?"

3. Have students rate themselves on the Student Success Skills Self-Evaluation scale. Go through each item one at a time with the group. Ask, "How many had a 4–5 on item one? How about a 2–3? A 1?" Ask for events tied to ratings. "What happened that led to your rating?" This process usually takes 10–15 minutes and can take longer if some events are highly charged with emotion and need more time. You and the group are scanning these mini stories for 1–3 events to role-play for the next part, the group session.

Middle

1. Ask group members to help decide on 1–3 events for the group to role-play. Look for events with the most common ground among group members.

2. Ask the person with the chosen situation to become the director and choose 1–3 group members to help act out the story. The director plays herself or himself and shows/tells the other actors what to do/say. General guidelines for setting the scene and directing the story include answering the following questions. Give these questions on a card to the person who is acting as director.

ROLE-PLAY QUESTIONS

- What is the setting (where and when)?
- Who are the main characters and how do they feel at the beginning of the story?
- What is the problem?
- What happens first?
- What are the feelings and reactions of the other characters?
- What do the characters do to try and solve the problem?
- How does the story end and how are the characters feeling?

Limit role-play prep to 2–3 minutes and role-play to 2–3 minutes.

3. After the role-play, have the group discuss the pros and cons of how the director handled the situation and explore alternative ways to handle the situation.

4. Both supportive and corrective feedback/coaching are needed to help people improve. Model the sandwich approach: give supportive feedback (bread), then corrective feedback (the meat), then finish with supportive feedback (the bread).

5. Ask students to use a go-round to share positives about the role-play—"I liked the way you . . .". Then do another go-round for coaching feedback—"You may want to consider . . .".

6. Have group members act out alternative ways of handling the situation, and get group feedback as to strengths and things that may need changing.

End

Ask the students to complete the Progress Monitoring sheet for math and English/language arts. Keep the completed sheets in each student's folder. Ask students to share in pairs how they are doing in these two classes and set a goal for continued improvement.

Ask group participants to share something they learned or relearned today and something about how they can use it this week.

Preview the next meeting.

Session 6
Topic: How taking care of yourself affects school performance

Resources

- Student folders
- Life Management Scale handouts
- Progress Monitoring handouts
- Index card with role-play questions

Beginning

1. Ask students to tell you some things they remember from last meeting. Ask, "Who used something we talked about last week during the week? How did it go?"

2. Ask students to rate themselves from 1–5 on the Life Management Scale. Have a folder for each student with a blank Life Management Scale and the completed forms from Session 2 and Session 4. After completing the form ask students to share in pairs similarities and differences they noticed between today's rating and the ratings several weeks ago.

3. Discuss the connection between performance in school and with friends and the other seven items on the list. Discuss how energy and mood are affected by exercise, sleep, diet, social support, and doing well in school. Discuss the connection between stress and the same items.

4. Discuss the notion of monitoring these items as a way to see connections and to gain knowledge about how their bodies and minds interact to affect how they feel and act.

Middle

1. Ask group members to pick one situation either about school this past week or peers/social life this past week to explore through role-play.

2. After a go-round of hearing a brief description of a situation from each member, have the group vote on a topic to role-play that has the most common ground among group members.

3. Ask the person with the chosen situation to become the director and choose 1–3 group members to help act out the story. The director plays herself or himself and shows/tells the other actors what to do/say. General guidelines for setting the scene and directing the story include

answering the following questions. Give these questions on a card to the person who is acting as director.

ROLE-PLAY QUESTIONS

- What is the setting (where and when)?
- Who are the main characters and how do they feel at the beginning of the story?
- What is the problem?
- What happens first?
- What are the feelings and reactions of the other characters?
- What do the characters do to try and solve the problem?
- How does the story end and how are the characters feeling?

Limit role-play prep to 2–3 minutes and role-play to 2–3 minutes.

4. After the role-play, have the group discuss the pros and cons of how the director handled the situation and explore alternative ways to handle the situation. Have group members act out alternative ways of handling the situation and get group feedback as to strengths and things that may need changing. Both supportive and corrective feedback/coaching are needed to help people improve. Model the sandwich approach: Give supportive feedback (bread), then corrective feedback (the meat), then finish with supportive feedback (the bread).

5. Ask students to use a go-round to share positives about the role-play—"I liked the way you . . .". Then do another go-round for coaching feedback—"You may want to consider . . .".

End

Ask the students to complete the Progress Monitoring sheet for math and English/language arts. Keep the completed sheet in each student's folder.

Ask group participants to share something they learned or relearned today and something about how they can use it this week.

Preview the next meeting.

Session 7

Topic: Transferring what you learn to daily life

Resources

- Student folders
- Student Success Skills Self-Evaluation handouts
- Progress Monitoring handouts
- Index card with role-play questions

Beginning

1. Ask students to tell you some things they remember from last meeting. Ask, "Who used something we talked about last week during the week? How did it go?"

2. Ask students to rate themselves on the Student Success Skills Self-Evaluation scale. Go through each item one at a time with the group. Ask, "How many had a 4–5 on item one? How about a 2–3? A 1?" Ask for events tied to ratings. "What happened that led to your rating?" This process usually takes 10–15 minutes and can take longer if some events are highly charged with emotion and need more time. You and the group are scanning these mini stories for 1–3 events to role-play for the next part of the group session.

Middle

1. Ask group members to help decide on 1–3 events for the group to role-play. Look for events with the most common ground among group members.

2. Ask the person with the chosen situation to become the director and choose 1–3 group members to help act out the story. The director plays himself or herself and shows/tells the other actors what to do/say. General guidelines for setting the scene and directing the story include answering the following questions. Give these questions on a card to the person who is acting as director.

ROLE-PLAY QUESTIONS

- What is the setting (where and when)?
- Who are the main characters and how do they feel at the beginning of the story?
- What is the problem?
- What happens first?
- What are the feelings and reactions of the other characters?
- What do the characters do to try and solve the problem?
- How does the story end and how are the characters feeling?

Limit role-play prep to 2–3 minutes and role-play to 2–3 minutes.

3. After the role-play, have the group discuss the pros and cons of how the director handled the situation and explore alternative ways to handle the situation.

4. Both supportive and corrective feedback/coaching are needed to help people improve. Model the sandwich approach: Give supportive feedback (bread), then corrective feedback (the meat), then finish with supportive feedback (the bread).

5. Ask students to use a go-round to share positives about the role-play—"I liked the way you . . .". Then do another go-round for coaching feedback—"You may want to consider . . .".

6. Have group members act out alternative ways of handling the situation, and get group feedback as to strengths and things that may need changing.

End

Ask the students to complete the Progress Monitoring sheet for math and English/language arts. Keep the completed sheet in each student's folder. Ask students to share in pairs how they are doing in these two classes and set a goal for continued improvement.

Ask group participants to share something they learned or relearned today and something about how they can use it this week.

Preview the next meeting.

Session 8
Topic: Spotlighting, evaluation

Resources

- Index cards or sheets of paper
- Group Evaluation form (page 10)

Beginning

Ask, "Who used something we talked about last week during the week? How did it go?"

REVIEW LIFE OF GROUP

1. Briefly go over each topic you've covered during the last seven weeks, asking for what students remember.
2. Then ask the following questions:
   - What are some of the most important things you have learned about yourself?
   - What has been the most helpful part of this group for you?
   - What is a goal you have set for yourself?

Middle

ACCEPTING AND GIVING COMPLIMENTS

1. Hand out index cards or sheets of paper. Each person is to write down at least one thing he or she admires, likes, or appreciates about each of the other group members.
2. Spotlight: Ask each group member to say directly to the "spotlighted" person, with eye contact: "[person's name] one thing I admire, like, or appreciate about you is . . .". Explain and give examples of the types of qualities you are asking the students to think of and how to say and receive them. Ask students not to use appearance compliments such as "I like your shirt, shoes, hair," etc., but rather qualities or actions.
3. After each comment, the spotlighted person says "thank you," nothing else. (Be sure you get in on this—it feels good.)

End

1. Process the spotlighting activity. How did it feel receiving compliments? Giving compliments?
2. Students complete anonymous evaluation.
3. Concluding remarks. Invite students to make individual appointments if they want. Remind them of the monthly follow-up sessions.

1.2
Refusal Skills

| Grade Level: High School | Time Required: 8 Sessions | Author: John P. Huerta |

Purpose

The purpose of this group is to help students develop or strengthen the social and self-management skills needed to resist requests that involve possible harm, danger, or negative consequences. The group is designed to provide students with a practical model for saying no to negative peer pressure. The five-step model leads students through a logical decision-making process and provides practice and coaching feedback through role-play.

Logistics

GROUP COMPOSITION

Students grades 9–12 mixed with regard to activity level and behavior control. Avoid loading group with only overactive behavior problem students. Students need multiple models of appropriate behavior. Groups with only behavior problem students usually do not show significant gains in prosocial behavior. Mixed groups are generally very effective.

GROUP SIZE

6–8 students

GROUP TIME PER SESSION

45–60 minutes

NUMBER OF SESSIONS

Eight, with optional booster sessions spaced approximately one month apart after regular group ends; sessions 5, 6, 7 follow the same format.

Recommended Resources

Full bibliographic details for these publications are included in the Bibliography at the end of this book.

Brigman and Earley, 1991: *Group Counseling for School Counselors.*

Goldstein and McGinnis, 1997: *Skillstreaming the Adolescent.*

McWhirter et al., 1998: *At Risk Youth: A Comprehensive Response.*

Moote, Smythe, and Wodarsky, 1999: *Social Skills Training with Youth in School Settings.*

O'Rourke and Worzybt, 1996: *Support Groups for Children.*

Weisz et al., 1995: "Effects of psychotherapy with children and adolescents revisited."

Session 1
Topic: Situations involving peer pressure

Resources
- Paper and pencils/pens

Beginning

Review the purpose of the group (this has been covered individually during the screening). The three goals of Refusal Skills are:

- to keep your friends
- to stay out of trouble
- to have fun

The refusal-skills group is designed to give students a practical model for saying no to negative peer pressure. The five-step model leads the student through the process of logical decision making, thereby generating positive alternatives to peer pressure. The teaching process involves role-playing and modeling each step of the skill to students, helping them practice, and coaching them throughout the learning experience.

Go over number of meetings, time, and place.

INTRODUCTIONS

Ask students to interview a partner and find out the following: name, two things they do for fun, birth order (oldest, youngest, middle, only) and one thing they are looking forward to this year. "Be prepared to introduce your partner to the group in one minute." Ask students to introduce partners. Ask other students to listen for similarities and differences and to point these out as the introductions progress.

GROUP RULES

Ask, "What rules do we need to work together, feel safe, and enjoy ourselves?" Be sure rules include: confidentiality (you own what you say and can share that with anyone, but what others say stays in the group); respect for others' opinions (no put-downs); the right to pass. Secure group consensus on each group rule.

Middle

1. Ask students to describe a situation in which teenagers have a hard time saying no. As this is the first meeting, students should write a situation on a sheet of paper without their name on it. The group leader can then read the situations and lead into discussion.

2. Ask students to discuss the personal effects that peer pressure has on them. Introduce the concept of inclusion, the need to belong, as a basic need of teens, and the power that the need to belong has over their choices and behavior.

3. Ask, "Is it possible to say no and still meet the three goals of the Refusal Skills model?" Solicit from group experiences of resisting peer pressure, and discuss whether or not they also achieved the three goals.

   Note: This is an important time for the group leader to model respect for opinions, and use facilitation skills to involve everyone, connect ideas, and create a safe climate for sharing thoughts and feelings.

End

1. Ask the group to summarize the purpose of the group and meeting times and places.

2. Ask each student to complete the sentence, "One thing I am looking forward to in this group is . . .", and share with a partner. After partner sharing, ask for volunteers to share with the whole group.

3. Preview next meeting.

Session 2
Topic: Refusal-skills model

Resources
- Refusal Skills: Steps to Take handout

Beginning

NAME GAME

Use the name game to validate each person as a member of the group. Go around and have each member share his/her name and an animal that has qualities that the student admires. Ask each student to briefly state which qualities the animal has that they admire. Use linking and connecting skills to show the universality of many of the qualities. Each person repeats the names of previous students and their animals before sharing their own. Group leader goes first. Ask for volunteers at the end to say everyone's name and animal.

REVIEW

Review the three goals of Refusal Skills.

Middle

1. Introduce the Refusal Skills model by passing out the Refusal Skills: Steps to Take handout and explaining the steps. The five steps are:

   1. Ask questions.
   2. Name the trouble.
   3. Identify the consequence.
   4. Suggest an alternative, then start to leave.
   5. Keep the door open.

2. Describe a personal situation to illustrate the five-step model, reviewing each step and explaining how each step was helpful. Each step of the model assists in decision making and consequently may influence friends positively by giving them more information. Specifically:

   I. **Ask questions.** Determine if it is a situation that will involve trouble. Encourage students not to be afraid to ask "dumb" questions. Too many times we get in trouble or make poor decisions because we don't think—we just do. Step 1 ensures that at least one person in the group will encourage others to think about the situation.

   II. **Name the trouble.** Too many kids base decisions on faulty information, e.g., "It's not burglary if the window is open." (A worksheet

is provided for Session 3 primarily to gather information and to discuss what is right and wrong.)

   III. **Identify the consequences.** Decide what you will be risking and express your thoughts. Again, many students do not consider all of the consequences of a decision. Step 3 encourages them to consider not only the legal but also the social, personal, and health consequences of a decision. Many groups may be influenced positively by Step 3; in that case, the student has effectively resisted peer pressure just by getting his or her friends to think.

   IV. **Suggest an alternative, then start to leave.** If a person still finds himself/herself being pressured after the first three steps, then he or she needs to suggest an alternative and leave. This step is the key to saying no and still achieving the three goals. It is very important to teach that one should not engage in an argument or discussion over the merits of the negative or positive alternative. The good guys do not always win these arguments, so don't even start. Suggest something positive and then leave. Many kids are looking for a way out, and while a positive alternative may not sway the whole group, there are many who are looking for something that will not involve trouble. (The worksheet for Session 4 is designed to generate alternatives.)

   V. **Keep the door open.** Encourage students not to put down or threaten the group that they are leaving if they want to achieve the three goals. However, many may choose to end a friendship if the stakes are too high.

3. Choose a low-level peer-pressure situation suggested by the group and role-play. The group leader should take the roles of the "good guy" and the "bad guy" in order to ensure proper modeling at the start of the learning process. In subsequent role-plays, the counselor plays the bad guy and the students play the good guy. The counselor offers corrective feedback (coaching) after each role-play, first asking other group members for their evaluation. After the role-play, discuss whether the five steps were followed and whether or not the "good guy" achieved the three goals.

End

1. Ask the students to recite the five steps of the Refusal Skills model.

2. Ask them to complete the sentences, "One thing I learned today was . . ." and "One way I can use what I learned this week is . . .".

3. Ask students to share answers with a partner. Then ask for volunteers to share with the whole group.

4. Preview next meeting.

Name_____ Date _____

Refusal Skills: Steps to Take

1. **Ask questions**—"*Why . . . where . . . ?*" Determine if it is a situation that will involve trouble.

2. **Name the trouble**—"*That's . . . .*" Tell your friend the real or legal name of the trouble.

3. **Identify the consequences**—"*If I get caught . . . .*" Tell your friend what you will be risking: legal, family, school, self-image, job, and health.

4. **Suggest an alternative, then start to leave**—"*Why don't we . . . ?*" Suggest something else that is fun.

5. **Keep the door open**—"*If you change your mind . . . .*" Leave, and invite your friend to join you if he/she decides to come later.

Session 3
Topic: Consequences, role-play

Resources
- Consequences—What Might Happen handout

Beginning
1. Review the five steps of the refusal skills model.
2. Ask who has had a chance to use the model. After each example, ask students to provide positive feedback and suggestions for alternative ways to use model.

Middle
1. Ask students to work in pairs to complete the Consequences—What Might Happen handout.
2. After pairs have finished, have the whole group go over each situation and reach consensus on the answers to ensure that everyone has correct information.
3. Ask for student volunteers to role-play the "good guys," and the counselor plays the "bad guy" in peer situations that the group has suggested. (The National PTA has gone on record as being opposed to students role-playing the "bad guys," since this provides practice in negative behavior. We strongly recommend that you have students role-play only the "good guys" when the role-play involves controversial issues or illegal activities. It is important to choose relatively easy situations at first to ensure initial student success. Situations that have attractive alternatives are usually the best. If necessary, the group leader can "freeze" the action if a student gets stuck. Freeze the action, solicit help or suggestions from the group, and then continue. The group leader can take the role of a coach during the role-play to help the "good guy" effectively resist peer pressure.
4. After the role-play, ask other group members to provide positive and corrective feedback to the volunteer. Include in the feedback whether the five steps were followed and whether or not the "good guy" achieved the three goals.

End
1. Ask students to share in pairs their endings to the statements, "One thing I learned today was . . ." and "One way I can use it this week is by . . .".
2. After pair sharing, ask for volunteers to share with the group.
3. Preview next meeting.

Name_____ Date _____

Consequences—What Might Happen?

Directions: For each of the troubles below, list the consequences. Also, fill in the legal name for that trouble, if any. In the last row of the Trouble column, write a situation of your own. Complete the consequences for that situation, too.

TROUBLE	CONSEQUENCES				
Situation	Legal	School	Family	You	Others
Taking a CD from a store without paying					
Smoking pot					
Skipping school					
Getting drunk with friends					
Cheating on a test					
Painting words on a public building					

         Group Counseling for School Counselors: A Practical Guide

Session 4
Topic: Alternatives to giving in

Resources
- Alternatives handout

Beginning

REVIEW

1. Ask student to share what they remember from the last meeting.
2. Review the five steps in the Refusal Skills model.
3. Ask student to share examples of them using refusal skills during the week.

Middle

1. Ask students to work in pairs to complete the Alternatives handout.
2. When all group members have completed the worksheet, the group goes over each item to generate multiple alternatives for each situation.
3. Students volunteer to role-play the "good guys," and the counselor plays the "bad guy" in peer situations that the group has suggested. It is important to choose relatively easy situations at first to ensure initial student success. Situations that have attractive alternatives are usually the best. If necessary, the group leader can "freeze" the action if a student gets stuck. Freeze the action, solicit help or suggestions from the group, and then continue. The group leader can take the role of a coach to assist the "good guy" to effectively resist peer pressure.
4. After the role-play, ask group members to provide positive and corrective feedback to the volunteer. Include whether the role-play included the five refusal skills steps and met the three goals of the Refusal Skills model.
5. The group leader can guide other group members to demonstrate alternative ways of handling the role-play situation and receive feedback from the leader and the group. These multiple models situations are the best learning experience for the development of new skills.

End

1. Ask students to share with a partner their completion of the statements, "Today I learned . . ." and "One way I can use what I learned is . . .".
2. Preview next meeting.

Name_____ Date_____

Alternatives

Directions: Work with a partner to complete this sheet. For each place listed in the first column, suggest an alternative course of action, and a way to say this to your friend without damaging your friendship. There are also blank lines in each "Your friend wants to . . ." column. Use these to write other risky choices a friend might want to make. Suggest alternatives for these choices, too.

Place	Your friend wants to . . .	"Why don't we . . ."	How do you say it and still keep your friend?
Class	1. cheat on a test. 2. copy someone's homework. 3. pass notes. 4. _____		
Cafeteria	1. have a food fight. 2. steal lunch money. 3. _____ 4. _____		
On the weekend	1. sneak out of your house late at night. 2. have a party when your parents are out of town. 3. go to a keg party. 4. _____		
Parking lot	1. get high. 2. steal tapes from someone's car. 3. _____ 4. _____		
After school	1. smoke cigarettes. 2. leave without paying the bill at a restaurant. 3. _____ 4. _____		

   Group Counseling for School Counselors: A Practical Guide

Sessions 5, 6, 7
Topic: Role-play using new refusal skills

Resources

- Alternatives handout from Session 4
- Refusal Skills Practice Sheet handout

Beginning

REVIEW

1. Ask students to review the five steps of the Refusal Skills model and the three goals.
2. Ask for volunteers to share their use of the model during the week.
3. Temperature check: Ask each student to rate how he or she is feeling and his/her energy level on a scale of 1–10, where 1 is low and 10 is high. Using the same scale, have students rate the past week. Give each student about one minute to elaborate on his or her rating.

Middle

Note: Building new skills takes time and repetition. In these three sessions, make sure all group members have opportunities to role-play and receive feedback.

1. Have students suggest peer situations for role-playing; students volunteer to role-play the "good guys," and the counselor plays the "bad guy." Situations that have attractive alternatives are usually the best. If necessary, the group leader can "freeze" the action if a student gets stuck. Stop the action, solicit help or suggestions from the group, and then continue. The group leader can take the role of a coach to assist the "good guy" in effectively resisting peer pressure.
2. After the role-play, ask group members to provide positive and corrective feedback to the volunteer. Include whether the role-play followed the five refusal skills steps and met the three goals of the Refusal Skills model.
3. The group leader can guide other group members to demonstrate alternative ways of handling the role-play situation and receive feedback from the leader and the group. These multiple models situations are the best learning experience for the development of new skills.

End

1. Ask students to share with a partner their completion of the statements, "Today I learned . . ." and "One way I can use what I learned is . . .".
2. Preview next meeting.

Name_____ Date_____

Refusal Skills Practice Sheet

Directions: Work with a partner to choose one place and one situation that might call for refusal skills. Use what you have learned about refusal skills to complete all the columns.

Place	Your friend wants you to . . .	Ask questions: Why? Where? etc.	Name the trouble.	Identify consequences.	Suggest an alternative and start to leave.	Keep the door open.

34   *Group Counseling for School Counselors: A Practical Guide*

Session 8
Topic: Spotlighting, evaluation, closure

Resources

- Index cards or sheet of paper
- Group Evaluation form (page 10)

Beginning

Ask, "Who used something we talked about last week during the week? How did it go?"

REVIEW LIFE OF GROUP

Briefly go over each topic you've covered during the last seven weeks, asking for what students remember.

Then ask the following questions:

1. What are some of the most important things you have learned about yourself?
2. What has been the most helpful part of this group for you?
3. What is a goal you have set for yourself?

Middle

ACCEPTING AND GIVING COMPLIMENTS

1. Hand out index cards or sheets of paper. Each person is to write down at least one thing he or she admires, likes, or appreciates about each of the other group members.
2. Spotlight: Ask each group member to say directly to the "spotlighted" person, with eye contact: "[person's name], one thing I admire, like, or appreciate about you is . . ."

Explain and give examples of the types of qualities you are asking the students to think of and how to say and receive them. Ask students not to use appearance compliments such as "I like your shirt, shoes, hair," etc., but rather qualities or actions.

3. After each comment, the spotlighted person says "thank you," nothing else. (Be sure you get in on this—it feels good.)

End

1. Process the spotlighting activity. How did it feel receiving compliments? Giving compliments?
2. Students complete anonymous evaluation.
3. Concluding remarks. Invite students to make individual appointments if they want. Remind them of the monthly follow-up sessions if any are planned.

1.3
Anger Management/Taking Control

Grade Level: High School	Time Required: 8 Sessions	Author: Anya F. Koszas

Purpose

To help students develop coping strategies to manage stress and anger appropriately. Students learn to

- Recognize the feelings and physical signs of anger.
- Understand their anger management style.
- Identify what triggers their anger.
- Deal with their anger in constructive ways.
- Prevent inappropriate ways of dealing with anger.
- Practice effective ways of dealing with anger.

Logistics

GROUP COMPOSITION

Students grades 9–12 mixed with regard to activity level and behavior control. Avoid loading group with only overactive behavior problem students. Students need multiple models of appropriate behavior. Groups with only behavior problem students usually do not show significant gains in prosocial behavior. Mixed groups are generally very effective.

GROUP SIZE

6–8 students

GROUP TIME PER SESSION

45–60 minutes

NUMBER OF SESSIONS

Eight, with optional booster sessions spaced approximately one month apart after regular group ends

Recommended Resources

Full bibliographic details for these publications are included in the Bibliography at the end of this book.

Brigman and Earley, 1991: *Group Counseling for School Counselors.*

Bete, 1997: *When Anger Heats Up.*

Eggert, 1994: *Anger Management for Youth.*

Guidance Club for Teens, 1993: *Anger, Temper Tantrums and Violent Emotions* (videocassette).

Korb-Khalsa, Azok, and Leutenberg, 1991: *Life Management Skills II.*

Kramer, 1994: *The Dynamics of Relationships.*

Peterson, 1995: *Talk With Teens About Feelings, Family, Relationships, and the Future.*

Rizzon-Toner, 1993: *Stress Management and Self-Esteem Activities.*

Schilling and Dunne, 1992: *Understanding Me.*

Taylor, 1994: *Anger Control Training for Children and Teens.*

Vernon, 1989: *Thinking, Feeling, Behaving.*

Session 1
Topic: Getting acquainted

Resources
- Index cards
- Box, bowl, or bag to hold cards

Beginning

WELCOME MEMBERS TO GROUP

Emphasize the meaning of "Don't be controlled" (name of group). Introduce yourself and explain the purpose of the group. *Example:* "All of us get angry, and it's how we respond to our anger that matters. We will learn what causes our own anger and we will learn and practice with group members good ways to respond to anger. We will ask you to give your own real-life examples of how you have responded to anger recently and—with the help of group members—we will help you figure out better ways to respond to anger.

"The group meets eight times, same place, same time, every week. As I mentioned when I met with each of you individually, there are three ways people get to participate in this group: 1) you heard about the group and thought it sounded good and signed up; 2) your parent heard or read about it and wanted you to check it out; 3) your teacher thought you'd enjoy it and that you'd be able to benefit from being in the group.

"As you probably know, this group is open to everyone. You don't have to have a problem with your anger to be here. We are here to learn about ourselves and to help others in dealing with life's problems that make us angry."

INTRODUCTIONS

Have students pair up and have them interview their partners to learn their names, what they like to do, and what they hope to get out of the group. Then have each student introduce his/her partner, based on the interview.

Middle

GROUP RULES

Ask, "What are some rules you think would help our group run better? I've found it's helpful to have a few rules to make our group run smoothly." Make sure to include the following:

1. Anything we talk about here is confidential—you own what you say but we do not talk about what anyone else says outside the group.

2. We do not want to make anyone uncomfortable. You have the right to say "pass" if you do not want to share your opinion on something.

3. One person talks at a time—the rest of us listen.

4. We respect each other's right to have different opinions even if we do not agree—no put-downs.

5. Share the time—no monopolizing "talk time." Ask for additional suggestions—get a group consensus on all rules.

GET ACQUAINTED

Say to students, "One of the most important parts of working in a group is getting to know one another and feeling comfortable and psychologically safe. We can begin that process by using these questions as discussion starters. Take a card from the bowl as it is passed around, read it to the group, and respond. Then we can hear what others think about the same question. I'll start."

Put the following questions on 3 × 5 cards and place in a bowl or box to pass around the circle.

- I trust people who . . .
- I can tell someone cares about what I am saying by the way they . . .
- Some feelings I have about starting this group are . . .
- I hope the group . . .
- When I first meet someone I usually . . .
- When I get angry I usually . . .
- Learning to control anger is important because . . .
- Taking good risks like being willing to share how you think and feel helps build good relationships because . . .
- I admire people who . . .

End

1. Ask students to share in pairs what they learned about the group and each other today and what they are looking forward to doing/learning in the group. Ask volunteers to share with whole group.

2. Ask students to review what the purpose of the group is, how many meetings, and so forth.

3. Preview the second meeting.

Session 2

Topic: Understanding what anger is: self-assessment

Resources

- Anger Management Self-Assessment handout

Beginning

REVIEW

Ask students to complete the sentence, "Something I remember from last meeting is . . .".

Briefly discuss anger triggers. Include the importance of knowing what your main triggers are so that you can prepare to handle them constructively.

Ask students to complete the sentence: "One of my top anger triggers is . . .".

Middle

1. Have students complete the Anger Management Self-Assessment handout. Encourage them to be honest. This is confidential information. They will do another self-assessment at the end of group and compare results for themselves.

2. Ask students to share their answers in pairs.

3. Lead the whole group in a discussion of the five items. Ask questions to help students clarify specifics related to each item, such as for 1, "How do you know when you are angry—what are the physical, mental signals?" And for 2, "What is your style—your predictable pattern?"

4. As the group discusses each item, ask participants to look for similarities and differences. Ask connecting questions such as, "Who noticed some similarities or differences in Jim's answers to what we have heard so far?" and "How many of you have had that experience or feel that way?" Especially have students explore why each of the questions is important to understand—the benefits to them— and get them to start sharing constructive anger management styles.

End

1. Ask students to share, in pairs, their responses to the statement, "One thing I learned or relearned that I can use right away is . . .".

2. Ask students to notice their anger triggers and anger response styles this week and be ready to share these with the group next week.

Name_____ Date_____

Anger Management Self-Assessment

Directions: Please rate yourself according to the following scale:

1	2	3	4	5
never	once in a while	often	most of the time	always

	1	2	3	4	5
1. I know when I am angry.	1	2	3	4	5
2. I am aware of my own anger style.	1	2	3	4	5
3. I know what triggers my anger.	1	2	3	4	5
4. I feel I deal with my anger in constructive ways.	1	2	3	4	5
5. My anger gets me in trouble.	1	2	3	4	5

Session 3
Topic: Understanding anger styles

Resources

- Anger Styles handouts—Stuffers, Escalators, Problem Solvers
- Anger Diary handout

Beginning

REVIEW

1. Ask the group, "What were some things we did last week in here?"
2. Share in pairs examples from the week of anger triggers and anger responses. Ask for volunteers to share with whole group.

Middle

1. Discuss what "stuffing" is. Encourage members to share a situation in which she/he "stuffed" anger, why, and the consequences. Distribute the Anger Styles: Stuffers handout.
2. Discuss "escalating." Share a situation in which a member or someone they know "escalated" to anger, why, and the consequences. Distribute Anger Styles: Escalators handout.
3. Discuss the "problem solver" approach—an assertive approach. Distribute the Anger Styles: Problem Solvers handout.

End

1. Ask students to share in pairs, "One thing I learned or relearned that I can use right away is . . .".
2. Ask students to notice their anger response styles this week. Give each student a copy of the Anger Diary and ask them to use it this week and to be prepared to share examples next week.

Name_____ Date_____

Anger Styles: Stuffers

Stuffing—Passive	Escalating—Aggressive	Problem Solving—Assertive

Stuffers tend to avoid direct confrontation.

Stuffers tend to deny anger. They may not admit to themselves or to others that they are angry. Stuffers may not be aware that they have the *right* to be angry.

A. Which of the following reasons for stuffing apply to you?

____ 1. Fear of hurting/offending someone

____ 2. Fear of being disliked or rejected

____ 3. Fear of losing control

____ 4. Feeling it's inappropriate (not OK) to be angry

____ 5. Feeling unable to cope with such a strong, intense emotion

____ 6. Fear of damaging/losing a relationship

____ 7. It's a learned behavior (but, it can be unlearned!)

____ 8. Trying to use a different style than the one I was raised with

B. What are some other reasons people stuff anger?

9. _____

10. _____

C. Consequences/problems associated with stuffing:

1. The anger comes out regardless.

2. Stuffing impairs relationships.

3. Stuffing compromises physical and mental health.

4. _____

5. _____

D. When would it be appropriate to take a passive approach and temporarily stuff anger?

_____

_____

_____

Name_____ Date_____

Anger Styles: Escalators

| Stuffing—Passive | Escalating—Aggressive | Problem Solving—Assertive |

Escalators try to control with anger and rage.

> Escalators tend to blame and shame the provoker.
> Escalating often leads to abusive situations.

A. Which of the following reasons for escalating apply to you?

____ 1. Feeling "I have no other choice"

____ 2. To demonstrate an image of strength/power

____ 3. To avoid expressing underlying emotions

____ 4. Fear of getting close to someone

____ 5. It's a learned behavior (but, it can be unlearned!)

____ 6. Lack of communication skills

B. What are some other reasons for escalating?

7. _____

8. _____

C. Consequences/problems associated with escalating:

1. The desired results may be short-term.

2. It may lead to physical destruction.

3. Escalating impairs relationships.

4. Escalating compromises physical and mental health.

5. Escalating can have legal ramifications.

6. _____

7. _____

D. Are there times when escalating would be appropriate? _____

_____

_____

_____

Name_____ Date _____

Anger Styles: Problem Solvers

Stuffing—Passive	Escalating—Aggressive	Problem Solving—Assertive

Problem solvers try to find a win-win solution.

> Problem solvers tend to try negotiation to right a wrong.
> Problem solvers tend to confront the situation/person respectfully but directly.

A. Which of the following reasons for problem solving apply to you?

___ 1. Feeling "I have a choice and I choose to show strength/power in a positive way"

___ 2. To demonstrate self-respect and respect for others

___ 3. To avoid the negative consequences from stuffing or escalating

___ 4. Knowing that sharing of feelings is essential to getting close to someone

___ 5. Problem solving is a style of handling anger that can be learned.

___ 6. The communication skills needed to be a problem solver are helpful in many other areas of life.

B. What are some other reasons for the problem-solving style of handling anger?

  7. _____

  8. _____

C. Consequences/problems associated with problem solving:

  1. Results tend to be long-term.

  2. Problem solving promotes positive physical and mental health.

  3. Problem solving improves relationships.

  4. _____

  5. _____

  6. _____

D. Are there times when problem solving would not be appropriate? _____

  _____

  _____

  _____

Name_____ Date_____

Anger Diary

Directions: For the next week, use this Anger Diary every day to keep track of what causes you to become angry, and the way you respond. Make extra copies of the diary as needed, or use the categories to make your own diary pages. At the next group meeting, bring at least three situations that caused you anger, and your responses to them. Be prepared to share excerpts from your diary with the group.

Date _____ Time _____

First symptom(s): _____

_____

_____

What triggered your anger response? _____

_____

_____

Your response: _____

_____

_____

+/− Generally, do you think you did well or not so well? _____

_____

_____

What was something you did well in this situation? _____

_____

_____

Is there something you can do in the future to better manage your anger? What? _____

_____

_____

Group Counseling for School Counselors: A Practical Guide

Session 4
Topic: Understanding uncontrolled anger sequence

Resources
- Completed Anger Diaries from Session 3
- Uncontrolled Anger Sequence handout
- Index cards with role-play questions
- Anger Diary handout

Beginning
1. Review anger styles discussed at last session.
2. Ask for volunteers to share a situation from their anger diaries when they felt angry and discuss briefly how they handled the situation, how they felt about how it ended, and any ideas for improvement for the future.

Middle
1. Using student examples of anger situations, teach the Uncontrolled Anger Sequence: triggers, thoughts, feelings, behavior, and consequences. Use the handout to help students gain a better understanding of the sequence of events when anger is experienced.
2. Ask volunteers to share personalized answers from each area. Ask students to listen for similarities and differences and use your connecting and linking skills to facilitate the discussion. The focus should be on building the ability to judge constructive vs. destructive ways of handling anger.
3. Ask the group members to pick one situation either about school this past week or peers/social life this past week to explore through role-play. Look for a situation that many group members can identify with.
4. Ask the person with the chosen situation to become the director and choose 1–2 group members to help act out the story. The director plays herself/himself and shows/tells the other actors what to do/say. General guidelines for setting the scene and directing the story include answering the following questions. Write these questions on an index card, then give the card to the person who is acting as the director.

ROLE-PLAY QUESTIONS

- What is the setting (where and when)?
- Who are the main characters and how are they feeling at the beginning of the story?

- What is the problem?
- What happens first?
- What are the feelings and reactions of the other characters?
- What do the characters do to try and solve the problem?
- How does the story end and how are the characters feeling?

Limit role-play prep to 2–3 minutes and role-play to 2–3 minutes.

5. After the role-play, have the group discuss the pros and cons of the way the director handled the situation and explore alternative ways to handle it. Have group members act out alternative ways of handling the situation and get group feedback as to strengths and things that may need changing.

Note: Discuss giving feedback/coaching. Both supportive and corrective feedback/coaching are needed to help people improve. Model the sandwich approach: Give supportive feedback (bread), then corrective feedback (the meat), then finish with supportive feedback (the bread).

Example: "John, I liked the way you stood up for yourself and did not get pushed around. One thing you may want to consider changing is saying what you have to say in a calmer voice, without yelling, but still getting your message across. With your self-confidence I think you will develop the assertiveness skills very quickly."

Ask students to use a go-round to share positives about the role-play—"I liked the way you . . .".

Then do another go-round for coaching feedback—"You may want to consider . . .".

End
1. Ask students to think of what they discovered or learned today and how they can use it this next week. Share with partner first, then share with group.
2. Give each member another copy of the Anger Diary and ask them to record at least one example this week and bring it to group next time for discussion.

Name_____ Date_____

Uncontrolled Anger Sequence

1. **Triggers:**

Something happens, like you get criticized, and you get angry.

What are some things that push your button? What causes you to get upset? To lose it? (For example, bossing, yelling, "jumping on your back" when you haven't done anything, getting rejected.)

_____

_____

_____

_____

What are some things you've observed that make others mad?

_____

_____

_____

_____

2. **Thoughts:**

We evaluate when our buttons get pushed; we think certain things, like "What a jerk!" or "How could I be so stupid?" or "He shouldn't act like that!" or "I can't take it anymore!" or "Jerk! Unfair! Terrible! Awful! Shouldn't be! They'll pay!"

These thoughts are triggered by our attitudes, our beliefs, our biases!

What thoughts or ideas usually come to your mind when the triggers we identified happen to you?

_____

_____

_____

_____

Write down some things you usually tell yourself—your self-talk (for example, "I'm going to show him" or "_____!") _____

_____

_____

_____

(continued)

Name_____ Date_____

Uncontrolled Anger Sequence *(continued)*

3. **Feelings:**

> Our thinking produces feelings! We feel the way we think.

So, how do you usually feel in the situations we identified?

Emotionally? (For example, anger is a secondary feeling that is aroused by other feelings, such as hurt, scared, attacked, mad, and frustrated.)

_____

_____

_____

Physically? (For example, what happens in parts of your body when you get really upset emotionally?)

_____

_____

_____

4. **Behaviors:**

> Upset feelings generate actions!

What do you do? How do you usually respond behaviorally? For example: Run! Fight! Attack! Cry! Withdraw!

_____

_____

_____

_____

5. **Consequences:**

> Negative behaviors usually result in negative consequences.

What are some consequences you often experience for getting out of control?

_____

_____

_____

_____

Session 5

Topic: Building skills—assertiveness and managing your anger

Resources

- Completed Anger Diaries from Session 4
- Index cards from Session 4
- Assertiveness handout
- Be Assertive handout
- Anger Diary handout

Beginning

REVIEW

Ask students what they remember from last meeting.

REPORT ON ANGER DIARY

Ask for examples from students' anger diaries. Focus on how they managed each situation and how they felt about the way it ended. Get feedback from group members and brainstorm alternative ways of managing similar situations in the future.

Middle

1. Discuss the handout on assertiveness. The beliefs that underlie each style—passive, aggressive, and assertive—are the keys to maintaining these styles. Since assertiveness is the most appropriate and healthy style for managing anger in most situations, it is important to spend time on clarifying the unintentional or intentional negative effects of the underlying beliefs of the other two styles. As usual, getting examples from the group of real-life situations of each style helps bring this discussion energy and interest.

2. Next, use the three situations from the Be Assertive handout to check for understanding of these three styles of managing anger.

3. Last, choose an example from the group to role-play each of the three ways—passive, aggressive, and assertive. Get as many group members involved in the role-plays as possible and ask the group to give feedback to the role-players on their performance. Use the setting cards from last week to help the director give background information about the situation.

End

1. Ask students to think of what they discovered or learned today and how they can use it this next week. Share with partner first, then share with group.

2. Give each member another copy of the Anger Diary. Ask them to record at least one example this week and bring it to group next time for discussion.

Name_____ Date _____

Assertiveness

Aggressive people:

- intentionally attack, take advantage of, humiliate, hurt, put down, or depreciate other people.
- act on the belief that others are not as important as they are.

The aggressive person's mottos are:

"Get them before they get you."
"How you play doesn't count, only that you win."
"Never give a sucker an even break."

Example:
As you leave a store after purchasing something, you realize that you have been shortchanged 65 cents. You hurry back into the store and loudly demand 65 cents, adding a derogatory comment about cashiers who can't add.

Passive people:

- permit others to take advantage of them.
- discount themselves and act as if others are more important than they are.

The passive person's mottos are:

"I should never make anyone feel uncomfortable, resentful, or displeased, except myself."
"I should never disappoint anyone or cause anyone to disapprove of me."

Example:
As you leave a store after purchasing something, you realize that you have been shortchanged 65 cents. You pause to decide if 65 cents is worth the effort. After a few moments of indecision, you decide not to cause a hassle, and leave.

Assertive people:

- express themselves openly and honestly to communicate their needs, wants, or feelings, without discounting the wants, needs, or feelings of others.

The assertive person's mottos are:

"We all have the right to ask for what we want."
"We all have the right to refuse a request."

Example:
As you leave a store after purchasing something, you realize that you have been shortchanged 65 cents. You go back, get the attention of the clerk, display the change you received, and state that you were shortchanged 65 cents.

Name_____ Date _____

Be Assertive

Directions: Decide which responses are assertive (AST), aggressive (AGG), or passive (PAS). Label them accordingly.

> *Situation:* Your parents tell you they don't want you to stay out past 1 A.M. on weekends, and you aren't pleased with the decision.

_____Response 1: You say nothing but are really angry and consider staying out later anyway.

_____Response 2: You confront your parents, saying that everyone else gets to stay out later and that they are just mean and old-fashioned. You say you hate living in their prison and you don't see why they have to make life so miserable for you.

_____Response 3: You tell your parents you think that, because you are 16, you should be able to stay out later at least once in a while. You ask them nicely if they will consider letting you do it sometimes.

> *Situation:* Your boyfriend or girlfriend stands you up.

_____Response 1: You call him/her and say firmly, but not in an angry tone, that you are upset that he/she didn't call and don't like to be treated like that. You tell him/her that, if there is a problem in the relationship, you'd like to discuss it but that you don't want to be treated so disrespectfully.

_____Response 2: You call him/her and, in an angry tone of voice, say that he/she is the most inconsiderate person you have ever dated, that you never want to see him/ her again, and that you think he/she is a real jerk.

_____Response 3: You don't say anything, but you are upset and act very cool and aloof the next time you see him/her. When he/she asks you what the matter is, you say nothing is wrong.

> *Situation:* You get a bad grade on a test, and you think that the teacher was unfair in grading it.

_____Response 1: You do nothing about it.

_____Response 2: You ask the teacher nicely if you could discuss the test. You indicate that you think your answer to the first question is right and request politely that he or she reconsider the response and the grade.

_____Response 3: You push your paper in front of the teacher and angrily accuse him or her of being unfair. You tell the teacher that you want your answer looked at again because you know you are right.

Session 6

Topic: Building skills—practicing managing your anger

Resources

- Completed Anger Diaries from Session 5
- Coping with Anger handout
- Anger Diary handout
- Index cards with setting questions from Session 4

Beginning

REVIEW

Ask students what they remember from last meeting.

REPORT ON ANGER DIARY

Ask for examples from students' anger diaries. Focus on how they managed each situation and how they felt about the way it ended. Get feedback from group members and brainstorm alternative ways of managing similar situations in the future.

Middle

1. Use the Coping with Anger handout to teach a model for effective anger management that includes positive self-talk. Go through the six steps one at a time, reading each out loud and brainstorming other self-talk possibilities.

2. Role-play scenarios. Ask students to write an anger-provoking situation on a piece of paper. Place it in a hat. Choose one situation. Use the setting cards to help the director give background information. After the role-play, ask group members to identify other effective techniques that would help the individual manage his/her anger constructively in the future.

End

1. Ask students to think of what they discovered or learned today and how they can use it this next week. Share with partner first, then share with group.

2. Give each member another copy of the Anger Diary. Ask them to record at least one example this week and bring it to group next time for discussion.

Name_____ Date_____

Coping with Anger

C **Calm down**

Say "Calm down, I can handle this. It won't help to blow up."

Other positive self-talk statements:

_____

_____

_____

_____

O **Overcome**

Say "I can overcome my automatic thinking—this isn't awful, dreadful, terrible, or catastrophic. I can handle this."

Other positive self-talk statements:

_____

_____

_____

_____

P **Problem solve**

Say "What are my best alternatives? What is my plan for this type of situation? Stop and think—there are always alternatives."

Other positive self-talk statements:

_____

_____

_____

_____

_____

(continued)

     Group Counseling for School Counselors: A Practical Guide

Name_____ Date_____

Coping with Anger *(continued)*

I Invite

Say "Invite creative thinking. Invite respect. Don't insult."

Other positive self-talk statements:

_____

_____

_____

_____

N Negotiate

Say "When I am angry it is important to think win-win—to negotiate. Don't get into the negatives, the blaming, the put-downs—they lead nowhere."

Other positive self-talk statements:

_____

_____

_____

_____

G Go for it!

Say "Good job. Way to go! You are getting better and better at this anger management stuff."

Other positive self-talk statements:

_____

_____

_____

_____

Session 7
Topic: Steps to coping with anger

Resources

- Completed Anger Diaries from Session 6
- Coping with Anger handout from Session 6
- Index card with setting questions

Beginning

REVIEW

Ask students what they remember from last meeting.

REPORT ON ANGER DIARY

Ask for examples from students' anger diaries. Focus on how they managed each situation and how they felt about the way it ended. Get feedback from group members and brainstorm alternative ways of managing similar situations in the future.

Middle

1. Review the Coping with Anger handout from last week to prepare for a role-play. Choose a situation from examples provided by students when they shared situations from their anger diaries.

2. Ask the person with the chosen situation to become the director and choose 1–2 group members to help act out the story. The director plays himself/herself and shows/tells the other actors what to do/say. General guidelines for setting the scene and directing the story include answering the following questions. Give these questions on a card to the person who is acting as the director.

ROLE-PLAY QUESTIONS

- What is the setting (where and when)?
- Who are the main characters and how are they feeling at the beginning of the story?
- What is the problem?
- What happens first?
- What are the feelings and reactions of the other characters?
- What do the characters do to try and solve the problem?
- How does the story end and how are the characters feeling?

Limit role-play prep to 2–3 minutes and role-play to 2–3 minutes.

3. After the role-play, have the group discuss the pros and cons of how the director handled the situation and explore alternative ways to handle it.

4. Let different group members take the lead role to provide multiple models of effective anger management. Be sure to ask about their self-talk. Have the group give feedback on the various ways of managing the situations.

End

Ask students to think of what they discovered or learned today and how they can use it this next week. Share with partner first, then share with group.

Session 8
Topic: Closing/evaluation

Resources
- Anger Management Self-Assessment handout (page 39)
- Group Evaluation form (page 10)
- Refreshments

Beginning

REVIEW
Ask students what they remember from last meeting.

SELF-ASSESSMENT
1. Distribute self-assessment sheets. Students complete a new one.
2. Return to students the self-assessment they completed at the beginning of the group. Ask students to compare both.

Middle
1. Ask them to share their conclusions from the pre-group and post-group inventory with a partner.

Ask them to share positive gains and areas they would like to continue to work on.
2. With the whole group, ask students to complete the statements "The most important thing I have learned about managing my anger is . . ." and "One way that I have improved in managing my anger is . . .".
3. As students share their answers to these two questions, ask the group if anyone wants to give some positive feedback to the person.

End
1. Complete group evaluation form. Stress confidentiality of information, and the fact that it will help you with your next anger management group.
2. Let students know that you are available to meet with them and that you will get the group together again in one month to check on their progress.
3. Share refreshments as a group.

1.4
Loss/Bereavement

| Grade Level: High School | Time Required: 8 Sessions | Author: Doreen Cammarata |

Purpose

Typically, adolescents repress their feelings or express them behaviorally; consequently, school work and participation in school activities are often affected. Therefore, the primary goal of the support group is identifying, validating, and encouraging expression in constructive ways. Another goal is to commemorate the life of the departed and to inspire the bereaved individual to continue to live, love, and learn, knowing that time will bring healing.

Logistics

GROUP COMPOSITION

Students in grades 9–12 who have recently (within the past year) experienced the death of an immediate family member. Students within 1–2 grade levels of one another may be grouped together.

GROUP SIZE

6–8 students

NUMBER OF SESSIONS

Eight

Background Information for the Grief Group Facilitator

Grief support groups address the significance of loss experienced by adolescents upon the death of someone close to them. The complexity of issues brought upon specifically by the impact of a death loss is quite unique. Although this grief shares similarities with the grief associated with other kinds of loss or separation (e.g., divorce), it is imperative to note that grief support groups are designed for those individuals who have experienced death loss. Careful screening of members and consents for minors must be done. Individuals experiencing other kinds of loss or separation should be referred to appropriate groups.

Before beginning a support group, the facilitator must acknowledge his or her own death issues. Any self-disclosure should be limited to promoting group rapport and group cohesion. Be aware that a variety of feelings may arise for the facilitator throughout the sessions; the facilitator's knowledge of his or her own limits and the perception that sharing must be for the betterment of the group are critical. Creating a safe and loving atmosphere is paramount. Collegial consultation along with continued education is always encouraged.

Encouraging grieving teens to externalize their grief is vitally important. It is crucial that professionals working with these groups are cognizant of the very specific and complex needs of grieving adolescents. Therefore, it is recommended that the facilitator of these groups have grief training, counseling experience, and group skills training.

A portion of this chapter is derived from the work and research that my colleague, Jeri Williams, and I completed while working for The Hospice of Martin and St. Lucie Inc.

Recommended Resources

Full bibliographic details for these publications are included in the Bibliography at the end of this book.

Buscaglia, 1982: *The Fall of Freddie the Leaf.*

Gootman, 1994: *When a Friend Dies.*

Grollman, 1993: *Straight Talk About Death for Teenagers.*

Grollman, 1995: *Bereaved Children and Teens.*

Hipp, 1995: *Help for the Hard Times.*

Kübler-Ross, 1974: *On Death and Dying.*

Oates, 1993: *Death in the School Community.*

O'Rourke and Worzybt, 1996: *Support Groups for Children.*

Traisman, 1992: *Fire in My Heart Ice in My Veins.*

Session 1

Topic: Getting acquainted, explanation of journaling

Resources

- Folders for use as student journals

Beginning

INTRODUCTION

Introduce yourself, discuss the purpose of the support group, allow the group members an opportunity to get to know one another, and establish informed consent.

"Welcome to this loss group. Each of you has experienced the death of someone close to you. It is my hope that throughout our sessions you will come to find this environment a safe place to share your feelings. We will be learning about the grief process along with constructive ways in which to cope with grief. I will stress in here that there is no right or wrong way to grieve but healthy and unhealthy ways to cope with our individual grief. Together we will try to uncover what works for each of you and how you may implement that in your life."

"Today, I'd like to start off by breaking into pairs and interviewing one another. Find out the following five things about your partner, then introduce him or her to the large group. Find out your partner's name, where he or she is from, whom he or she lives with, something that makes your partner sad, and something that makes your partner happy."

Having members introduce one another is likely to promote a level of trust in the group. The early phase of a group is critical to create a trustworthy and safe environment for the members.

Middle

1. Discuss the important ground rules set for the group. Explain confidentiality and its limits.

Encourage each member to share as he or she feels comfortable, and stress that no one is ever forced to share. Accentuate the significance of respecting fellow group members by actively listening and using nonjudgmental statements toward one another.

"You own what you say but not what others say. Anything others share in here should be kept among the group members and expressed only during group time. You may share what you say with whomever you choose. I will keep confidential everything any of you say. The most important exceptions to confidentiality occur if you pose a threat to yourself or to anyone else. In all other instances confidentiality is accepted and maintained."

2. Introduce the concept of journaling thoughts and feelings.

Hand out folders to be used as journals and have students write their names on them. Explain that at the end of each session you will collect these and that members are welcome to keep an additional journal at home which may be added to this at any time.

End

First through their journals and then through sharing in the large group, have students respond to the following statements:

"I feel . . . about coming to this group."

"Something I hope to get out of this group is . . ."

"Today I learned . . ."

Session 2
Topic: Trust, sharing losses

Beginning

Have students complete the statement, "My week was . . . and I'd like to share . . .".

Middle

1. Begin discussion on trust. Have members define trust and its importance in this group in comparison to other environments. An optional activity is a trust walk. Have the members pair up. One is blindfolded while the other leads him or her on a short walk. Then have the pairs alternate roles.

   "At various times in our lives we place trust in other people. Share how it feels to have someone place trust in you and/or to be the one putting trust in another."

2. Allow members to brainstorm the meaning of loss. Have them identify the losses they have endured in their lives, including the current death. At this time give each member an opportunity to talk about who died, when, how, and the way in which the group member found out about the death. If there is a strong level of comfort, members can also share what has been most difficult for them since the death.

   "Let's brainstorm what loss is and list all the types of losses that we can think of. After this we will take a closer look at the loss that has brought each of you to this group."

After the discussion the facilitator could say the following:

"Loss is when we no longer have something or someone that is meaningful to us. We will be discussing our reactions to loss in the coming weeks, but for today, let us take some time to speak about the death of our loved ones. Let's go around the room and share who died, when, how, and the way in which you found out about the death. If you would like, you can also share with the group what has been most difficult for you since the death."

Provide each member a chance to speak. Not everyone will feel comfortable talking. Try to encourage participation but allow for the members to share at their own comfort level. It may be wise to start by asking for a volunteer and then go around the room. Empathy and caring skills should be utilized at this time.

End

First through their journals and then through sharing in the large group, have students respond to the following statements:

"I learned . . ."

"I can see that I need to . . ."

Session 3
Topic: Stages of grief

Resources
- Chart paper

Beginning

Have students respond to the statement, "Today I feel . . .".

REVIEW

Ask members to recall the definition of loss. Give members an opportunity to discuss if they have been utilizing a journal outside the group. Have them share whether the journal has been a helpful tool for them.

Middle

"Today we are going to learn about grief. Grief is a normal reaction to loss. Theorists have created various labels and tools to help educate people about grief. I'd like to show you one model and get your feedback about it."

List on a chart Dr. Elisabeth Kübler-Ross's stages of grief: denial, anger, bargaining, depression, and acceptance. Explain to the members that not everyone experiences each of these stages, and a person may not gradually move through these stages, starting at denial and ending at acceptance. Rather, this was designed as a guide to understanding some of the most common symptoms experienced in grieving individuals. It is just as common for people to revisit a stage once they have moved through that stage as it is for some to skip over various stages. People vacillate between stages, and the length of the stages will vary according to the individual. Accentuate to your group that everyone grieves differently and that there is no right or wrong way to grieve.

Have students share their reactions: "Which of these stages can you identify with?"

Linking members by looking for and pursuing common themes within the group will strengthen group cohesion. Through empathizing and reflecting, the facilitator can encourage members to explore their feelings. Be prepared for and sensitive to group members expressing intense emotional reactions. It is likely that your members will be in very different places with their grief so you may ask them to recall how they felt right after the death occurred as opposed to their current feelings.

End

First through their journals and then through sharing in the large group, have students respond to the following statements:

"I learned . . ."

"I see that I need to . . ."

Session 4
Topic: Reactions to grief

Resources
- Blackboard/Whiteboard or chart paper
- Video on teen grief (recommended: *Teen Grief: Climbing Back*)

Beginning
Have students respond to the statement, "This week I felt . . .".

REVIEW
Ask members to recall the stages of grief.

Middle
1. "Let's create a list of grief reactions and emotions that each of us has experienced. Break into small groups and come up with as many as you can think of; then we will share your responses in a large group."

   Allow small groups time to complete the activity. Then, on a blackboard or chart, list the groups' responses, along with the following symptoms of grief in older children and teens:

difficulty concentrating	truancy
forgetfulness	accident proneness
poor schoolwork	overeating/under-eating
lowered grades/ performance/effort	experimentation with drugs/alcohol
insomnia or sleeping too much	seeming depressed
reclusiveness or social withdrawal	sexual promiscuity
antisocial/destructive behavior	staying away/running away from home
negative risk-taking	talk of or attempted suicide
resentment of authority	nightmares/symbolic dreams
overdependence	drastic change in interests/friends
regression	
frequent sickness	

"When we look at the behaviors listed, we can immediately identify the majority of them as being negative. In the weeks to come I will point out positive gains we can experience from grief. However, I feel it is important that each of you is aware of all the ways in which one may react to grief."

Disclosing a personal experience can assist your members by validating their reactions. An example I have utilized from my own personal losses is as follows:

"I recall when I was thirteen and a very close cousin of mine died of leukemia. I had many strong reactions like those we've listed. I felt so alone and misunderstood. It wasn't until someone explained to me that I was experiencing grief that I began to feel some relief."

2. Show a video on teen grief. I recommend *Teen Grief: Climbing Back*.

   "Let's take a look at a video and see how some others who have experienced loss are reacting."

3. After the video, have members discuss their reactions. Stress how this group, like the group viewed on the video, can help members to grow in a positive direction. Accentuate the healthy coping mechanisms displayed by the group members on the video. Ask group members to take notice throughout the next week of all the ways in which each of them is dealing with their grief.

End
First through their journals and then through sharing in the large group, have members respond to the following statements:
   "I learned . . ."
   "I relearned . . ."
   "I need to . . ."

Session 5
Topic: Dealing with grief, memory boxes

Resources
- Student folders
- Magazines
- Scissors
- Paper clips

Beginning
Have students respond to the statement, "This past week something I noticed about the way I'm coping with my grief is . . .".

REVIEW
Briefly review the symptoms of grief discussed in the prior meeting.

Middle
1. "Today in large group let's identify some constructive ways to deal with our grief. Specifically, refer to what kinds of things you can do that may be healthy."

   Have members disclose their reactions. Add to the group's responses by suggesting the following: Make a scrapbook or collage, write poetry or stories about your loved one, write a letter to your loved one, plant flowers or a memory tree, have friends and family write or tell you about special memories, keep something that reminds you of your loved one in a special place, pray, visit the grave, cry to release your tears, play sports or do something physical to release your anger, seek individual grief counseling.

2. "We keep referring to the importance of memories. It is obvious that after someone we love dies we tend to value time spent with them before the death. Things that may trigger our memories include pictures, songs, smells, being at a specific place, objects, etc. The activity we are about to do is making a memory box. This will take us until next session to complete. While we work on this, I would like you to spend time talking with those around you about some of your memories. For next week please bring in a picture or a written memory of your loved one, along with some music that reminds you of him/her."

   Members can begin their memory boxes by cutting out pictures and/or words from magazines that remind them of the deceased. Have students paperclip them and leave in their folders until next week.

End
First through their journals and then through sharing with the large group, have students respond to the following statements:

"I learned . . ."

"One way I can use what I learned is . . ."

Session 6
Topic: Rituals

Resources

- Small boxes
- Collage materials
- Glue sticks
- Tape and/or CD player

Beginning

Have students respond to the statement, "I feel happy when . . .".

REVIEW

Allow students time to express their reactions to last week's session.

Middle

1. While playing music that members brought to session, allow time to complete memory boxes. Instruct members to decoupage all the magazine pictures and words from last week onto their boxes.

2. Go around the group and have members share either about the memory object that they brought in or the pictures and words they chose for their boxes.

3. "Our society utilizes various services for memory rituals. Funeral services, memorial services, and services of remembrance are all types of ritual services that help grieving individuals obtain closure or reach acceptance after the death of a loved one. If you attended any service for your loved one, please share what it was like, how you felt about going, and anything you would have changed about it."

Encouraging group members to share about these experiences may evoke intense emotions. Responding genuinely with warmth and caring will create an atmosphere that encourages members in releasing their grief, and will ultimately assist them in healing from their loss.

End

First through their journals and then through sharing in the large group, have students respond to the following statements:

"I learned . . ."
"I relearned . . ."
"I need to . . ."

Session 7
Topic: Bibliotherapy, preparing for termination

Resources

- Book about death (recommended: *The Fall of Freddie the Leaf*, by Leo Buscaglia)
- List of grief-related resources available for students
- Gains from Loss handout

Beginning

Have students respond to the statement, "Over the past sessions I have felt that . . .".

REVIEW

Allow members time to process some of the previous material discussed in the group.

Middle

1. Read a book to the members about death. Recommended is *The Fall of Freddie the Leaf*, written by Leo Buscaglia.

2. Have group members share their individual interpretations of the meaning of the story. In addition, encourage them to discuss any other books on the topic of death that they have read. Provide members with a bibliotherapy list of appropriate grief books from the resource list at the beginning of this chapter, along with any others gathered from your local library or bookstores.

3. "As we approach our last meeting, I would like you to think about how you feel about the work you have done in these sessions and if you wish you had done anything differently. In addition, I would also like you to reflect upon how you feel about the group coming to an end and identify individuals outside the group from whom you can receive support."

Preparing group members for termination will help them make a sustained effort to review and think through the specifics of the work they have done. The facilitator can explore the issue of separation and encourage members to look for support in their relationships outside the group. Specific plans for follow-up work and evaluation should be made and confirmed during the last session.

4. "Before closing today's session I would like to highlight some of the long-term gains that you may experience from working through your loss. The following list is taken from research done by an unknown author; it is titled 'Gains from Loss.'" Distribute the Gains from Loss handout.

End

First through their journals and then through sharing in the large group, have students respond to the following statements:

"I learned . . ."

"One way I can use what I learned this week is . . ."

Name_____ Date_____

Gains from Loss

1. There is generally a strengthening effect on children/adolescents who have experienced a serious loss and worked through it.

2. They see themselves as "survivors," despite adverse situations.

3. They recognize the importance of family, friends, and life as gifts to be cherished, not taken for granted.

4. They are generally more sensitive and compassionate than most other children/adolescents.

5. They have faced grown-up issues early and tend to mature faster.

6. They often have a broader, more developed perspective on life.

7. They are generally more aware of pain and suffering in others.

8. They are the best examples for other kids/adolescents who are hurting and feel hopeless. Many of them become peer counselors or go into helping professions.

9. Many develop a stronger, deeper faith.

10. The healing usually draws siblings closer together.

11. These children/adolescents have learned successful coping skills that can be used to get them through any future losses.

Session 8
Topic: Review, share, close

Resources
- Group Evaluation form (page 10)

Beginning
Have students respond to the statement, "I hope . . .".

Middle
1. "Today will be our last consecutive session. I would like to confirm a follow-up date exactly one month from now. If anyone feels that he or she would like to schedule an individual appointment with me prior to that meeting, please feel free to do so at the end of our session today or as needed."

   One way of maximizing the chance that members will receive lasting benefits from the group is to arrange a follow-up session. This is especially true for grieving adolescents. As the adolescent progresses through developmental phases, he or she will experience the grief in a new way. Providing ongoing support is highly beneficial for these individuals.

2. "As a closing activity, I would like each of you to close your eyes and imagine all the events during the time we've been together. Play back the most significant events in your mind as if watching them on a videotape. What impressions are the strongest for you? What do you recall most clearly? What had the most meaning for you? Take a few moments. When you are ready, open your eyes and allow yourself to share with the rest of the group what you are recalling."

   Allow each member ample time to share responses.

3. Written evaluation (see Group Evaluation form).

End
Return folders that were used as journals to the members and have them share the following in the large group:

"Something I learned from being in this group is . . ."

1.5
Divorce/Changing Families

Grade Level: High School	Time Required: 6 Sessions	Author: Mary Mills

Purpose

To help students find healthy ways to manage the stress and turmoil that usually accompany parent divorce.

Students learn about the typical thoughts, feelings, and issues adolescents experience when their parents divorce. The focus is on building communication and coping skills to help students deal effectively with this serious life stressor.

Logistics

GROUP COMPOSITION

Students in grades 9–12 who have recently experienced the divorce of their parents

Students who are within 1–2 grade levels may be grouped.

GROUP SIZE

6–8 students

GROUP TIME PER SESSION

45–60 minutes

NUMBER OF SESSIONS

Six, with optional booster sessions spaced approximately one month apart after regular group ends

Recommended Resources

Full bibliographic details for these publications are included in the Bibliography at the end of this book.

Admunson-Beckman and Lucas, 1989: "Gaining a foothold in the aftermath of divorce."

Alpert-Gillis, Pedro-Carroll, and Cowen, 1989: "The Children of Divorce Intervention Program."

Cordell and Bergman-Meador, 1991: "The use of drawings in group intervention for children of divorce."

Crosbie-Burnett and Newcomer, 1990: "Group counseling children of divorce."

Garvin, Leber, and Kalter, 1991: "Children of divorce."

Grych and Fincham, 1992: "Interventions for children of divorce."

Jackson, 1998: *When Your Parents Split Up.*

Marta and Laz, 1997: *Rainbows: Facilitator Component Module.*

O'Rourke and Worzybt, 1996: *Support Groups for Children.*

Rose, 1998: *Group Work with Children and Adolescents.*

Session 1
Topic: Sharing family situations

Resources
- Sentence Completion 1 handout

Beginning
1. Review the purpose of the group. (Purpose was covered in pre-group screening, and permission letter was given at that time.)
2. Explain that students who have experienced the divorce or separation of their parents have found group sessions such as this helpful because they can share their feelings with students who have similar experiences; and that feeling alone, confused, angry, ashamed are all normal feelings and represent the different stages that we go through when we have a breakup in our family. The purpose of this group is to help students find healthy ways to manage the stress and turmoil that usually accompany parent divorce or separation.

INTRODUCTIONS
Ask students to interview a partner and then introduce the partner to the group. Find out: name, grade, birth order (oldest, youngest, middle, only), and one thing the partner does to cope with stress. After interviews are complete ask students to introduce their partners.

GROUP RULES
Ask students to develop rules for group to ensure that everyone feels safe sharing ideas and feelings.

Be sure to include: Right to pass, no put-downs, and confidentiality (you own what you say and can share with whom you like, but you do not own what others say and should keep everyone else's comments in the group).

Middle
1. After introductions, use a go-round to hear from each student a brief summary of family situation (how long parents separated or divorced, with whom students are living, and their biggest family concerns at this time). This is an important time for the leader to use facilitation skills to link/connect/universalize similar ideas, feelings, and situations and to model effective listening and respect/caring.
2. Distribute Sentence Completion 1 handout. Have students discuss these three questions in pairs.
3. Then have pairs share with the group what it was like to discuss the sentences with their partner. Next, go through each sentence and ask volunteers to share their ideas/feelings.

End
1. Use a go-round and have each group member complete the following statement: "Today in group, I learned . . .".
2. Preview next meeting.

Name_____ Date_____

Sentence Completion 1

Directions: Complete each of the following statements.

1. When I first found out that my parents were getting a divorce, I felt _____

   _____

   _____

   _____

   _____

   _____

   _____

   _____

2. One thing that has improved since the divorce/separation is _____

   _____

   _____

   _____

   _____

   _____

   _____

3. One thing that I miss is _____

   _____

   _____

   _____

   _____

   _____

   _____

Session 2
Topic: Coping with stress

Resources

- Stress Coping Self-Monitoring handout
- Folders for students
- Sentence Completion 2 handout

Beginning

1. Introduce the Stress Coping Self-Monitoring sheet.

   "When a family goes through a divorce or separation it is usually a very stressful time for all family members.

   "Our feelings and energy are indicators of how we are coping with the stress. The self-monitoring sheet can help you keep track of your stress level and improve your stress coping skills."

2. Go over the seven items with the group and have them fill out the form as you go. Next have them share their responses with a partner.

3. Last, have volunteers share what it was like for them to share these answers with their partner.

PROCESS FOR USING THE STRESS COPING HANDOUT

1. Provide a folder for each student. Throughout the course of this group, you should have students complete the Stress Coping handout each week and compare it with previous weeks to look for patterns.

2. When students have completed the Stress Coping handout, have them pair-share two or three of the most significant items from the Stress Coping sheet.

3. Use "How many of you" questions for each item, asking for raise of hand or thumbs-up. *Example:* "How many rated mood/feelings for the week at 7 or more or at 4 or below?"

   "How many rated mood higher this week than last?"

4. Discuss the connection between mood and energy and the other items. Note that we have a lot of control over items 3–7. These in turn have a lot of control over items 1–2.

   Spend 5–10 minutes per session on this very important activity.

Middle

1. Ask group members to discuss in pairs Sentence Completion 2 handout.

2. Ask pairs to share answers with group.

3. Next, ask individuals to write anonymous "Dear Abby" letters to be turned in and discussed at the next session. The letter should reflect a current problem the student is experiencing because of the changes in the family. Collect the letters in a box and keep for next time.

End

1. Ask students to share with partner their response to these two sentence stems: "Today in group, I learned . . ." and "One way I can use what I learned is . . .". Ask for volunteers to share answers with entire group.

2. Preview next meeting.

Name_____ Date_____

Stress Coping Self-Monitoring

Directions: Rate each of the following on a 1–10 scale, where 1 is the lowest/negative and 10 is the highest/positive.

1. Feelings and moods My most positive feelings were _____ and were connected to high points: _____ (experience events)	1 2 3 4 5 6 7 8 9 10
My most negative feelings were _____ and were connected to low points: _____ (experience events)	1 2 3 4 5 6 7 8 9 10
2. Energy My average energy level for the last week: My energy level for today/right now:	1 2 3 4 5 6 7 8 9 10 1 2 3 4 5 6 7 8 9 10
3. Food/Nutrition _____ I ate better/more healthily this week compared to my usual. _____ I ate worse/less healthily this week than usual.	1 2 3 4 5 6 7 8 9 10 1 2 3 4 5 6 7 8 9 10
4. Exercise _____ I exercised at least 3 times this week for at least 30 minutes each time.	1 2 3 4 5 6 7 8 9 10

(continued)

Group Counseling for School Counselors: A Practical Guide

Name_____ Date _____

Stress Coping Self-Monitoring *(continued)*

5. Sleep Check all that apply: _____ I got 7–10 hours of sleep most nights. _____ I have trouble going to sleep. _____ I wake up and can't go back to sleep. _____ I sleep 10 or more hours regularly.	1 2 3 4 5 6 7 8 9 10
6. Fun How much fun I had this week:	1 2 3 4 5 6 7 8 9 10
7. Social support My level of social support this week with friends: with family:	1 2 3 4 5 6 7 8 9 10 1 2 3 4 5 6 7 8 9 10

Name_____ Date_____

Sentence Completion 2

Directions: Complete each of the following statements.

1. One way I have changed since the divorce/separation is _____

   _____

   _____

   _____

   _____

   _____

   _____

   _____

2. The biggest change since the divorce/separation has been _____

   _____

   _____

   _____

   _____

   _____

   _____

3. Something I still do not understand is _____

   _____

   _____

   _____

   _____

   _____

   _____

   _____

Group Counseling for School Counselors: A Practical Guide

Session 3
Topic: Dear Abby (problem solving)

Resources
- Student folders
- Stress Coping Self-Monitoring handout (page 70)
- "Dear Abby" letters written during Session 2

Beginning
1. Go over the seven-item Stress Coping Self-Monitoring handout with the group and have them fill out the form as you go.
2. Have students share their responses with a partner.
3. Last, have volunteers share any patterns they discovered from looking at this week's and last week's stress coping handout.

Middle
1. Discuss the "Dear Abby" letters. This is a chance to introduce problem solving and to reinforce healthy alternative ways to manage difficult situations.

   Sample questions for discussion include: What would you do in that situation? How would that alternative affect you, others? What else could you do? Who agrees that this alternative would be a good one? Who thinks there are some problems with this alternative? What are they?

2. Choose a situation that has a lot of common ground and set up a role-play to demonstrate positive ways to handle it.
3. Ask for a volunteer to take the lead role. The lead role person then selects students to play the other role(s).
4. Ask students to evaluate the role-play, sharing positives first, then ideas for improving how the situation was handled.
5. Have students with the best alternatives role-play how it would go.
6. Again, have the group give feedback.

End
1. Ask students to share with partners their responses to these two sentence stems: "Today in group, I learned . . ." and "One way I can use what I learned is . . .". Ask for volunteers to share answers with entire group.
2. Preview next meeting.

Session 4
Topic: Communicating with parents

Resources

- Student folders
- Stress Coping Self-Monitoring handout (page 70)

Beginning

1. Go over the Stress Coping Self-Monitoring handout with the group and have them fill out the form as you go.
2. Next have them share their responses with a partner.
3. Last, have volunteers share any patterns they discovered from looking at this week's and the last two weeks' stress coping questions.

Middle

1. Ask the group to discuss the following statements.

   "I can tell if Mom/Dad is really listening to me when . . ."

   "When I have something bothering me, I let them know by . . ."

   "When they start giving advice, I feel . . ."

   "I am willing to listen to them if . . ."

   "The best time to talk with Mom/Dad is . . ."

   "When the parent I am visiting makes negative comments about my other parent, . . ."

2. Discuss with students appropriate times to talk with parents. Talk about adult moods and the best way to introduce a topic.

ROLE-PLAY

1. Ask students to choose a situation to role-play based on today's discussion.
2. Choose a situation that has a lot of common ground and set up a role-play to demonstrate positive ways to handle it.
3. Ask for a volunteer to take the lead role. The lead role person then selects students to play the other role(s).
4. Ask students to evaluate the role-play, sharing positives first, then ideas for improving how the situation was handled.
5. Have students with the best alternatives role-play how it would go.
6. Again, have the group give feedback.

End

1. Ask students to share with partner their responses to these two sentence stems: "Today in group, I learned . . ." and "One way I can use what I learned is . . .". Ask for volunteers to share answers with the entire group.
2. Preview next session.

Session 5
Topic: True-false questionnaire

Resources
- Student folders
- Stress Coping Self-Monitoring handout (page 70)
- True-False Questionnaire

Beginning
1. Go over the Stress Coping Self-Monitoring handout with the group and have them fill out the form as you go.
2. Next have them share their responses with a partner.
3. Last, have volunteers share any patterns they discovered from looking at this week's and the last three weeks' stress coping questions.

Middle
1. Introduce the True-False Questionnaire. Ask pairs to discuss and reach consensus on each item.
2. Next, ask pairs to report their conclusions to the group. Invite the group to discuss possible positive and negative consequences to various answers given.

ROLE-PLAY
1. Choose a situation that has a lot of common ground and set up a role-play to demonstrate positive ways to handle it.
2. Ask for a volunteer to take the lead role. The lead role person then selects students to play the other role(s).
3. Ask students to evaluate the role-play, sharing positives first, then ideas for improving how the situation was handled.
4. Have the students with the best alternatives role-play how they would go.
5. Again, have the group give feedback.

End
1. Ask students to share with partner their response to these two sentence stems: "Today in group, I learned . . ." and "One way I can use what I learned is . . .". Ask for volunteers to share answers with the entire group.
2. Preview next meeting.

Name_____ Date _____

True-False Questionnaire

Directions: Decide whether each statement below is true or false. Mark statements "T" for true or "F" for false.

1. _____ Parents who don't love each other should stay together for the sake of the children.

2. _____ Parents should tell their children why they are getting a divorce.

3. _____ If your parents are divorced, it is likely that when you grow up, you will get a divorce.

4. _____ The parent that you visit should not have rules or make you work.

5. _____ One parent should not make negative comments about the other parent.

6. _____ Your stepparent has no right to discipline you.

7. _____ Children should be included in the decision of whom the parent remarries.

8. _____ Children should not let their parents know how they feel about the divorce.

9. _____ A child should try to make up for the parent who has left by taking on extra responsibilities and being an emotional support to the parent he or she is living with.

10. _____ Children should be able to decide which parent they want to live with.

       Group Counseling for School Counselors: A Practical Guide

Session 6
Topic: Review, spotlighting, closure

Resources

- Student folders
- Stress Coping Self-Monitoring handout
- Index cards or sheets of paper
- Group Evaluation form (page 10)

Beginning

1. Go over the Stress Coping Self-Monitoring handout with the group and have them fill out the form as you go.
2. Next, have them share their responses with a partner.
3. Last, have volunteers share any patterns they discovered from looking at this week's and the last four weeks' stress coping questions.
4. Review the previous five small group sessions. Then ask the following questions:
   - What are some the most important things you have learned about yourself?
   - What has been the most helpful part of this group for you?
   - What is a goal you have set for yourself?

Middle

ACCEPTING AND GIVING COMPLIMENTS

1. Hand out index cards or sheets of paper. Each person is to write down at least one thing he or she admires, likes, or appreciates about each of the other group members.
2. Spotlight: Ask each group member to say directly to the spotlighted person, with eye contact: "[Person's name], one thing I admire, like, or appreciate about you is . . .".
   Explain and give examples of the types of qualities you are asking the students to think of and how to say and receive them. Ask students not to use appearance compliments such as "I like your shirt, shoes, hair," etc., but rather qualities or actions.
3. After each comment, the spotlighted person says "thank you," nothing else. (Be sure you get in on this—it feels good.)

End

1. Process the spotlighting activity. How did it feel receiving compliments? Giving compliments?
2. Students complete anonymous evaluation.
3. Concluding remarks. Invite students to make individual appointments if they want. Remind them of the monthly follow-up sessions if any are planned.

1.6
Pregnancy Education

Grade Level: High School	Time Required: 6 Sessions	Author: Maryanne Brannigan Grimes

Purpose

To provide factual information on the birthing process to pregnant teens

To educate students about options and alternatives available to pregnant teens

To provide a safe atmosphere for pregnant teens to explore their feelings concerning their pregnancy

Logistics

GROUP COMPOSITION

Pregnant girls. Also, statistics show that 50 percent of all pregnant teens drop out of school. I have found this to be true. For this reason, teen mothers might be invited to join.

GROUP SIZE

7–8 students

GROUP TIME PER SESSION

45–60 minutes

NUMBER OF SESSIONS

Six, with optional follow-up sessions

GROUP RULES

1. Everything that is said is confidential.
2. No question is stupid.
3. Don't press your values/beliefs on other group members.

Recommended Resources

Full bibliographic details for these publications are included in the Bibliography at the end of this book.

DiClemente, 1992: *Adolescents and AIDS.*

Hechinger, 1992: *Fateful Choices.*

McWhirter et al., 1998: *At Risk Youth.*

Miller et al., 1992: *Preventing Adolescent Pregnancy.*

Musick, 1993: *Young, Poor, and Pregnant.*

Session 1
Topic: Get acquainted

Resources

- Get Acquainted handout
- 3 × 5 index cards
- Pencils
- Grapes, bowl

Beginning

GRAPE ACTIVITY

Give each student a grape. Have students examine their grapes and get to know them. Then have them put the grapes back in a bowl. Shake them up and ask the students to find "their" grape. Usually they aren't sure if they're finding the right grape. It's difficult to know someone unless you learn about him or her—looking at the surface isn't always enough.

Middle

1. Distribute the Get Acquainted handout.
2. Allow students five minutes to complete the sheets.

3. Have students form pairs and discuss their answers with their partners.
4. After sufficient time has passed, have students form a circle and introduce their partners to the group.
5. Talk about group rules. If students would like to add another one or two, allow them to do so. Keep the rules simple.
6. Going around the circle, have students complete the statement, "I hope to get/gain/learn _____ from this group . . .".
7. Give students index cards to write down any questions they might be too embarrassed to verbalize. (Using index-card questions, modify future lesson plans as needed. You may want to address a few of these questions during each session, and allow several more opportunities for students to write anonymous questions.)

End

Each student completes the following sentence: "Today I learned . . .".

Parent Letter

Dear Parent:

   Your daughter, _____, has expressed an interest in being involved in a pregnancy education/support group.

   The group will meet once a week and will allow your child to meet with other pregnant teens. The group will be led by a trained counselor who is skilled in promoting a safe atmosphere for communication. The basic ground rule is strict confidentiality.

   Students involved in the group will miss class once a week (during a different class period each week) and have agreed to make arrangements in advance to remain current in their class work.

   If you would like further information on this group please feel free to contact me at

_____.

Counselor

_____

Please sign below if you agree to allow your child to participate in this group.

_____

Name_____ Date_____

Get Acquainted

Directions: Answer the following questions and then share the information with your partner.

1. What is your name? Are you the oldest, middle, youngest, or only child in your family? _____
   _____

2. Who are you most like in your family? Why? _____
   _____

3. Who do you think loves you most in the world? (can be more than one person)
   _____
   _____

4. What do you enjoy doing in your spare time? _____
   _____

5. What do you like best about yourself? _____
   _____

6. If you could change one thing about yourself, what would it be, and why?
   _____
   _____

7. Where do you think you'll be in five years, and what do you think you'll be doing?
   _____
   _____

8. Whom are you depending on most right now? _____
   _____

Session 2
Topic: Pregnancy quiz, egg babies

Resources

- Hard-boiled eggs—half marked with pink dots, half with blue
- Small wicker baskets to carry eggs in
- Pregnancy Quiz handout

Beginning

REVIEW

In the last session students learned each other's names and a little about each other. Have each student recall something she remembers about a member of the group.

Middle

1. Students will each reach into a bag and select a hard-boiled "egg baby." If it has a blue dot, it's a boy; if it has a pink dot, it's a girl. Allow students to draw faces on their babies and ask them to talk about what they think their real baby will look like. Evaluate students' reality level by listening to how they describe what their babies will look like in the future.

2. After students have finished decorating their egg babies, explain the rules for the egg-baby assignments.

   (a) Students must keep their eggs with them at all times, or they must hire a responsible babysitter.

   (b) Students must keep a realistic diary of feedings, diaper changes, and hours of sleep.

   (c) They will report back to the group in a week.

3. Hand out the pregnancy quiz and allow time for students to complete it.

4. Discuss correct/incorrect answers and clear up any misconceptions.

5. Ask if there is anything else students would like to discuss.

6. End with the open-ended statement, "What I liked most/least about this session was . . .".

PREGNANCY QUIZ ANSWERS

1. T
2. F Pregnancy is not a time to diet. The developing baby needs nutrients to grow.
3. T
4. F Anything you feel the effects of, the baby can feel the effects of. It is dangerous to use drugs or alcohol.
5. F You should consult your doctor before continuing your regular exercise program, but exercise is a good habit that usually can be continued during pregnancy.
6. F In many ways the first three months are the most important. Bad habits should be corrected.
7. F Most women report that they feel tired more during the first three months than they do during the rest of the pregnancy.
8. T
9. F Do not feel intimidated by doctors or nurses. Ask.
10. F Smoking during pregnancy can reduce oxygen to the developing fetus and can result in low birth weight.

End

Students complete the following: "Today I was surprised that . . .".

Name_____ Date _____

Pregnancy Quiz

Directions: Put a **T** on the line if the statement is true, an **F** if the statement is false.

_____ 1. A woman must eat carefully to supply adequate protein, carbohydrates, and fat to the fetus.

_____ 2. A woman can safely diet during pregnancy.

_____ 3. Common discomforts of pregnancy include nausea, constipation, heartburn.

_____ 4. It is okay to use drugs or alcohol during pregnancy as long as it is in moderation.

_____ 5. You should stop exercising when you find out you are pregnant.

_____ 6. The first three months of pregnancy are the least important, so you may continue old habits without care.

_____ 7. During the first three months of pregnancy the mother will probably have extra energy.

_____ 8. Prenatal vitamins guarantee that the mother receives needed nutrients.

_____ 9. Because you are a teen, you have no rights concerning your health care.

_____ 10. Smoking is not harmful to the developing baby.

Session 3
Topic: Personal Issues

Resources

- Personal Issues handout
- Pencils

Beginning

Each student in the circle will briefly tell the group about her last doctor's appointment and what she learned.

Middle

1. Moving around the circle, have each student report on her egg-baby experience.
2. Discuss with students the differences between this activity and real life. (Pregnant teens are often unaware of the realities of having a baby. They imagine a dream-like existence after the baby is born. Your goal as group leader is to help them understand the reality of having a baby.)
3. Using the Personal Issues handout, ask the questions one at a time and allow students time to answer.
4. End with a summary of the discussion and, if necessary, what question the group will begin with next week.
5. This lesson plan may be used for two sessions if trust level is high and students do not get through all the questions. Modify future lesson plans accordingly.

End

Students complete the sentence, "Today I learned . . .".

Name_____ Date _____

Personal Issues

Be prepared to discuss the following questions with the group.

1. Do you have any definite plans for after the birth of the baby?

2. How has your relationship with the father of the baby changed since you found out you were pregnant?

3. How did your parents react when you told them you were pregnant, and how has your relationship with them changed since you told them?

4. Have you lost any friends because you are pregnant? Have your friends supported your decisions concerning this pregnancy?

5. Do you see yourself any differently than before you became pregnant?

6. Are you planning on staying in school? If yes, how will you manage school and your baby? If no, what will you be doing instead?

7. Are you receiving regular prenatal care, and with whom?

8. What are you most afraid of concerning this pregnancy?

9. How do you think having a baby will change your life?

10. If you could change one thing in your life right now, other than being pregnant, what would it be?

Session 4
Topic: Relaxation, labor and delivery

Resources

- Relaxation tape or exercise
- Guest speaker from hospital, clinic, birthing center, Lamaze, or Better Birth Foundation

Beginning

Using any relaxation tape or relaxation exercise, have students learn the value of relaxation. Remind them that this will be useful when they go into labor.

REVIEW

Have students talk about something they learned from the last session.

Middle

1. Have a guest speaker from a hospital, clinic, or birthing center show pictures of the fetus and the stages of labor and delivery, and explain them. The speaker should also tell students about the kinds of painkillers that are available and their effects.

2. Students will ask the speaker questions. (Students may have so many questions that you may want to lengthen the session or have one speaker to discuss the developing fetus and one to discuss the labor process.)

End

Each student completes the following: "Today I was surprised about . . ."

Session 5
Topic: Teen mother presentations

Resources

- Two or three teen mothers (don't get them all from your school), including:
  A teen mother who dropped out of school
  A teen who gave her baby up for adoption

Beginning

REVIEW

Have students talk about something they learned from the last session.

Play a round of "telephone." Make up a story about yourself and include details. Have students whisper the message from one to another, and have the last student tell the message to the group. The message has usually been altered. Explain to the students that listening to "others" rather than to the actual source of information is usually the reason for misconceptions. That is why you are providing them with the source of information: teen mothers who will tell them about their experiences.

Middle

1. Remind students of the values rule and confidentiality rule.

2. Ask each mother to tell her story, including the decision-making processes that she went through. Ask that each include how she feels about those decisions now. Also ask those who kept their babies to talk about their responsibilities and how they manage school, or to share their feelings about dropping out if that was their choice.

3. Allow students time to ask questions. If students don't have enough time to answer/ask all the questions that they need to, you may ask the mothers if they feel comfortable giving out their phone numbers so that students can call with further questions.

End

Students complete the statement, "Today I learned . . .".

Session 6
Topic: Closure, evaluation

Resources

- Envelopes
- Strips of paper with group members' names on them. Make enough so that each student has a strip with every other group member's name on it.
- Pregnancy Group Evaluation form

Beginning

Hand each student strips of paper with group members' names on them. Have each write a positive message or wish to each girl. Collect all the messages and sort them by name, then give each group member an envelope of wishes.

Middle

1. Remind students that because this is the last session, they can deal with new material on an individual basis with the counselor.
2. Ask if there are any unresolved issues that should be dealt with before the group ends.

End

1. Allow students to share feelings about the group's end.
2. Have students complete group evaluation.
3. Make arrangements with individuals to meet their specific needs.

Note: Use the results of the evaluations to modify future groups.

Name_____ Date_____

Pregnancy Group Evaluation

Directions: Please answer these questions as honestly as possible. Your answers will help us to modify future groups.

1. Was the group what you expected it to be? _____
_____

2. Did you receive all the information you needed from group sessions? If not, what should be added?
_____
_____

3. Would you prefer to meet individually with your counselor to discuss your situation, or do you prefer group sessions?
_____
_____

4. Which group sessions were most helpful? _____
_____

5. Which sessions were least helpful, and why? _____
_____
_____

6. What can you suggest that would improve the group experience? _____
_____
_____

7. Do you feel that pregnancy support/education groups should be offered to pregnant teens in the future?
_____
_____

8. On a scale of 1 to 10, 10 being the best, how would you rate the overall group experience?

   1   2   3   4   5   6   7   8   9   10

1.7
Transition—The Buddy System

Grade Level: Freshmen and Seniors in High School	Time Required: 7 Sessions	Author: Gayle Kelley

Note: For an additional plan for students who are transitioning into new schools, see Part 4 in this volume, Group Plans for All Levels (page 289).

Purpose

The purpose of this group is to team a senior who previously had difficulties in school—such as academic failure, attendance, and/or peer relationships—with a freshman having similar difficulties.

GOALS AND OBJECTIVES

- To aid freshmen/seniors in enhancing self-empowering beliefs
- To improve peer relationships
- To give students a better understanding of the skills necessary for a successful high school career
- To improve communication skills
- To improve academic performance
- To facilitate students' ability to request help when needed
- To help students recognize problem areas and seek appropriate help
- To encourage student participation in extracurricular/community activities
- To help students access and better understand their feelings
- To help students recognize how the need for approval shapes behavior, thoughts, feelings, and actions
- To facilitate sharing ideas for success

Logistics

GROUP COMPOSITION

Freshmen having some difficulty in school (academic, social, etc.) and seniors who coped with similar problems

GROUP SIZE

8–12 freshmen plus 8–12 seniors

GROUP TIME PER SESSION

45 minutes

NUMBER OF SESSIONS

Seven

Method

- Request names of freshmen and seniors from teachers, administrators, and counselors.
- Ask seniors if they would like to be a buddy. Ask freshmen who need support if they would like to have a buddy. (Seniors participating in the Buddy System frequently have had previous training as peer helpers. In addition, they will have 2–5 training sessions according to their need. Ongoing training as the program progresses is tailored to the specific needs of the buddies, i.e., tutoring skills, encouragement skills, and listening/problem-solving skills. For a listing of specific peer-training materials, see the Resources listed at the end of this section.)
- Team the senior and the freshman based on the information available (sex, same number of courses failed, attendance problems, similar home situations, etc.) so that a common bond can be more readily formed.
- Give a permission slip to both seniors and freshmen, and relate details and purpose of the program.
- After permission slips have been returned, issue a group pass to each student.

Sample Pass to Buddy Group

Dear _____

This is your pass to the group meetings on the below listed dates. Please check in with your teacher and then come directly to the counselor's office. We will start right after the bell. Please have your teacher initial this pass before coming to group.

Session #			
1	Wednesday, (month, day)		1st period
2	_____		2nd period
3	_____		3rd period
4	_____		4th period
5	_____		5th period
6	_____		6th period
7	_____		TBA

See you Wednesday.

Note: Many teachers find it very helpful to know the exact day the students will be absent from their class. They record it on their attendance register and find that on some days, due to various school functions, activities, group meetings, prearranged absences, etc., they would be wise to plan an alternate lesson rather than have a majority of students miss an important lecture or test. This is helpful in creating a cooperative atmosphere between teachers and the counseling department.

Scheduling

Sessions 1 and 2 should take place in the same month. Sessions 3, 4, and 5 should take place once a month. Sessions 6 and 7 should take place in the same month. All group sessions after Session 1 include seniors and their freshman buddies.

The primary activity will occur between seniors and freshmen outside of group sessions. The basic assumption is that the freshmen will listen, relate to, and incorporate information from the seniors more readily than from "just one more adult." The meetings may occur in any number of locations, such as the peer counselor/leader room, media center, classroom after school, the individuals' homes, or perhaps a local favorite such as McDonald's or Burger King.

The purpose of the group sessions is to bring together these individuals and introduce activities that will stimulate ideas that they can use for themselves or with their buddy. The activities are experiential and designed to have the students use various methods of identifying and solving problems.

The counselor may wish to have both freshmen and seniors meet together for all sessions. If this is done, the counselor needs to schedule separate meetings for the freshmen and seniors at least every other month.

The purpose of having freshmen and seniors meeting separately is to have time to process the buddy meetings without the buddy being present. It has been found that problems may be occurring and the buddy does not address the issue because the other buddy is present. Also, buddies may simply feel that it is not a problem of any major concern that needs to be addressed to the group. However, if a session is limited to just freshmen or just seniors, these problems can be addressed. The counselor must ask for concerns of the group members: Does their buddy seem to be giving too much advice, or is he/she not keeping appointments with them? Once the conversation begins, both positive and negative comments are expressed concerning the buddies. The group process begins so that the others can offer what has worked for them or say that the problem also exists for them.

The counselor may wish to have every other session one in which freshmen and seniors meet separately. Any number of arrangements can be used so that not only is the cohesiveness of the group members considered, but so also is the need for discussion of their buddies without hesitation or embarrassment.

Seniors will be required to keep a log or calendar to record contacts with the buddy. Seniors may contact the counselor at any time to discuss a buddy or to ask for additional study information.

Evaluation

The Buddy System is designed to start a few weeks after the beginning of a semester and to conclude a few weeks before the end of that same semester. Therefore, all pre-assessments of attendance and grades are based on the previous semester. All post-assessments are based on the final grades and attendance of the current semester.

A pre-behavior rating scale and self-esteem inventory, such as the Cooper-Smith Self-Esteem Inventory, should be distributed/administered at the beginning of the group (preferably before Session 1). The post-assessments of the same should be distributed/administered at the conclusion of the group sessions.

Seniors	Freshmen
Pre- and Post-Assessments	Pre- and Post-Assessments
Grades	Grades
Self-esteem	Self-esteem
	Attendance
	Behavior Rating Scale

Data on the freshmen are necessary for the accountability of the group. The additional data on the seniors are optional, but may provide pertinent information concerning the effectiveness of the program for seniors as well as freshmen.

Recommended Resources

Full bibliographic details for these publications are included in the Bibliography at the end of this book.

Brigman and Earley, 1990: *Peer Helping*.

Myrick, 1998: *Development Guidance and Counseling*.

National Peer Helpers Association.

Tindall, 1995: *Peer Counseling*

Parent Letter

Dear Parent:

At _____ High School we are constantly trying to improve our services to students and parents. Your son or daughter has been selected for a Support for Freshman Transition project called The Buddy System. This project pairs seniors with freshmen to provide mentoring. Seven small-group sessions are conducted by the school counselor. Additional mentoring time is encouraged for each pair. We will be monitoring grades, attendance, and behavior to determine the success of the project.

If you have any questions, or do not want your child involved in this project, please inform me by calling _____.

Sincerely,

Counselor

My son or daughter, _____, has my permission to attend the pilot Buddy System project. I understand that my student will miss no more than one class period of each subject (the group will rotate the meeting through the six class periods). The student is responsible for obtaining work that he/she will miss due to the group meeting.

_____   _____
               signature   date

Session 1
Topic: Introduction, ground rules, and guidelines

Resources
- Paper and pencils
- For seniors—Buddy System Criteria
- Poster board or chart paper
- Buddy System contract

For the first session, meet with seniors separately and then meet with freshmen.

Beginning

INTRODUCTION

Begin by explaining the purpose of the Buddy System and the group rules (confidentiality, attendance, no put-downs, and one person talking at a time). Also explain that whether in large-group session or in buddy session, the peer must report to the counselor and the counselor must report any information that might be viewed as a threat or potential threat to the life of the individual or another (this includes but is not limited to suicide; drug abuse; physical, emotional, or sexual abuse; or threats on the life of another) according to the policy set forth by the school.

Middle

Use the following activity to introduce group members to one another and to facilitate group cohesiveness.

THE INTERVIEW

1. Have students get into pairs. Supply each person with a sheet of paper and pencil. The first person interviews the second person so that the first person can introduce the second person to the group. (Allow three to four minutes.) Then the second person interviews the first person.

   When interviews are complete, begin with a volunteer to introduce his/her partner to the group. Continue around the circle. (Leader may preface activity by stating that we probably all feel uncomfortable introducing ourselves, so we will allow someone else to help us.)

2. From information gleaned from introductions, discuss similarities among group members. Continue discussion with the following questions:

- How do you feel about being chosen for the program?
- How do you feel about the nature of the program?

   Seniors: What do you think you can contribute to this freshman?

   Freshmen: What information or help do you want from this senior?

3. **Seniors:** Go over some of the techniques of information giving. Remind them not to give advice. Review use of I-messages, as opposed to you-messages; listening skills; use of feeling words. Supply seniors with a list of feeling words as well as a packet of study skills/test-taking information, log, and any other materials suitable for use.

   Freshmen: Have students make a list of the problems they encountered last semester that interfered with their academic/social success. What problems are they now encountering? Process their responses as a group and encourage them to share their responses with their senior buddies. (Leader writes problems on poster board to use in Session 6.)

End

Review similarities from introductions. Briefly restate ground rules. **Freshmen:** Have them review the kind of help they hope to receive from buddy. **Seniors:** Have them review the kind of help they hope to give buddy.

Double-check on names with "Good-bye _____" activity. Ask each student to turn to the person on the right and say "good-bye" and then that person's name. Repeat the process with the person on the left.

HOMEWORK

Seniors: Give students a copy of the Buddy System Criteria. Have them keep a record of sessions with buddy; include weekly grades, attendance, and goal. Remember the criteria established for the recording of sessions.

Freshmen: Keep a record of weekly grades and attendance. Distribute the Buddy System contract to students. Have them complete it and keep in their folders.

Name_____ Date_____

Buddy System Contract

I understand:

_____ that I have made a commitment to attend the group for consecutive sessions.

_____ that attendance will be taken in group and it is my responsibility to report to the group room and be ready to begin on time.

_____ that it is my responsibility to make arrangements in advance with classroom teachers for any work that I may miss by being in group.

_____ that it is my responsibility to keep what others say and do in group confidential.

_____ that the group leaders will also keep confidential what I say and do in group, involving other people only when they become concerned for my health, safety, or welfare.

_____ that all school policies regarding acceptable behavior apply to the group.

_____ that I am responsible for completing all assignments that are part of the group.

Signed: _____

(Student)

Name_____ Date_____

Buddy System Criteria

These are the requirements for a senior meeting with a freshman buddy.

1. There should be a meeting twice a week, preferably at the beginning of the week and near the end of the week. Occasionally, the meeting time may be limited to only once a week due to schedules and other difficulties. This should not occur more than twice for the entire length of the group session.

2. Seniors may use their scheduled meeting time for peer counseling, tutoring, support, or just building a rapport. Any problems such as abuse (within the family, or the individual abusing self or substances), suicide, or other major areas of concern should always be reported to the counselor immediately.

3. Seniors should feel free to consult with the counselor, teacher, or other professional support staff to obtain material, information, or support for helping their buddy. (They may ask the counselor for material for test-taking skills, a teacher for information regarding problem-solving techniques for a particular subject area, the media specialist for tutoring materials.)

4. Seniors will keep a record of their sessions with their buddy, using the Buddy Session Record form.

5. Seniors will give the record of these sessions to the Buddy System counselor at scheduled meetings or as directed by the counselor at times other than scheduled meetings. The counselor may wish to keep the record or simply review and return it to the senior.

Buddy Session Record

Name of Senior Buddy _____

Name of Freshman Buddy _____

Date and time	Location	Focus of session*	Attendance during last week	Weekly grades in core subjects	Behavior for last week	Next scheduled session's date, time, and location	Anticipated topic of next session

*Main focus of session—tutoring in math, peer counseling related to school, friends, etc.

Session 2
Topic: Commonalities, introducing buddy pairs

Resources

- Refreshments
- List of senior/freshmen buddy pairs

Preparation

Before beginning this session, you need to match senior and freshman buddies. Use information such as gender, similarity of home situations, similarity of school changes—e.g., attendance, similarity in number/type of courses failed, to make the best possible buddy pair matches.

Beginning

INTRODUCTION

Welcome both freshmen and seniors. Begin by stating the purpose and ground rules of the group. Preface the activity by stating that the activity will help us relax with one another and learn some interesting things about one another.

Middle

DOUBLE LINE

1. Begin by forming a double line with an equal number of students on both sides. Each line alternates seniors and freshmen. Each set of partners has 14 seconds to answer a question, 7 seconds each. ("Stop" will be called after 7 seconds as a signal to switch. Then "Move one person" will be called and the line on the right of the leader moves ahead one person (end person comes around to other end). Here are possible questions:

   - If you could spend an hour with a famous person, who would it be, and why?
   - If you had to live somewhere else for a year, where would it be?
   - Who is your hero/heroine, and why?
   - If you had to change your first name, what would the new one be, and why?
   - What is one thing about school you like and one thing you dislike?

   - What subject in school are you best at, and why?
   - What is one thing that makes you happy, and why?
   - What is your favorite (TV program, food, musical group, pastime, color, season, etc.), and why?
   - If you had to move to Pakistan next year, what would you miss most about the place where you now live?
   - What one change would you most like to see in our society?

   Allow the line to move completely through at least one time (more if you have time and see that the group is really enjoying the activity).

2. Discuss any similarities among students. Ask them to raise hands if their partner started a topic they would like to go back and discuss some more, or that they found interesting or funny. Remind them that making new friends is often very easy once you have something to talk about or share. The buddy system will give them an opportunity to share with one another.

End

EXCHANGE OF NAMES

Call names of buddy pairs. Ask students to write down their buddy's full name, address, phone number, schedule of classes and teachers (room numbers if possible), and list of after-school events in which they are participating (include days and practice times).

SUMMARY

After giving the buddy pairs ample time to exchange information, ask the group to remember that confidentiality extends into the buddy sessions with one another. Encourage them to continue with fellowship. Give homework assignment. Enjoy snacks and mingle.

HOMEWORK

Same as assignment from Session 1. Tell groups to wear slacks or shorts to next meeting.

Session 3
Topic: Cooperative skills, problem-solving skills

Beginning

Ask students to state their name and the problem areas in which they are working with their buddies. Allow for questions and any information-giving, as necessary.

Middle

ENTANGLEMENT

1. Students form a circle, arms crossed and outstretched in front of them. Each student reaches into center of the circle and grasps the hands of two people. (Make sure they are holding the hands of people other than those standing next to them.) Without releasing their grip, they must untangle the knot formed by the group. They should end up in a circle; however, some may be facing inward and some outward.

2. Ask the following questions: How did you feel at different times when untangling the knot? Use feeling words (e.g., confused, no direction, confident, excited when accomplished). What were some of the qualities of the people that helped untangle the group? Use feeling words (e.g., cooperation, leadership, acceptance, willingness to try). Relate these qualities to the buddy system.

End

Ask each person to state a feeling that came to them while tangling/untangling that might be a benefit in the process of helping/being helped by their buddy. *Example:* I need to be more accepting; buddy needs to be more excited about learning; etc.

Session 4
Topic: Feelings and our need for approval

Beginning

Have students share with the group successes with or concerns about buddy. Ask them to share how they or their buddy used what was learned in the last session.

Middle

"I AM"

1. This exercise is a series of unfinished statements. With the group in a circle, go around the room, having each member complete a different sentence with whatever comes to mind. Allow for a second or third round if participants are interested. Another alternative is to throw out several of the statements to the group as a whole. A discussion or elaboration may follow.

    I'm happiest when . . .

    In a group, I am . . .

    When I'm alone at home, I . . .

    Most people I know . . .

    I get angry when . . .

    What I want most in my life is . . .

    I often find myself . . .

    People who know me well think I am . . .

    I used to be . . .

    It makes me uncomfortable when . . .

    When people first meet me, they . . .

    When someone tries to bully me, I feel . . .

    When I'm on cloud nine, I feel . . .

    When someone praises my work, I feel . . .

    When I'm on a blind date, I feel . . .

    When people don't appreciate what I have done, I feel . . .

    When everyone is telling me what to do, I feel . . .

    When I'm loved, I feel . . .

    I have never liked . . .

    I trust those who . . .

    In a group, I am most afraid of . . .

    I respect . . .

    I feel irritated when . . .

    From past experiences, I believe teachers think I am . . .

    My family thinks that I am . . .

    What I like best at school is . . .

    Usually when the teacher calls on me, I feel . . .

    I would consider it risky to . . .

    I need to improve most in . . .

    It makes me proud . . .

    A good thing that happened recently was . . .

    Since last year, I have changed most in . . .

    Usually I don't like to talk about . . .

    People seem to like my . . .

2. Ask, "Did any of you not say your first thought because you were concerned about what others might think—that they might not approve of you or what you thought? Discuss how you felt when you realized that your first reaction might not be approved of by others. We all want the approval of others. How does this affect our conduct in class, study habits, projects, participation in class discussions, etc.? Do we always seek approval in positive ways? How so?

    "How does this discussion help you see yourself and help you relate to your buddy?"

End

Review the session, using students' statements about approval. Ask them to keep this session's discussion in mind while they silently respond to the following statement:

"Approval from others is more important to me than my own self-approval." (Respond with *strongly agree*; *agree*; *neutral*; *disagree*; or *strongly disagree*.)

Ask students to consider how their response relates to the way they approach academic/social activities (positive or negative). Ask them to keep their response in mind the next time a situation arises in which they withhold their first response or reaction (either positive or negative).

HOMEWORK

Write on paper an incident in which you changed your answer or behavior because of what others might think.

Session 5

Topic: Problem-solving skills, communication skills

Beginning

1. Ask for any questions or concerns.
2. Share homework assignment (how we changed an answer or action because of what others might think).
3. Have group discuss any common feelings or incidents.

Middle

BODY SCULPTURES

1. Introduce the concept of body sculptures. Using group members, sculpt a problem. (*Example:* A student talks to friend on phone while doing homework in the living room, where his little brother is playing a video game.) Place group members to show this scene. Discuss how you can actually see how this arrangement of people interferes with learning/studying. Resculpt with the friend waiting until the student finishes homework, the student in another room at a comfortable studying area/position, and the brother playing his video game in the living room. (This is a suggestion. Try to elicit a real problem from the group and sculpt it.)
2. Encourage other group members to discuss what is going on. *Example:* "Can you see anything that interferes with the student's studying? Can you see why his study efforts are being defeated? How can this be changed? Do it!"

3. Some problems may not lend themselves readily to sculpting, but an effort can be made. The idea is to visualize a problem and then change its direction. Others can learn from how a person changes his or her own personal situation.
4. "How did it feel to share the success of a problem conquered? How did it feel to 'look' at the problem? Could you 'see' why a situation might be difficult? When the situation changed, could you see as well as feel that the change was positive?"

End

Review what was learned in today's activity. Encourage group to visualize problems so that they can better work solutions. Suggest a problem area that they might work on next.

HOMEWORK

Ask the group to mentally sculpt a problem and then sculpt a solution. Ask them to write down the problem, the parts that contribute to the problem, and the solutions taken. *Example:*

Problem: Poor grades on homework

Parts that contribute: Friend on phone, brother playing game in same room, etc.

Solution: Have friend call later, study in own room or when brother is finished with game.

Suggest that visualizing a problem by sculpting with people or visualizing it on paper helps facilitate better solutions.

Session 6
Topic: Feelings, self-esteem, skills required for high school success

Beginning

Begin by sharing successes great and small.
Freshmen: How has your buddy helped you the most?
Seniors: How has your buddy improved? Do you think this is a worthwhile project? Why or why not? Any suggestions for the next group of buddies?

Middle

1. **Freshmen:** Bring out the list of problem areas from Session 1; cross off the successes. Ask students: "How does it feel to cross off some of the areas? How does it feel if some areas are still left?" (Words such as hopeful, small obstacles, inconvenient but obtainable, etc., will probably be used in discussing areas still left.)

   Seniors: Go over some of the communication skills taught in Session 1. Ask each senior how he/she used these skills with buddy.

2. Discuss: "How does it feel to have the group sessions over, as well as the buddy system? How can you use what you have learned now that the program is over?" (Encourage lots of feeling words.)

End

Each person takes a turn at completing the sentence stem, "At the beginning of the Buddy System I . . . but now I . . .". Process the feelings from the stem. Give an invitation to the total group get-together (Session 7).

HOMEWORK

Bring a goodie to share for the get-together.

Session 7
Topic: Peer relationships, group termination

Beginning

1. Both freshmen and seniors attend this meeting. Arrange the chairs in a large circle, and have buddy sit next to buddy.

2. Begin by stating that this is the final session of the Buddy System. Ask each buddy to say his/her own name and how he/she feels about helping or having been helped. Encourage open discussion. Point out similar problems and successes among buddy pairs.

Middle

1. Give each person a pen or pencil and a piece of paper. Ask buddies to write each other a thank-you note, mentioning specific instances that helped them or that they enjoyed. After notes are written, ask them to hold the notes until the conclusion of the session.

2. Discuss: "How did you feel as you wrote the note?" (Awkward, too much to say and not enough paper, embarrassed, nothing to say, etc.)

3. Would you recommend that the Buddy System be used again? Why or why not? List on paper the pros and cons.

4. Read pros and cons aloud after all the contributions have been made. Ask if the group agrees. Discuss with the group whether the Buddy System should be used again.

End

Ask each student to finish with a word or two of praise for his/her buddy (helpful, energetic, cooperative, knowledgeable, tries, works hard, creative, responsible, loads of patience, etc.). After all have had a chance to praise their buddy, the thank-you notes are exchanged. As students exchange notes, encourage them to share successes as they snack on refreshments and enjoy the fellowship of all the buddies.

HOMEWORK

Ask the group members to remember the lessons presented and to continue working on more successes. Since most of them have enjoyed the group, encourage them to become active in extracurricular/community activities. These activities will provide continued enjoyment, friendship, and success.

Part 2:
Middle School Group Plans

2.1
Academic and Social Support:
Student Success Skills

Grade Level: Middle School and High School	Time Required: 8 Sessions	Authors: Greg Brigman and Barbara Earley Goodman

Purpose

To provide support for underachieving students with the aim of improving academic performance

Logistics

Ten weekly group meetings, each lasting approximately 40 minutes, followed by monthly booster sessions Six–eight students per group

Background Information

Every school has students who are performing below their ability. These students may exhibit any or all of the following characteristics and behaviors: apathy, discouragement, disruptive behavior, slow learning, attendance problems, home problems, low motivation, or learning skills deficits.

This field-tested group plan has worked successfully with many students who fit one or more of these profiles.

The following steps are helpful for building success into your group program:

1. Ask teachers to identify students who are underperforming and not already receiving support services.

2. Invite students in for a pre-group screening. During the pre-group screening, explain the benefits of participating, discuss expectations for participation, help students begin to set goals, and answer any questions students may have. Use the Student Contract that follows to clarify the level of commitment you are asking of students.

3. Make sure the program is voluntary.

4. Inform parents about the benefits of the academic support group and ask them to sign a permission and commitment form, like the one on page 110.

5. It is very helpful to have parent-teacher conferences, telephone contact, and conferences with students individually as adjuncts to the group.

When these steps are followed, it is likely that students will rate this group experience as positive and helpful—and that their report cards will show marked improvement. This has been the case for the authors when conducting these groups.

Finally, some background information is important to keep in mind as you plan your academic support group:

A review of the research literature involving school counselor interventions with low-achieving and underachieving elementary-, middle-, and high-school students by Wilson (1982) and confirmed by Prout and Prout (1998) included the following:

1. Group counseling seems to be more effective than individual counseling.

2. Structured group programs are more effective than unstructured programs.

3. Group programs lasting eight weeks or less had positive results in only one of five programs evaluated. Of nine programs lasting between nine and twelve weeks, five were effective; however, six of eight interventions lasting more than twelve weeks were successful.

4. Programs in which children volunteered for treatment were more successful than programs with nonvoluntary participants.

5. Programs that combined counseling and study skills were most effective.

Recommended Resources

Full bibliographic details for these publications are included in the Bibliography at the end of this book.

Brigman and Earley, 1991: *Group Counseling for School Counselors.*

Brown, 1999a: "Improving academic achievement."

Brown, 1999b: *Proven Strategies for Improving Learning and Academic Achievement.*

Goldstein and McGinnis, 1997: *Skillstreaming the Adolescent.*

Hattie, Biggs, and Purdie, 1996: "Effects of learning skills interventions on student learning."

Lee, Winfield, and Wilson, 1991: "Academic behaviors among high-achieving African-American students."

McWhirter et al., 1998: *At Risk Youth.*

Masten and Coatsworth, 1998: "The development of competence in favorable and unfavorable environments."

Moote, Smythe, and Wodarsky, 1999: *Social Skills Training with Youth in School Settings: A Review.*

O'Rourke and Worzybt, 1996: *Support Groups for Children.*

Wang, Haertel, and Walberg, 1994: *Educational Resilience in Inner City America.*

Student Contract

I, _____, have agreed to join this group because

_____

_____

_____

I agree that:

_____ I will attend the group each week.

_____ I will share my ideas and feelings in group. I also have the right to pass.

_____ I will set reasonable grade goals for myself and work to achieve them.

_____ I will be present at school every day unless I am sick.

_____ I will do my homework each night.

_____ I will use an assignment notebook daily.

_____ I will turn all assignments in on time to avoid any zeros.

_____ I will use a folder or notebook for each subject.

Name: _____

Date: _____

Parent Letter—Student Success Skills

Dear Parent:

Your child, _____, has indicated an interest in participating in our Student Success Skills group. The purpose of the group, which meets once per week for 10 weeks, is to help students strengthen the skills needed to be successful academically. This is a voluntary program that has been helpful to students who have participated in the past. We hope you will support your child's decision to participate.

Attached is a copy of a contract your child has signed indicating his/her commitment to follow through on eight specific behaviors. We are also asking each parent to commit to the six specific behaviors on the attached sheet (although we realize that you may already be using these behaviors). Please complete the Suggestions for Parents form and return it to the counselor.

We are available to talk with you about your child's progress, and we appreciate your willingness to work with us to make this a good year for your child. Please let us know if you have questions about this program or anything else.

Sincerely,

School Counselor

Suggestions for Parents

_____ I will talk with my child in an encouraging manner about the Student Success Skills group and I support my child's commitment to the Student Contract.

_____ Together my child and I will decide on a specific study time and location that is free from distractions.

_____ I will sit down with my child for 10 minutes at the beginning or ending of the study time to review what was learned in each class that day and to find out if homework was assigned.

_____ I realize that school assignments are my child's responsibility and that I am not expected to do my child's homework or projects.

_____ I will arrange a conference with my child's teachers or counselor for suggestions on what to do at home to support my child's academic success.

_____ I will meet with my child at least once a week to discuss his/her progress.

I support my child's decision to participate in the Student Success Skills group and I commit to doing the six suggestions listed above.

Student Name: _____

Parent Signature: _____

Session 1
Topic: Self-evaluation, getting acquainted

Resources

- Student Self-Evaluation handout

Beginning

INTRODUCTION

1. Ask students to form pairs and interview each other in preparation for introducing their partner to the group. Pairs ask each other name, birth order (oldest, youngest, middle, only), and two things they do for fun.

2. Pairs introduce partners to group and group listens for similarities and differences.

3. Explain group purpose to students. *Example:* "We wanted to support you in being successful in school. We have a plan that has worked for students your age. For the next 10 weeks we are offering a group that will include activities on:
   - goal setting
   - tips to make learning faster and easier
   - communicating with your teacher
   - organization
   - motivation

   We will also be sending a letter to your parents explaining the group and asking them to encourage your efforts to improve."

GROUP RULES

Ask students to suggest rules for the group to work together well. Get consensus on any that you adopt. Ask a student to write these down. Make sure you include the following:

- Respect other's opinions—no put-downs.
- We encourage sharing ideas but you have the right to pass.

- Confidentiality—You own what you say and can tell who you want. You do not own what others say; what others say stays within the group.

Middle

1. Distribute the Student Self-Evaluation handout. Let the group know that each week they will go over these items and learn how to use problem solving to improve in any area where they are not doing as well as they would like.

2. Ask students to rate each of the 11 statements on a scale of 1–4. These are behaviors associated with students who are successful in school and who get along well with others. If students are willing to improve in these behaviors they will be more successful academically and socially.

3. Go through the statements, asking for ratings from each student. This usually generates discussion. You will need to keep the focus on accepting responsibility instead of blaming a teacher or others.

4. Let students know that the group meetings will address areas they feel need improvement.

Note: Repeated exposure to concrete examples of how to perform these essential skills is the core of this group. If deficits in reading and/or math are present it is advisable to also involve the student with tutoring.

End

1. Ask students to summarize purpose of group.

2. Ask students to write a specific goal based on one of the 11 areas from the Student Self-Evaluation form for this week.

3. Students share their goals with the group. After each goal is shared, have the entire group say in unison, "You can do it [name of student], go for it!"

4. Preview some of the areas of focus in the coming meetings.

Name_____ Date _____

Student Self-Evaluation

Directions: Rate yourself on a scale of 1–4 on each item below. Follow the rating system listed here.

1. outstanding   2. above average   3. satisfactory   4. needs improvement

I listen carefully and follow directions.	1	2	3	4
I participate in class discussion.	1	2	3	4
I know when and how to ask questions when I'm unsure or don't know.	1	2	3	4
I work well in small groups.	1	2	3	4
I get along well with others in class.	1	2	3	4
I read all assignments and understand what I read.	1	2	3	4
I complete work assigned on time; I do not get zeros.	1	2	3	4
I have at least one dependable study buddy in each class whom I can call at home for help.	1	2	3	4
I have a system to help me remember important facts and concepts, such as making an outline, putting key information on note cards, or concept mapping.	1	2	3	4
I know what to expect on tests and have a study plan that begins several days in advance, instead of cramming the night before.	1	2	3	4
I keep a list of test grades and other grades for each course in my course folder and I know how my teacher calculates my final grade.	1	2	3	4

Session 2
Topic: Goal setting, grade monitoring, student success training

Resources

- Student Success Training Goal handout
- Student folders
- Grade Monitoring Form
- Optional: tape recorder and blank tapes

Beginning

1. Ask students to record grades for the week on the Grade Monitoring Forms in their folders.
2. Ask students to respond in a go-round to the statements: "My name is . . . and one thing that is going better is . . ." and "I could make better grades if . . .".

REVIEW

1. Ask students to share what they remember about last meeting.
2. Ask students to report on last week's goals.

Middle

GOAL SETTING

1. Introduce Student Success Training. You can read aloud the script located at the end of this plan or tape record it beforehand.

   Tell students, "This script presents techniques used by high achievers in sports, school, and business. Three techniques you should pay attention to: relaxation training, goal setting, and picturing success. Following the script, you will be asked to write a specific goal and a plan to reach it."

2. Ask students to sit comfortably with eyes closed. Then play the tape or read the script.
3. After presenting the script, ask students to write a goal and plan as directed on the tape, using the Student Success Training Goal handout.
4. Have students share their goals and plans. They can divide into groups of 2–4, or share with the whole group. You should critique the goals and plans as to how clear, definite, and specific they are.

End

1. Ask students to write an ending to the following statements. Ask them to share their answers with a partner. Then ask for volunteers to share what they wrote.

   "Today I learned . . ."

   "My goal for next week is . . ."

2. Students share their goals with the group. After each goal is shared the entire group says in unison, "You can do it, [name of student], go for it!"
3. Preview next meeting.
4. Remind students to bring the signed parent commitment form to the next session.

Student Success Training Script

Hello, this is your Student Success Training material. Student Success Training has many similarities to the training used by top athletes around the world. Many U.S. Olympic and professional athletes use the skills that you will be learning about in Student Success Training. Learning how to set clear, definite, and possible goals, learning how to design programs that help you achieve those goals, and learning how to keep your motivation up are the keys to Student Success Training.

Succeeding in school is one of the main ways young people learn that they are capable and can compete successfully in the world. We all want to be successful. Students who have given up on being successful in school sometimes offer phony reasons for not trying. They say, "Oh, I don't care if I get bad grades," or "School's not important to me." Don't fall for these lines. Remember, everyone wants to be successful. Students who don't try in school usually have given up because they are scared—scared they won't do well even if they try their best. They have bought the idea that they can't learn. What they need is a new plan and the courage to try again.

Listen closely: Each of you can be successful in school. Each of you can learn the key facts of any course. It may take you a shorter or longer time than someone else, but each of you can learn. You own the most fantastic computer ever made: your brain. We are made to be lifetime learners.

We have built-in curiosity to make learning fun. Do you know that boredom is an unnatural state? Boredom is the lack of curiosity. If you often find yourself bored, it simply means you haven't yet learned to use that incredible learning machine, the brain. The good news is that you can learn to use it well. Today you will learn, or relearn, several skills that will help you get more out of your incredibly sophisticated brain. You will learn a process for setting clear, definite, and possible goals, and you will learn the steps in relaxation training that will help you use your creativity.

To begin, I would like you to follow my instructions for a relaxation-training exercise. Evidence suggests that we can speed up our learning when our body and mind are relaxed and calm. Therefore, anyone wanting to make learning easier and faster will want to master these simple steps in relaxation training and use them regularly. The exercise will last about 12 minutes. At the end of that time, I will ask you to do two things: First, rate how deeply you allowed yourself to relax; and second, write out a specific goal that is important to you.

Let's begin. Get into a comfortable position, close your eyes, uncross your arms and legs, and take several slow, deep breaths. These should be gentle and noiseless; the person next to you should not be able to hear you breathe. Now you are going to go through the main muscles in your body and tell them to relax. The key is to put your attention where you want to relax and imagine the muscles relaxing.

I want you to start with the muscles in your forehead and eyes. Name the part and tell it to relax. For example, say "Forehead and eyes, relax," then imagine them letting go. Feel the release. Next, tell your jaw and neck to relax. Feel them relaxing and letting go.

When you learn to relax the muscles in your face and neck, the rest of your body follows. Now, tell your shoulders and arms to relax. If you don't feel them relaxing immediately, then imagine that they are deeply relaxing. Your body will follow your thoughts.

Now, tell the muscles in your upper back and chest to relax and let go.

Now, tell your stomach and lower back to relax and let go.

Now, tell your thighs and knees to relax and let go.

Now, tell your calves, ankles, and feet to relax and let go.

Now, continue to breathe slowly, deeply, and gently as I tell you how to train your mind to relax. To relax your mind, you use your imagination. First, I would like you to picture yourself in a very relaxing, soothing, comfortable, and safe place. This place may be familiar to you, like your room at home, a treehouse in the woods, or a favorite spot at the beach. Or it can be a place you create. As you picture yourself in this resting place, pay attention to what you can see and hear around you. Also notice what you can feel and smell. Let all of your senses be aware of this pleasant and peaceful place.

Now that your body and mind are relaxed, I'd like to guide you through creating a clear, definite, and possible goal for yourself. Setting specific goals and picturing yourself achieving those goals gives your brain a map for success. Right now, I want you to pick one school subject in which you have a test coming up between four and seven days from today. Pick a subject that you would like to do well in. Remember, the test must be between four and seven days from now. This short-term time frame will give you a chance to practice your success plan right away.

After you choose the subject, decide the letter grade that you would like. This letter grade should be no more than one letter above your average test grade in this subject. For example, let's say you choose science as the subject that has a test coming up in five days, and your average test grade so far has been C. Set your goal as a B for this test. I will give you a few moments to decide on a subject and letter-grade goal.

Now that you have a clear goal, the next step is to develop a plan that will allow you to reach your goal. A good plan will include where you will study, what you will study, when you will study, and how long you will study. It is also useful to identify people or resources that can be helpful to you while you are learning the material.

Learning for most people is faster and easier when you have few or no distractions, so choose a place that is quiet. If you prefer music playing in the background, it should be instrumental—that is, without lyrics. Picture yourself sitting in a place after school that would be the best place to study.

Knowing what to study makes all the difference. You should know the type of test and the pages in the text that the test covers, and you should be sure to have an accurate set of notes and teacher handouts. Picture yourself starting today at the study place you have chosen, reviewing your notes and readings for the upcoming test. Write down any questions you have about any of the material you don't understand. See yourself asking your teacher about any questions from your studying, before class or after class or when the teacher asks if there are any questions.

The key to doing well on tests lies in reviewing notes and readings each day. It only takes a few minutes to go over the key points. Picture yourself reviewing the key points from your notes and reading at your study place for a few minutes, starting today and including each day between today and the test day.

Now, finally, I want you to picture yourself feeling confident as you sit down to take the test, knowing that you have stuck to your plan and are prepared. Picture yourself handing in your test, feeling sure that you did well. Picture yourself getting your test paper back with the grade you chose as your goal. See yourself smile, feeling good about achieving your goal.

Picturing successful completion of a goal is a key skill. Many top athletes, businesspeople, and students use this skill regularly. It can help you reach your goals.

In just a moment, I will ask you to open your eyes. After going through a relaxation-training exercise, as you just have, you can expect to feel relaxed, alert, and energized. The more you practice, the better the results. After I ask you to open your eyes, I will ask you to do three things. Now, open your eyes, feeling alert and awake.

First, rate how relaxed you were during the exercise on a 1–10 scale, 10 being the most relaxed. Write this number down. Second, write down the goal you chose, the subject, the letter grade, and the place and amount of time per day you plan to study. And third, now that you have a clear, definite, and possible goal, go achieve it and experience the good feelings that come when you succeed.

Name_____ Date_____

Grade Monitoring Form

Subject _____

Last report period grade	Goal for this report period	Midterm grade for this report period	Final grade

Date	Homework	Quiz	Test	Project/Report

Strategies to help reach goal:

1. Study for tests ahead of time.

2. Get high grades on homework.

3. Have a study buddy.

4. Turn in extra credit.

5. Use note cards/outline/concept map for key concepts.

Name_____ Date _____

Student Success Training Goal

Course: _____

1. Set a goal.

    Goals that are:

    1. clear

    2. have a definite time limit; and

    3. are reasonable

    have the best chance of being achieved.

    > My Grade Goal for this course this six weeks is _____ (A, B, C).

2. Develop a study plan.

    Be sure to include:

    - amount of time
    - starting time
    - study place
    - how many days per week

    > *Example:* To study 20 minutes per day beginning at 4 P.M. in my room at least three days per week.

    > My study plan to achieve this goal:
    >
    > _____
    >
    > _____
    >
    > _____
    >
    > _____
    >
    > _____

    Good luck on reaching your goal!

Session 3
Topic: Student success skills

Resources

- Student Success Skills Guide to Scoring in the Game of Academics handout
- Student Self-Evaluation handout (page 112)

Beginning

1. In a go-round ask students to complete the sentences, "My name is… and the way I feel about school this week is . . ." (give a number between 1 and 10, where 1 is awful and 10 is wonderful). "I feel this way because . . ."

2. Students share progress they made on the goals they set last meeting.

Middle

STUDENT SUCCESS SKILLS GUIDE TO SCORING IN ACADEMICS AND SELF-EVALUATION

1. Briefly go over the Student Success Skills Guide to Scoring in the Game of Academics. (This is an awareness activity rather than a time for skill teaching.) Ask students to evaluate their strengths and areas of weakness as you go through the various sections.

2. Next, ask students to discuss in pairs the following three statements:

   "One of my academic strengths (strong points for doing well in school) is . . ."

   "One reason I sometimes make bad grades is . . ."

   "The most important thing I can do to take responsibility for making good grades is . . ."

3. Ask pairs to share answers with the group. Ask group for feedback on answers.

4. Ask for a show of hands after each strength and each reason for making bad grades is given.

Those who share the strength or reason should raise their hands. Which answers show "taking responsibility"?

5. Discuss the positive power of taking responsibility. It is important to show the benefits to students of their taking responsibility, i.e., academic improvement, stress reduction, social gains, parent relations, and so forth.

6. Go through the Student Self-Evaluation form item by item, asking students to rate each on a 1–4 scale. Ask for show of hands on each item. How many had 3–4? Discuss how the first three items (listening, participating, asking questions) are connected.

7. Discuss the fact that if you are doing well on the first three, you can have more fun with the next two (working in small groups and getting along with others).

8. Ask students to write a goal for the week based on one of the 11 areas discussed.

9. Collect parent letter. Ask students how their parents reacted and if they sat down and discussed the checklist.

End

1. Ask students to discuss in pairs the following two sentences:

   "Today I learned . . ."

   "My goal for next week is . . ."

2. Students share their goal with group. After each goal is shared, the entire group says in unison, "You can do it [name of student], go for it!"

3. Preview next meeting.

Name_____ Date _____

The Student Success Skills Guide
to Scoring in the Game of Academics

1. **How to improve concentration and memory**

   (a) Space out review, rather than cramming.

   (b) Use graphic organizers: Outlines, concept maps.

   (c) Use the index card method: Put one key term/concept per card. Use cards several days in advance for repeated review.

   (d) Use memory techniques for key terms, i.e., acronyms, memory location techniques, associations.

   (e) Make information meaningful.

      1. Ask questions.

      2. Find something interesting.

      3. Anticipate questions teacher will ask.

   (f) Use several types of learning.

      1. Reading

      2. Writing

      3. Listening

      4. Speaking

2. **Preparing for tests**

   (a) Read material and take notes.

   (b) Answer review questions; put key terms in notes.

   (c) Reduce class and reading notes to 1–2 pages, then to note cards.

   (d) Go over these 1–2 pages/note cards 5–10 times, spaced over 2–3 days.

(continued)

Name_____ Date_____

The Student Success Skills Guide
to Scoring in the Game of Academics *(continued)*

(e) Find out all you can about the test.

  1. What kind—i.e., short answer, multiple-choice, essay, matching, etc.

  2. Make up a practice test.

  3. Ask your teacher about the test.

(f) No new reading within 24 hours of test, if possible. Instead, have notes organized by the night before and only review.

(g) Picture yourself doing well.

3. **Taking tests**

(a) Use slow breathing to relax.

(b) Look over the test; answer easy questions first.

(c) Go back to hard items; look for clues; eliminate wrong answers; take educated guesses.

(d) Go for items with the most points first.

(e) Budget your time.

4. **How to avoid test anxiety**

(a) Overlearn the details, facts.

(b) Know all you can about the test—see #2(e).

(c) Use a practice test—make up your own or ask teacher.

(d) Have a test-taking strategy and follow it—see #3 above.

(e) Imagine yourself taking the test and doing well.

(f) During the test, use nickel-breathing technique: breathe in slowly to a count of five; hold for five counts; exhale slowly to five counts; repeat five times. (Practice before test day.)

Session 4
Topic: Handling conflicts, role-play

Resources

- Student Self-Evaluation handout (page 112)
- Grade Monitoring handout (page 116)
- Student folders
- Paper and pencils
- Chart paper

Beginning

1. Ask students to record grades for the week on the grade monitoring forms in their folders.
2. Ask students to respond in a go-round to the statements:

   "My name is . . ."

   "One thing that is going better is . . ."

   "What I have the most trouble with is . . ."

REVIEW

1. Ask students to share what they remember about last meeting.
2. Ask students to report on last week's goals.

Middle

HANDLING CONFLICTS

1. Ask students to write down typical problems either that they have had with other students at school or that they notice lots of other students have with each other at school. Ask them not to put their names on the list. Tell them you will collect everyone's ideas in a moment and the group will discuss: (a) if they agree that the problem is typical and (b) some possible solutions.
2. Collect lists of problems. Read each one and ask if it is a typical problem for this age group. List on a flip chart all the agreed-upon typical problems. Ask the group members to rank the top three problems in terms of how interested they would be in having the group discuss possible solutions.
3. Lead a discussion on possible solutions for the top three problems selected. Use a brainstorming technique. List all offered solutions on chart paper or blackboard/white board. Then go back and have

the group code each one as "H," helpful, or "HA," harmful to self or others. *Note:* Some will be rated as both. Have the group decide if the helpful side outweighs the harmful side.

4. Ask group to divide into pairs and plan a role-play for one of the three problems. The role-play should include one of the helpful solutions. Allow approximately five minutes for planning.
5. Ask each pair to present their role-play. Ask the rest of the group to discuss how realistically the problem and solution were portrayed and to demonstrate additional suggestions for handling the problem. The leader can also demonstrate various positive alternative ways to handle the situation or coach students in different ways to act. *Note:* It is the role-play and coaching that make this a powerful learning activity.

STUDENT SELF-EVALUATION

1. Go through each of the seven items, reading them aloud and asking students to rate how they did that week. Ask, "Who rated that item 'Good,' who rated it 'OK,' who rated it 'Needs to improve'?"
2. Use the items to stimulate discussion and to clarify problem areas that need to be addressed.
3. Use group problem solving by asking students to brainstorm solutions to problems students bring up as you move down the list. Role-playing solutions to problems is a valuable way to help students learn alternative strategies for handling difficult situations. The problem solving can also include how to handle the social problems that come up during the group meetings.

End

1. Ask students to write an ending to the following two statements. Ask them to share their answers with a partner. Then ask for volunteers to share what they wrote.

   "One thing I learned today was . . ."

   "One way I can use what I learned today is . . ."

2. Preview next session.

Session 5
Topic: Asking questions, role-play

Resources
- Student Self-Evaluation (page 112)
- Grade Monitoring form (page 116)
- Student folders
- List of web sites for study help, references

Beginning
1. Ask students to record grades for the week on the grade monitoring forms in their folders.
2. Ask students to respond in a go-round to the statement:

   "My name is . . . and one thing that is going better is . . ."

REVIEW
1. Ask students to share what they remember about last meeting.
2. Ask students to report on last week's goals.

Middle

ASKING QUESTIONS
1. Students sometimes don't ask questions in class when they don't understand something because they're afraid they'll look dumb. If you know when and how to ask questions, you can look smart even when you don't understand something.

   When Ask: "When are the best times to ask your teacher questions about assignments?" Some recommended times are:
   - before class;
   - when the teacher asks, "Are there any questions";
   - right after you miss a key point, assuming you have been listening and know how to look smart when you ask a question.
   - at the end of class.

   How The do's and don'ts of asking questions. Ask: "What are some ways to ask questions that might make you look dumb?"
   - Say "Huh?"
   - Say "What did you say?"
   - Ask "What are we supposed to do?" right after teacher gives instructions.
2. Go over with students the basics of looking good when asking questions:

- When asking a question, let the teacher know you heard part of what was said. "Ms. Jones, I understand about . . . and I heard you say . . ., but where I lost you was . . . . Could you say a little more about that?"
- Let the teacher know you care. "Mr. Smith, I want to understand this point, but I'm really having a hard time. Could you explain it once more, please?"

Both examples include nonverbal messages—tone of voice, facial expressions, and body language—that must match the verbal message of sincerity in order for questions to be received positively.

ROLE-PLAY
1. Have students set the scene—teacher, class, subject. One student plays the teacher and begins lecturing or giving directions. Another student models looking smart when asking a question.
2. Try several variations—Beginning of class, after teacher asks "Are there any questions," as soon as student misses a key point, and end of class.
3. Brainstorm other ways to be sure students know what to do on an assignment or what to study for a test, e.g., check with a friend, call a study buddy.
4. Brainstorm and create a list of web sites that provide tutoring help or easy references. Check with your school media center or public library ahead of time for examples.

STUDENT SELF-EVALUATION
1. Go through each of the seven items, reading them aloud and asking students to rate how they did that week. Ask, "Who rated that item 'Good', who rated it 'OK', who rated it 'Needs to improve'?"
2. Use the items to stimulate discussion and to identify problem areas that need to be addressed.
3. Use group problem solving by asking students to brainstorm solutions to problems raised by group members as you move down the list.
4. Role-playing solutions to problems is a valuable way to help students learn alternative strategies for handling difficult situations. The problem solving can also include how to handle the social problems that come up during the group meetings. The idea is for all participants to move to 3–4 range on all 11 topics.

End

1. Ask students to write an ending to the following two statements. Ask them to share their answers with a partner. Then ask for volunteers to share what they wrote.

   "One thing I learned today was . . ."

   "One way I can use what I learned today is . . ."

2. Preview next session. Direct students to bring their social studies text to the session.

Session 6
Topic: How to approach any reading assignment

Resources

- How to Approach Any Reading Assignment handout
- Student Self-Evaluation handout (page 112)
- Grade Monitoring form (page 116)
- Student folders
- Student social studies text

Beginning

1. Ask students to record grades for the week on the grade monitoring forms in their folders.
2. Ask students to complete the following statements:

   "When people talk to me, I like for them to . . ."

   "A person who talks all the time makes me feel . . ."

   "When people give me unwanted advice, I feel . . ."

   "I trust people who . . ."

   "I am willing to listen to others if . . ."

REVIEW

1. Ask students to share what they remember about last meeting.
2. Ask students to report on last week's goals.

Middle

READING STRATEGIES

1. Go over the How to Approach Any Reading Assignment handout with students.
2. Guide students through an upcoming chapter in their social studies book, using the reading handout.

Note: It is essential to use student text and current chapter with the reading strategies. Students need to practice the strategies in context; simply going over these strategies without a proper context is not effective. It would be ideal if you could work with the teachers and have them reinforce these or similar strategies with their entire class.

STUDENT SELF-EVALUATION

1. Go through each of the seven items, reading them aloud and asking students to rate how they did that week. Ask, "Who rated that item 'Good', who rated it 'OK', who rated it 'Needs to improve'?"
2. Use the items to stimulate discussion and to clarify problem areas that need to be addressed.
3. Use group problem solving by asking students to brainstorm solutions to problems students bring up as you move down the list.
4. Role-playing solutions to problems is a valuable way to help students learn alternative strategies for handling difficult situations.
5. The problem solving can also include how to handle the social problems that come up during the group meetings. The idea is for all participants to move to 3–4 range on all 11 topics.

End

1. Ask students to write an ending to the following two statements. Ask them to share their answers with a partner. Then ask for volunteers to share what they wrote.

   "One thing I learned today was . . ."

   "One way I can use what I learned today is . . ."

2. Preview next session. Direct students to bring their math text to the next session.

Name_____ Date _____

How to Approach Any Reading Assignment

There are many ways you can improve your understanding of what you read. We recommend that you have a clear step-by-step approach that can be easily followed.

1. **Develop an overview** of the reading. Ask yourself, "What are this section's key points?" To begin to get the "big picture" of what the section is about:

   - Look at any pictures, graphs; read captions.
   - Read introduction paragraph and summary paragraph.
   - Read questions, if any, at the end of the section.
   - Look over the vocabulary list.
   - Look at boldface headings. Turn each heading into a question you will answer when you read the section.

2. **Read the section.** As you read, mentally answer the questions you made up from each heading. Make a list of any terms you don't understand. As you finish each subsection, mentally summarize the main ideas.

3. **Review what you have read.** Look over questions and key terms at the end of the section. If you cannot answer them, return to the section where they are covered and reread. Before leaving the section, be sure you can answer the *W* and *H* questions:

   who, what, when, where, why, and how.

(continued)

Name_____ Date_____

How to Approach Any Reading Assignment *(continued)*

The chart below summarizes these steps and indicates the percentage of comprehension we gain as we progress through each step.

How to Make Remembering What You Read Easier		
Preview 10–20% comprehension	**Read** 50–80% comprehension	**Review** 85–98% comprehension
1. Look at pictures, graphs, charts, read captions.	1. Read to answer questions.	1. Go back to questions and try to answer them mentally.
2. Read summary and questions.	2. Write down any boldface words or terms you don't understand.	2. For those you can't answer, refer to the text.
3. Read the headings, turning them into questions.	3. After reading each subsection, mentally summarize.	3. Make sure you answer all the *W* and *H* questions.

         Group Counseling for School Counselors: A Practical Guide

Session 7
Topic: Math checklist

Resources

- Grade Monitoring form (page 116)
- Student folders
- Math checklist handout
- Student Self-Evaluation handout (page 112)
- Student math text

Beginning

1. Ask students to record grades for the week on the grade monitoring forms in their folders.
2. Ask students to complete the following statements:
   "One reading tip I used this week was . . ."
   "One subject I am improving in is . . ."

REVIEW

1. Ask students to share what they remember about last meeting.
2. Ask students to report on last week's goals.

Middle

1. Present the Math Checklist by asking volunteers to read each point or paragraph aloud to the group. Stop after each section to discuss, asking for student opinions and experiences.
2. This is a good time to ask about who is being tutored or who may want a tutor. It is important to provide coordinating tutoring services when needed. This academic support group is not a substitute for skill training in reading or math. Specialists in each of these areas need to be involved if a deficit exists. Coordination with classroom teachers is an important part of the success of the Student Success Skills group program.
3. Ask students to generate any current problems in math. Process the handout, using the particular problems they bring up in the math book.
4. Have students get into pairs, going through math problems that are causing difficulty while using the strategies on the handout.

   Note: The handout can also be used by a peer tutor or adult tutor.

STUDENT SELF-EVALUATION FORM

1. Go through each of the 11 items, reading them aloud and asking students to rate how they did that week. Ask, "Who rated that item 'Good,' who rated it 'OK,' who rated it 'Needs to improve'?"
2. Use the items to stimulate discussion and to clarify problem areas that need to be addressed.
3. Use group problem solving by asking students to brainstorm solutions to problems students bring up as you move down the list.
4. Role-playing solutions to problems is a valuable way to help students learn alternative strategies for handling difficult situations. The problem solving can also include how to handle the social problems that come up during the group meetings. The idea is for all participants to move to 3–4 range on all 11 topics.

End

1. Ask students to write an ending to the following two sentences. Ask them to share their answers with a partner. Then ask for volunteers to share what they wrote.
   "One thing I learned today was . . ."
   "One way I can use what I learned today is . . ."
2. Preview next session.

Name_____ Date _____

Math Checklist

You can master the needed steps for any math problem. Use this problem-solving approach.

1. Pinpoint the type of math problems on which you are having difficulty.

2. Choose a problem. As you begin working, say out loud each step you are using.

3. When you cannot specify what you should do next or when you give the wrong step, stop. Find an example with an explanation in the text. Read this example aloud, step by step.

4. If no clear example is available, ask for help. Ask him or her to write out the necessary steps. Then try the problem again, using the steps presented.

Working math problems involves applying a series of steps in a set order. It makes it easier if you follow this simple two-step process.

(a) Write out the steps.

(b) Say the steps as you perform each operation, checking them off as you go.

Many difficulties in math occur because students have not mastered the basic four operations—adding, subtracting, multiplying, and dividing.

These four operations are like any skill. Mastering them requires repetition.

The sooner you master the four operations, the sooner math will become easier.

It is helpful to have someone check these basic operations when you notice errors. When you have trouble with computational skills, flash cards and sample problems can help you to master the skill.

Think of some of your favorite athletes, musicians, dancers, or artists. They have all put in a lot of time to master the basics. When you master the basics, in any area of life, then you have more control and freedom.

The first step is to determine where you need to strengthen your skills. The next step is to set a plan to work on building these skills to a mastery level. Then you get to enjoy using these skills and appreciating the good feeling that comes from being successful.

Session 8
Topic: Review, spotlight, evaluation

Resources
- Index cards or sheets of paper
- Group Evaluation form (page 10)

Beginning

Ask, "Who used something we talked about last week during the week? How did it go?"

REVIEW LIFE OF GROUP

1. Briefly go over each topic you've covered during the last seven weeks, asking students what they remember.
2. Then ask the following questions:
   - What are some of the most important things you have learned about yourself?
   - What has been the most helpful part of this group for you?
   - What is a goal you have set for yourself?

Middle

ACCEPTING AND GIVING COMPLIMENTS

1. Hand out index cards or sheets of paper. Each person is to write down at least one thing he or she admires, likes, or appreciates about each of the other group members.
2. Spotlight: Ask each group member to say directly to the "spotlighted" person, with eye contact: "[person's name], one thing I admire, like, or appreciate about you is . . .".
3. Explain and give examples of the types of qualities you are asking students to think of and how to say and receive them. Ask students not to use appearance compliments such as "I like your shirt, shoes, hair," etc., but to use qualities or actions.
4. After each comment, the spotlighted person says "thank you," nothing else. (Be sure you get in on this—it feels good.)

End

1. Process the spotlighting activity. How did it feel receiving compliments? Giving compliments?
2. Students complete anonymous Group Evaluation.
3. Concluding remarks. Invite students to make individual appointments if they want. Remind them of the monthly follow-up sessions.

Booster Session Generic Plan

Meeting once a month with the group after the weekly sessions end is a good way to maintain the gains the students have made and provides additional support for their continued growth. It also provides a way to monitor the long-term effect of participating in your groups.

Resources

- Grade Monitoring Form (page 116)
- Student Self-Evaluation handout (page 112)

Beginning

MOVEMENT, GROUP TEMPERATURE, REVIEW, AND GOAL REPORT

1. In a go-round ask students to rate how they are feeling on the "great, pretty good, not so good, really bad" scale. Be sure to check with any not so good or really bad to determine if follow-up is needed.

2. Ask students to fill out grade forms for the core subjects using grades from the last report card or midterm progress report. Turn in grade forms to you.

3. Ask students to share in a go-round their rating of how their grades are doing on a scale of 1–10, where 10 is great and 1 is poor.

Middle

STUDENT SELF-EVALUATION

1. Go through each of the 11 items, reading them aloud and asking students to rate how they did the past month. Ask, "Who rated that item 'Good,' who rated it 'OK,' who rated it 'Needs to improve'?"

2. Use the items to stimulate discussion and to clarify problem areas that need to be addressed.

3. Use group problem solving by asking students to brainstorm solutions to problems students bring up as you move down the list.

4. Role-playing solutions to problems is a valuable way to help students learn alternative strategies for handling difficult situations.

SOCIAL PROBLEM SOLVING

1. Ask students about problems that they have had with other students/teachers at school. Make a list.

2. Ask the group members to rank the top three problems in terms of interest to them for group to discuss possible solutions.

3. Lead a discussion on possible solutions for the selected top three problems. Use a brainstorming technique. List all offered solutions first. Then go back and have the group code each one as "H," helpful, or "HA," harmful to self or others. *Note:* Some will be rated as both. Have group decide if the helpful side outweighs the harmful side.

4. Ask group to divide into pairs and plan a role-play for one of the three problems. The role-play should include one of the helpful solutions. Allow approximately five minutes for planning.

5. Ask each pair to present their role-play. Ask the rest of the group to discuss how realistically the problem and solution were portrayed. Ask students to demonstrate additional suggestions for handling the problem. You can also demonstrate various positive alternative ways to handle the situation or coach students in different ways to act. *Note:* It is the role play and coaching that make this a powerful learning activity.

End

1. Ask students to write an ending to the following two sentences. Ask them to share their answers with a partner. Then ask for volunteers to share what they wrote.

   "One thing I learned today was . . ."

   "One way I can use what I learned today is . . ."

2. Preview next month's session.

Student Success Skills:
Positive Student Impact Frequency Table

It is useful to tally how many students brought their grades up and to share this with teachers and parents. A frequency table is helpful. A sample is shown below.

Many counselors also include a behavior rating by teachers as a measure of positive impact on student performance. One example of a K–12 nationally normed scale that closely mirrors the training of this group is the *School Social Behavior Scales* (Merrill, 1992). This instrument has subscales that measure academic competence and social competence.

Counselors are increasingly including pre/post nationally standardized achievement scores as indicators of positive impact.

Total number of students in Student Success Skills group: _____

Criteria for selection: _____

_____

_____

Number who brought at least one core academic subject up
at least one letter grade: _____

                                        percent of total: _____

Number who brought two or more core academic subjects up
at least one letter grade: _____

                                        percent of total: _____

2.2
Coping with Stress and Anger

Grade Level: Middle School and High School	Time Required: 8 Sessions	Authors: Wes Hawkins and Greg Brigman

Purpose

To help students develop coping strategies to manage stress and anger appropriately. Students learn:

- causes and personal triggers of anger
- appropriate ways to respond to anger
- an easy-to-use anger/conflict self-monitoring system
- a helpful social problem-solving model

Real-life situations are used to role-play various situations and practice new ways of responding to anger and stress.

Logistics

GROUP COMPOSITION

Students grades 6–8 mixed with regard to activity level and behavior control. Avoid loading group with only overactive behavior problem students. Students need multiple models of appropriate behavior. Groups with only behavior problem students usually do not show significant gains in prosocial behavior. Mixed groups are generally very effective.

GROUP SIZE

6–8 students

GROUP TIME PER SESSION

45 minutes

NUMBER OF SESSIONS

Eight, with optional booster sessions spaced approximately one month apart after regular group ends.

Recommended Resources

Full bibliographic details for these publications are included in the Bibliography at the end of this book.

Begun and Huml, eds, 1999: *Violence Prevention Skills: Lessons and Activities.*

Bloom, 1984: *Community Mental Health.*

Bowman et al., 1998: *Aggressive and Violent Students.*

Goldstein and Conoley, eds, 1997: *School Violence Intervention.*

Hawkins, 1986: *Circle of Friends Project.*

Kivel et al., 1997: *Making the Peace.*

Sunburst Communications: *When Anger Turns to Rage.* (videocassette)

Sunburst Communications: *When You're Mad! Mad! Mad!* (videocassette)

Sunburst Communications: *Handling Your Anger.* (videocassette)

Sunburst Communications: *Anger: You Can Handle It.* (videocassette)

Sunburst Communications: *Anger Management Skills.* (videocassette)

Taylor, 1994: *Anger Control Training for Children and Teens.*

Whitehouse et al., 1996: *A Volcano in My Tummy: Helping Children to Handle Anger.*

Wilde, 1995: *Anger Management in Schools.*

Wilde, 1994: *Hot Stuff to Help Kids Chill Out.*

Session 1
Topic: What's this group about; getting to know each other

Resources

- Chart paper/blackboard/whiteboard

Beginning

1. Introduce yourself and explain the purpose of the group.

   Example: "All of us get angry, and it's how we respond to our anger that matters. We will learn what causes our own anger and we will learn and practice with group members good ways to respond to anger. We will ask you to give your own real-life examples of how you have responded to anger recently and—with the help of group members—we will help you figure out better ways to respond to anger.

   "The group meets eight times, same place, same time, every week. As I mentioned when I met with each of you individually, there are three ways people get to participate in this group: 1) you heard about the group, thought it sounded good, and signed up; 2) your parent heard or read about it and wanted you to check it out; 3) your teacher thought you'd enjoy it and that you'd be able to benefit from being in the group.

   "As you probably know, this group is open to everyone. You don't have to have a problem with your anger to be here. We are here to learn about ourselves and to help others in dealing with life's problems that make us angry. Think of the group as 'keeping a cool head with a little help from your friends.'"

INTRODUCTIONS

Have students pair up and have them interview their partners in terms of their names, what they like to do, and what they hope to get out of the group. Then have each student introduce his/her partner, based on the interview.

Middle

GROUP RULES

1. Ask, "What are some rules you think would help our group run better? I've found it's helpful to have a few rules to make our group run smoothly." Make sure to include the following:

   - Anything we talk about here is confidential—you own what you say but we do not talk about what anyone else says outside the group.
   - You have the right to say "pass" if you do not want to share your opinion on something. We do not want to make anyone uncomfortable.
   - One person talks at a time—the rest of us listen.
   - We respect each other's right to have different opinions even if we do not agree—no put-downs.
   - Share the time—no monopolizing "talk time."

2. Ask for additional suggestions—get a group consensus on all rules.

ANGER STRATEGIES

1. Have students work in pairs to generate strategies that people their age use for dealing with anger. We are trying to generate typical strategies for handling anger. The strategies could be healthy and helpful or could be unhealthy and harmful.

2. Next have pairs report and list their strategies on a flip chart or board.

3. Have the group code each idea as "H" for helpful or "HA" for harmful.

4. Then ask group to choose the top 2–3 that represent how most people their age deal with anger.

End

1. Ask students to share in pairs what they learned about the group and each other today and what they are looking forward to doing/learning in the group. Ask volunteers to share with whole group.

2. Ask students to review what the purpose of the group is, how many meetings, and so forth.

3. Preview the second meeting.

Session 2

Topic: It's how you respond to anger that counts

Resources

- Prince Llewelyn and his Dog Gelert handout
- Life Problem Solver handout
- Monitor Your Anger handout
- Blackboard/whiteboard/chart paper

Beginning

1. Have students read the story of Prince Llewelyn of Wales and his beloved dog, Gelert. If they wish, they can use the lines at the bottom of the page to make notes about their reactions. Have them respond to the story and discuss if they have ever acted out of anger when they wished they hadn't.

2. Begin discussion by noting that we all become angry at times but it is how we respond that counts. Note that anger is like stress. We will always have it; what is important is how we **respond** to it. For example, Prince Llewelyn suffered the rest of his life because he acted in anger and killed his dog. Many past presidents (Carter, Clinton, Kennedy, Nixon) advise you not to act when you are mad or you are likely to make mistakes.

3. Note that the purpose of this group is to identify the ways we have responded to anger and, with group input, to identify other possible ways of responding to anger and discuss the outcomes.

Middle

1. Explain the Life Problem Solver handout. Model the use of the chart. Have students fill out how they responded when they last became angry.

2. After students have filled out the form, use the board and ask for volunteers to share how they responded to anger. Then identify other possible ways they could have responded.

3. Compare outcomes on the form to demonstrate that our responses to anger do affect outcomes.

4. List the different types of responses to anger and discuss with the group. Write the list on chart paper and post it on the wall for future sessions.

End

1. Have students complete the statement: "What I learned from group today was . . ."

2. Emphasize that responses to anger do affect the outcome—as with Prince Llewelyn.

LIFE GOAL* FOR NEXT WEEK:

Demonstrate how to use the Monitor Your Anger handout. For this week, students need only complete Step 1, keeping track of how many times they get angry each day. Ask students to use the handout to chart the number of times they become angry during the ensuing week.

* We chose to call this exercise a "Life Goal" instead of homework because the skills learned here are to be generalized in the student's environment as life skills.

Name_____ Date _____

Prince Llewelyn and his Dog Gelert

In the 13th century, the Prince of North Wales, Llewelyn, went hunting one day without his faithful hound, Gelert. Gelert usually accompanied his master, but for some unknown reason he stayed at the prince's castle this day. On the prince's return, he found Gelert stained and smeared with blood. Gelert joyfully sprang to meet his master. The prince started to greet Gelert, but then saw that the cot of his infant son was empty and smeared with blood. Swelling with anger, the prince plunged his sword into the faithful hound's side, thinking the dog had killed his son. Gelert yelped in extreme pain and, looking into his master's eyes, fell to the floor and died. The dog's dying cry was answered by a child's cry. Prince Llewelyn searched and discovered his son unharmed. Nearby lay the body of a mighty wolf, which Gelert had slain to protect the prince's son. The prince, filled with remorse and sadness, was said never to have smiled again. Gelert is buried in Beddgelert, Wales. This story is a memorial to the life of Gelert, the faithful hound.

_____

_____

_____

_____

_____

_____

Name_____ Date_____

Life Problem Solver

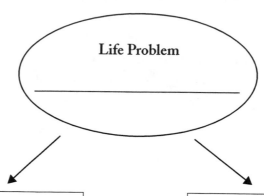

Life Problem

_____

How I Responded to Life Problem
_____ _____ _____ _____ _____ _____ _____

Other Ways I Could Have Responded to Life Problem
_____ _____ _____ _____ _____ _____ _____

Outcome of Response to Life Problem
_____ _____ _____ _____ _____ _____ _____

Probable Outcomes of Other Responses to Life Problem
_____ _____ _____ _____ _____ _____ _____

       Group Counseling for School Counselors: A Practical Guide

Name_____ Date _____

Monitor Your Anger

Directions:

1. Look at the chart below. Each time you become angry in a given day, put a dot in the row that corresponds to that day of the week. If it is the first time you got angry that day, put a dot in the "1" box for the day. If you get angry again on the same day, put a dot in the "2" box, and so forth.

2. Each time you get angry, write a brief description of the event/s that preceded your anger on the lines below. If you need more space, use the back of this sheet.

_____

_____

_____

_____

_____

_____

_____

3. At the end of the week, circle the highest dot you recorded for each day. Then draw a line to connect the circles.

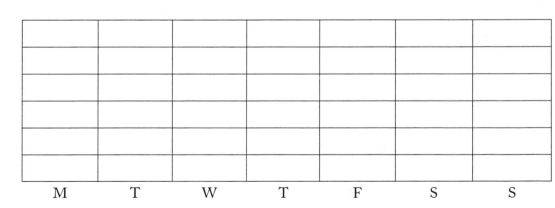

Session 3
Topic: What is my kind of anger?

Resources

- Blackboard/whiteboard/chart paper
- Completed Monitor Your Anger handouts from Session 2
- My Kind of Anger handout
- Monitor Your Anger handout (page 137)

Beginning

1. Have students complete the statement, "What I get mad about the most is . . .".
2. Review the Monitoring Your Anger results for the last week.

Middle

1. Begin discussion by noting that this time we want to identify our own anger and, specifically, what **causes** or **triggers** our anger. The emotion of anger often arises when we perceive that our rights have been violated or threatened. Fear of rejection and stress are two other leading causes of anger. Sometimes anger is a secondary feeling that follows a primary feeling. For example, if we are rejected and feel hurt we sometimes change from the primary feeling—hurt—to the secondary feeling—anger. It is important to understand where the anger is coming from. Another example of primary/secondary feelings connected to anger is depres-

sion. Sometimes people express their depression in the form of lashing out at others in anger. The purpose of today's group is to identify which types of events or stressors cause us to feel angry (e.g., disrespect for others, teasing, time pressure, loss, stress, etc.) and to practice good ways to respond so that we have the outcome we want.

2. Have students complete the My Kind of Anger handout.
3. When students have completed the handout, have them discuss their specific anger triggers.

End

1. Have students complete the statement, "What I learned from group today was . . .".
2. Using student responses, emphasize that each person has his/her own type of anger, in that each person usually has **predictable** types of triggers/stressors/events that produce anger. Note again that a first step in responding to and controlling one's anger is to identify the triggers that are specific to oneself.

LIFE GOAL FOR NEXT WEEK

List the times you became angry each day, as you did last week. This time also list **why** or **what event** made you angry on the Monitor Your Anger handout.

Name_____ Date_____

My Kind of Anger

Part I

Directions: Think back to times you have become angry. Place a check mark beside any situation in which you have felt angry.

_____ Grades or academic problems

_____ Interaction with friends

_____ Interaction with parents or family members

_____ Interaction with teachers

_____ Interaction with principal

_____ Teasing/bullying

_____ Put-downs by peers

_____ Time issue

_____ Test

_____ Others—Please list:

_____

_____

_____

Summarize your responses: _____

_____

_____

_____

Part II

What events/triggers/stressors happened to cause your anger?

_____

_____

_____

Part III

Is there a pattern in your anger responses?

_____

_____

_____

Session 4
Topic: Strategy for responding to anger

Resources

- The Coconut Grove Fire handout
- Completed Monitor Your Anger handouts from Session 3
- Life Problem Solver handout (page 136)
- Poster board/chart paper
- Monitor Your Anger handout (page 137)

Beginning

1. Have students read the Coconut Grove Fire handout.
2. Have them respond to the story and to the statement, "Talking about my problems when I am angry makes me feel . . .".
3. Review the Monitor Your Anger results for the last week.
4. Note that there are many ways to deal with anger, but ignoring anger is seldom effective. Learning to deal with our anger is a very important life skill. Not learning to deal with our anger can seriously affect our relationships and career in negative ways.

Middle

1. Using the Life Problem Solver, have a pair of students role-play responding to a past situation in which they wished they had managed their anger differently.
2. Brainstorm other strategies for effectively dealing with anger in this situation, then redo the role-play.

3. Use the role-play as a springboard for a discussion of effective ways to deal with the types of situations students identified last week using the My Kind of Anger form.
4. Put responses on posters and place on the wall for future sessions. This is an important session in which positive alternatives need to be identified. Some possible ideas for positively handling anger include:

   - take a "time-out" to cool down
   - think through how you want to respond
   - talk it over with a trusted friend, family member, teacher, counselor
   - check out your self-talk and change any non-helpful messages to healthy ones
   - talk it over with the person with whom you are angry after calming down
   - humor
   - physical activity
   - rest, relaxation

End

Have students complete the statement, "What I learned from group today was . . .".

LIFE GOAL FOR NEXT WEEK

Use or practice a strategy we have discussed today to deal with anger this week. Be ready to discuss it next group session in the Life Problem Solver strategy time.

Name_____ Date _____

The Coconut Grove Fire

In 1942, the Coconut Grove was a popular nightclub in Boston, Massachusetts, where crowds gathered to dance the night away. One fateful night, a large fire broke out in the nightclub. Hundreds of people died. Many of them died because the doors opened inwards. So many people were pressed against the doors that they couldn't be opened.

Many of those who survived the fire were in much emotional stress and grief. At the time, we didn't know how to help people who were exposed to a crisis such as this. A psychiatrist from Harvard was asked to study how to help these survivors. He found out that those survivors who could **talk about their feelings** felt less stress and suffered less psychological distress and illness than those who did not talk about their feelings.

This was a landmark study in mental health. It provided evidence that talking about problems is very important for mental health.

This study also served as the origin of the intervention teams that come to a school or community after a major crisis such as school violence, a hurricane, or a bus accident.

Session 5
Topic: Anger response strategy—keep-cool rules

Resources

- Completed Monitor Your Anger handouts from Session 4
- Keep-Cool Rules handout
- Posters from Session 4
- Monitor Your Anger handout (page 137)

Beginning

1. Have students respond to the statement, "There are times one has to deal with anger head-on. Those times are . . .".
2. Review the Monitor Your Anger results for the last week.

Middle

1. Review the fact that there are many ways to deal with anger, as indicated on the posters from last week.
2. Introduce the notion of **assertiveness**, respecting yourself and the other person, as one effective way to resolve conflicts.
3. Discuss the two extremes on either side of assertiveness: **passivity** and **aggression**. Being too passive means always avoiding conflict, not showing respect for yourself, and treating yourself like a doormat. Being aggressive means being too pushy, acting like a bully, and respecting only yourself and not the other person.

4. Draw an assertiveness continuum on the board to make this point and distinguish among passive, assertive, and aggressive. Ask group members to stand at the point along the continuum that represents how they usually handle conflict.
5. Next, brainstorm what each style looks like and sounds like: body language, voice, tone.
6. Last, discuss the social consequences of each style.

KEEP-COOL RULES

1. Explain how to use the Keep-Cool Rules.
2. Model the use of these rules to students using the Life Problem Solver (page 136) on a simulated problem.
3. Then, using the Life Problem Solver, have students role-play responding to a past anger situation or a simulated situation using the Keep-Cool Rules.

End

1. Have students complete the statement, "What I learned from group today was . . .".
2. Distribute Monitor Your Anger handout and ask students to complete it for the ensuing week.

LIFE GOAL FOR NEXT WEEK

Use or practice the Keep-Cool Rules to deal with your anger strategy with friends or family. Be ready to discuss during the next group session, using the Life Problem Solver.

Keep-Cool Rules

When you get angry, follow the four rules below:

1. **Stop! Cool down.**

   Do not respond if you are at an 8, 9, or 10 on the 1–10 anger scale. Take a time-out. Get out of the situation. Find a place to think.

2. **Think!**

   Review the situation and figure out why you are angry and what you can say/do that will lead to the outcome you want.

3. **Act!**

   Schedule a time to talk to the other person, or to a neutral person, if you need to vent first. If you need the help of another person, talk to the school counselor or peer mediation leader to set up a peer mediation meeting.

4. **Resolve!**

   Follow the steps below to resolve anger with another person:

   Step 1: Person who is angry (Person 1) expresses feelings and behavior to other person (Person 2): "I felt angry when you (state exact behavior) . . ."

   Step 2: Person 1 asks Person 2: "What did you think happened?"

   Discuss how each person perceived the situation and how each felt about it.

   Both persons should be able to restate the other's point of view and feeling.

   Step 3: Person 1 asks Person 2: "In the future, I would like for you to . . . .
   How does that sound to you?"

   Step 4: Person 2 responds. Repeat steps 1–4 until a resolution is reached that is satisfactory to both persons. Shake hands and say one positive comment to each other in dealing with this issue.

Session 6
Topic: Practice makes for cool heads

Resources

- Completed Monitor Your Anger handouts from Session 5
- Life Problem Solver handout (page 136)
- Poster board/chart paper
- Optional: video camera and TV/VCR
- Monitor Your Anger handout (page 137)

Beginning

1. Have students respond to the statement, "I used or practiced the Keep-Cool Rules last week to deal with anger involving . . . and found the Keep-Cool Rules to . . .".
2. Review the Monitor Your Anger results for the last week.
3. Tell students, "The purpose of today's group is to practice and figure out ways to use the Keep-Cool Rules at school, at home, and in our personal lives (romantic and platonic relationships). We will figure out ways to reduce barriers to use, etc."

Middle

1. Using the Life Problem Solver, have students fill out how they responded when they last became angry and how they can use the Keep-Cool Rules.

2. Discuss combining the direct approach of talking to the person with whom you are angry with other anger management strategies.
3. Have students brainstorm ways to make sure they use the Keep-Cool Rules (e.g., establish buddy system, call someone). Put responses on a poster and put on the wall for visual clues.
4. Role-play a few examples of group members' use of the Keep-Cool Rules, or situations they want to practice that are likely to come up this week.
5. Have group give feedback on steps.
6. Videotaping the role-plays and using the tape to give feedback is a very powerful way to teach these skills.

End

1. Have students complete the statement, "What I learned from group today was . . .".
2. Distribute Monitor Your Anger handouts for students to complete over the coming week.

LIFE GOAL FOR NEXT WEEK

Use or practice the Keep-Cool Rules to deal with your anger strategy with friends or family. Be ready to discuss during the next group session, using the Life Problem Solver.

Session 7
Topic: Making anger management part of your life

Resources

- Completed Monitor Your Anger handouts from Session 6
- Poster board/chart paper

Beginning

1. Ask students to respond to the statement, "People have control over how they respond to anger."

2. Review the Monitor Your Anger results for the last week.

3. Say to students, "People do have control over how they respond to anger. The strategies we have learned in this group are life skills, and the real importance of these skills is to use them long after this group is over, with friends, peers, parents, teachers, etc.

   "Family and friends and peers will be with us long after this group is finished. The purpose of today's group is to develop and put in place a plan for establishing conflict resolution areas at school, at home, and within the family. Note that this is much like a designated driver program—we will find a designated place in our school, home, or place with peers to resolve conflict in a positive way.

   "This may not seem cool to do, but how we solve problems in today's world is important. We see many adults, for example, yelling at each other, hitting each other, and even killing others. Sometimes even multi-million-dollar baseball players solve their problems on the baseball field by having a group punch-out, making ridiculous role models for our youth."

Middle

1. Have the group develop a plan to designate places at school (coordinated with school counselor), home, and with peers as a "designated conflict resolution areas." Have copies or large blown-up copies of the Keep-Cool Rules made for posting on the walls of the designated conflict resolution places.

2. Note that there are many ways to make sure we use the Keep-Cool Rules (e.g., put printed cards in wallet or purse, establish buddy system, call someone). Brainstorm plans for how group members can use the designated conflict management areas when needed.

3. Brainstorm other ideas from the group about managing anger and stress. Write these ideas on a poster, and post it on the wall for last session review.

End

Have students complete the statement, "What I learned from group today was . . .".

LIFE GOAL

As a group, put in place the designated conflict management area in your school. Individually, put it in place with your family. Use them—don't lose them.

Session 8
Topic: What we learned, how to use it

Resources
- Blackboard/writing board
- Index cards/paper

Beginning
Report on Life Goal from last week, which was: As a group, put in place the designated conflict management area in your school. Individually, put it in place with your family.

Middle
1. Hand out index cards or sheets of paper. Each person is to write down at least one thing they liked or appreciated about each of the other group members in helping him/her deal with anger.
2. Have each group member share those positive statements by spotlighting each group member.

3. When receiving compliments, the student must not negate the compliment but simply say "thank-you" or another positive response.

End
1. Have students singly respond to the statements, "What I have learned about responding to anger in this group is . . ."
   "I will use the strategies to respond to anger in the future because . . ."
2. Say good-bye, shake hands, and compliment each other for attending this group and trying to make the world a better place to live for others.
3. Remind group that you are available and that the group will meet in one month to review each person's progress in managing his or her anger.

2.3
Loss/Bereavement

Grade Level: Middle School	Time Required: 7 Sessions	Authors: Barbara Earley Goodman and Greg Brigman

Purpose

A loss group provides a support system for students who have experienced the death of a parent or other family member. These students may have difficulty accepting the death and expressing their feelings. They often act brave and believe the feelings will go away. They think no one understands. Frequently there are unresolved conflicts, feelings of abandonment, anger, and guilt. They may be in a stage of limbo, not able to move ahead because they feel as if their life is over.

Before the group begins, talk with each child in an individual session to let him or her know what the group is about and to learn what his or her particular situation is. Give students a parent letter to take home that explains the group and asks for a parent signature; see page 148 for a sample letter.

It is important that you feel comfortable with the topic of death before leading a group. There are many good books and journal articles on helping kids deal with loss. Since this topic involves deep feelings, we could not encourage anyone to attempt this group without doing background reading and having some experience leading other types of groups.

Know your own feelings about death. Tune in to your philosophy and beliefs, but be careful about discussing your religious beliefs with students. Look at the losses in your life and how you have dealt with them. Some introspection is helpful before you start leading group sessions. During the group, maintain an attitude of acceptance, concern, and caring. This environment of support allows the expression of sadness and promotes movement through the various stages of loss, which lead to healing.

If this group is meeting because of the death of a fellow student or a teacher, the leader could still use some of these lessons with a small group or a classroom but should perhaps modify the amount of time.

If there is a school crisis, assistance support groups could come from community therapists, hospital chaplains, mental health social workers, or other school counselors in the system.

Logistics

GROUP COMPOSITION

Students in grades 6–8 who have recently experienced the death of a loved one. Students who are within 1–2 grade levels may be grouped.

GROUP SIZE

6–8 students

GROUP TIME PER SESSION

45 minutes

NUMBER OF SESSIONS

Seven

Recommended Resources

Full bibliographic details for these publications are included in the Bibliography at the end of this book.

Buscaglia, 1982: *The Fall of Freddie the Leaf.*

Elkind, 1988: *The Hurried Child: Growing Up Too Fast Too Soon.*

Gootman, 1994: *When a Friend Dies: A Book for Teens About Grieving and Healing.*

Grollman, 1995: *Bereaved Children and Teens: A Support Guide for Parents and Professionals.*

Hipp, 1995: *Help for the Hard Times: Getting Through Loss.*

Kroen, 1996: *Helping Children Cope with the Loss of a Loved One.*

Kübler-Ross, 1974: *On Death and Dying.*

Le Shan, 1976: *Learning to Say Good-Bye: When a Parent Dies.*

Oates, 1993: *Death in the School Community.*

Romain, 1999: *What on Earth Do You Do When Someone Dies?*

Traisman, 1992: *Fire in My Heart Ice in My Veins.*

Parent Letter

Dear Parent:

Your child, _____, has chosen to participate in a group dealing with loss and grief. Often students experience a loss and are not prepared to cope with it. Children may suffer the loss of a parent, a sibling, a friend, or a classmate.

Loss is an issue that has deep impact on people. I hope that our discussions in school will be the beginnings of family discussions in the home.

If you have questions or anything you would like to share with me concerning your child or the counseling program, please call me at _____.

Counselor

Student's Signature _____

Parent's Signature _____

Session 1
Topic: Responses to death, bibliotherapy, journaling

Resources

- Optional: books on death, such as *What on Earth Do You Do When Someone Dies?* (Romain), *When a Friend Dies: A Book for Teens About Grieving and Healing* (Gootman), *Learning to Say Good-Bye,* or *Fire in My Heart Ice in My Veins*

Beginning

INTRODUCTION

Introduce yourself and explain the purpose of the group:

"This is a loss group, and I know that you have experienced a loss in your family. We'll be meeting each week at this time to share with each other how things are going and how you are feeling. This group will be a place where you can talk openly about how you are feeling.

"Sometimes your friends may not understand what you are going through and you may not have anyone to talk to. I have found in leading groups like this that students feel more comfortable talking about death when they realize others have had similar experiences."

SHARING THE SITUATION

"I'd like to begin by going around the group and having each of you state your name and what your particular situation is. Tell us who has died in your family, when it happened, and any details you would like to share with the group."

Talking about their situations in front of the group could stir deep feelings and emotions for some students. Be prepared to use your skills of reflective listening and group leadership.

Middle

1. Discuss with students how friends sometimes don't know what to say. "What are some of the responses you have received when your friends found out about the death?" (Students report that friends sometimes don't say anything, make inappropriate remarks, or ask questions about specific details of the death.)

   "Adults often offer platitudes: 'He's better off because he doesn't have to suffer,' or 'It was his time to go.' None of these exchanges helps us in our grief. Our friends want to help, but because they feel awkward and uncomfortable, they may say the wrong things. What would you like for your friends to say? What would be helpful? If someone you knew were to experience a death of someone close to him or her, what would you do or say?"

2. You may read aloud to the group some selections from books such as *What on Earth Do You Do When Someone Dies?* or *When a Friend Dies: A Book for Teens About Grieving and Healing.*

   Show students some books on death from your guidance library or the school library. Briefly explain each one, and let them check out the books to take home. You may read some passages aloud to the group. *Learning to Say Good-Bye* by Eda Le Shan is a helpful book to read to upper elementary, middle, or high school students.

3. Encourage students to keep a journal during the weeks that the loss group meets. The leader can provide the paper or notebook and allow time to begin writing while in the group. You may give a sentence stem or give an idea each time. *Fire in My Heart Ice in My Veins* is a journaling book for teens. Each participant could have his or her own copy and could continue the writing assignments after the group is over. Some examples of sentence stems are:

   - Our funniest time together . . .
   - Some things I remember you saying . . .
   - What it felt line going back to school after you died . . .
   - Helpful things that others have said or done . . .

End

JOURNAL WRITING

Ask students to think and write their endings to the following sentence stems. Then ask students to share what they would like with a partner. Last, ask volunteers to share with the whole group.

"Today I learned . . ."
"I relearned . . ."
"I was surprised that . . ."
"I can use what I learned this week by . . ."
Preview next session.

Session 2
Topic: Stages of grief

Resources
- Chart paper
- Student journals

Beginning
1. Ask students to share in a go-round their endings for the following statements:

   "My name is . . . and I wish . . ."

   "Some thoughts I have had this week are . . ."

   "A journal writing I would like to share with the group is . . ."

2. Ask students to review what they remember from the last session.

3. Ask if anyone used anything they got from the last session.

Middle
1. Begin discussion with the following. "In our lives we experience many kinds of losses, not just death. What are some other losses you have had?" Students often mention loss of friendships, moving, losing a favorite possession, losing a favorite teacher, having something stolen from them, or losing a pet. Allow students to discuss their particular situation and how they felt when it happened. "What were the feelings you experienced in the beginning, a little later, and when did you finally accept what happened?"

2. Let students know that people experience any kind of loss in stages. According to Dr. Kübler-Ross, in her book *On Death and Dying*, the stages of grief are:
   - denial
   - anger
   - bargaining
   - depression
   - acceptance

List these stages on a chart and have the group members personalize their situations and discuss how they went through or are going through the various stages, and in what order. A person in grief can move back and forth between stages, or can remain stuck in a stage before finally reaching the acceptance stage.

Ask each student: Which stage are you in now?

For those students who may not be in the acceptance stage, use your best empathy and caring skills to help them explore their feelings. Your goal is not to move them to the acceptance stage, but to allow them to state their feelings while you listen and remain there for them.

End

JOURNAL WRITING
Ask students to write in their journals their answers to these sentence stems. When they are done, ask them to share what they choose with the whole group.

"Today I learned or relearned . . ."

"I can see that I need to . . ."

Preview next session.

Session 3
Topic: Changes due to loss

Beginning

Ask students to share their responses to the statement, "My name is . . . and today I feel . . ."

REVIEW

1. Ask students to remember the five stages of grief.
2. Ask them what else they remember about the last meeting.
3. Ask them to share anything they have used from the group this past week.

Middle

THREE QUESTIONS

1. Say to students, "Today I would like to give each of you some time to share with us what is going on with you. As I talk with each person, the rest of you think about how your feelings and experiences are similar or different. Here are some questions I would like you to think about:
   - Since the loss occurred in your family, how has your life changed?
   - What is difficult for you right now?

   - What needs working on or needs to be improved?

2. Say, "Let me give you a minute to think about those questions and we'll begin when you're ready." Give thinking time. "Would someone volunteer to begin our discussion? Maria, you look like you're ready to begin. How has your life changed?"

3. Gently move through the questions, allowing enough time so every group member will have a chance to participate before the period is over.

4. Leave some time at the end of the session to explore similar experiences of other group members. Pull together the idea that everyone has situations that need to be improved, and perhaps some of these situations are normal in any family, not just grieving families.

End

1. Journal writing and sharing:
   "I learned . . ."
   "I relearned . . ."
   "I see that I need to . . ."
2. Preview next meeting.

Session 4
Topic: Memories

Beginning

"The high point of my week was when . . ."
"The low point was when . . ."

REVIEW

1. Spend time summarizing similar experiences that the group shared from last week's activity.

2. Ask for volunteers to share what they have used from the group this past week.

Middle

1. "Focus on a happy memory that you have of the person you have lost. Perhaps there was a vacation you shared, a funny experience, or an especially happy event. I'll give you some thinking time, and then we'll go around the circle and let each person share a happy memory." Have each group member share his or her happy memory. Process the activity by pointing out similarities, differences, and giving affirmation for sharing their personal experiences.

2. "If you could write a letter to that person right now, what would you like to say? Would you like to tell the person how you are doing, about a happy memory, or what you would like him/her to know?

    "What qualities did that person have that you want to have in your life? What messages about living did he or she give you, either with words or by how he/she lived?

"I'll give you some paper and time to think. When you're ready, begin your letter with 'Dear . . .' and write whatever you're feeling. This letter is private, so you won't have to share it with group unless you feel like it."

3. Allow time for everyone to finish the letter. Allow them to discuss the feelings they had while writing the letter. Permit those students who want to read their letter to the group to do so.

4. Sharing these memories often elicits tears and sadness. Sometimes students tune in to the loss of future happy times together. It's important for the counselor not to shut off the expression of sadness. This expression is one key to the healing process. Most people in the student's life are probably uncomfortable with these feelings and don't allow their expression.

End

1. Journal Writing:
    "I learned . . ."
    "I relearned . . ."
    "One thing I can use this week is . . ."

2. Ask students to talk to friends or family about their thoughts or experiences while attending this group.

3. Preview next meeting.

Session 5
Topic: Loss-related art activity

Resources

- Art supplies

Beginning

Ask students to finish the sentence stems:
"I feel happy when . . ."
"I feel sad when . . ."

REVIEW

1. Allow time for students to express how they felt during last week's activity.
2. Ask students to share their experience talking to friends or family about their thoughts or experiences while attending this group.

Middle

1. Provide art supplies and have students draw a picture of the pain associated with their loss. Explain, "The picture does not need to be realistic. You may use symbols, or colors, or simple shapes to express the pain you feel. No one else needs to be able to tell what the picture is about. You will know, and that is all that matters." Students and leaders who insist they have no artistic ability and are reticent about beginning this activity will get deeply involved once you are able to convince them to begin. They may also want to write a poem or short story to accompany their picture.

2. Have each person share his or her drawing with the group, and explain what it means and how he/she is feeling. Students may wish to display their drawings on a wall of the group room.

3. Discuss any books on death the students have read while participating in the group. Encourage them to share their readings and the group discussions with siblings and family members.

End

1. Ask students to discuss what it was like to draw their pain and to share their pictures.
2. Ask students to complete the following sentence stems:
   "Today I learned or relearned . . ."
   "I can see I need to . . ."
3. Preview next meeting.

Session 6
Topic: Rituals

Resources

- Small, soft ball
- Drawing supplies

Beginning

Hold a soft ball in your hand and complete this statement, "A way that I could help someone who is going through loss is . . .".

Throw the ball to a group member who repeats the sentence. Continue until each person has had a turn.

REVIEW

Allow time for students to talk about last week's art activity.

Middle

1. Have students discuss rituals of death: funerals, cremations, wakes, customs of sending flowers and bringing food to the home. Some cultures may have customs that are not familiar to other cultures. What is the importance of the rituals?

Be careful that students are respectful of each others' religions, beliefs, and customs. This discussion can help students understand and appreciate differences.

2. Ask students to draw three pictures using symbols and colors:

    (a) Their life before the loss

    (b) Their life now

    (c) Their life as they hope it will be in the future

3. Ask students to share their pictures with the group.

End

1. Ask students to share what it was like to draw and share today's pictures.

2. Journal writing: "One thing I can start doing now that will help me have the kind of future I want . . ."

3. Ask students to share journal writing.

4. Preview last session.

Session 7
Topic: Handling stress, evaluation, closure

Resources

- Optional: the Children's Stress Scale, in David Elkind, *The Hurried Child*
- Group Evaluation form (page 10)

Beginning

1. Have students complete the sentence, "I hope . . ."
2. Review last session.
3. Share how students are using what they are learning in group.

Middle

1. Losses and changes can create stress. Discuss with the group ways to handle stress. Encourage members to:
   - Get involved in physical activities
   - Develop solid social support networks with family and friends
   - Have a list of positive fun activities they can do in various time limits and at limited or no costs
   - Get enough sleep
   - Eat a healthy diet
2. You may want to look at the Children's Stress Scale, an adaptation of the Holmes Stress Inventory, which is found in David Elkind's book, *The Hurried Child*. Be careful in using this or any

survey. You don't want to cause alarm if a student scores high on the number of losses experienced in the past year. Rather, focus on positive activities—hobbies, physical exercise. Use the scale as an awareness technique, pointing out the importance of taking care of yourself to prevent stressful situations.

Some students remain in the shock stage for months. Often teachers expect these students to be back to normal after several weeks. It may take a year or longer for students to move to acceptance. The most important part of the healing process is to allow the person to express sadness. If someone cannot express sadness, long-term problems often result.

End

1. Ask students to complete written evaluation.
2. Have students respond to the statement, "Something I learned from being in this group is . . .".
3. Let students know that after the group is over, you plan to see each member individually in the next few weeks.
4. If some group members are in need of additional resources, have a conference with a family member and talk to him or her about counseling from a private therapist or community agency.

2.4
Divorce/Changing Families

Grade Level: Middle School	Time Required: 10 Sessions	Author: Barbara Earley Goodman

Purpose

To help students cope with the stress of parent divorce. Students are taught coping skills, and learn about how to constructively deal with typical issues associated with divorce. Bibliotherapy is used to stimulate sharing of thoughts, feelings, and positive coping strategies.

Parent divorce is a significant and growing issue effecting children's social and academic development. Parent divorce is one of the most stressful events that can happen to a child. Support groups have been found to be effective in helping students deal constructively with parent divorce and to be able to return their attention to academic performance and positive peer relations.

Before the group begins, talk with each child in an individual session to let him or her know what the group is about and to learn what his or her particular situation is.

The group leader should be comfortable with his or her own issues about divorce. Self-disclosure should be limited to promoting group rapport and cohesion.

Logistics

GROUP COMPOSITION

Students in grades 6–8 who have recently experienced the divorce of their parents. Students who are within 1–2 grade levels may be grouped.

GROUP SIZE

6–8 students

GROUP TIME PER SESSION

45 minutes

NUMBER OF SESSIONS

Ten

Recommended Resources

Full bibliographic details for these publications are included in the Bibliography at the end of this book.

Brown and Brown, 1986: *The Dinosaurs Divorce.*

Clark, 1998: *When Your Parents Divorce.*

Curran, 1983: *Traits of a Healthy Family.*

Gardner, 1971: *The Boys and Girls Book About Divorce.*

Heegaard, 1990: *When Mom and Dad Separate.*

Heegaard, 1993: *When a Parent Marries Again.*

Jackson, 1998: *When Your Parents Split Up.*

Margolin, 1996: *Complete Group Counseling Program for Children of Divorce.*

Schneider and Zuckerberg, 1996: *Difficult Questions Kids Ask and Are Too Afraid to Ask About Divorce.*

Stern and Stern, 1997: *Divorce Is Not the End of the World.*

Sunburst Communications, 1991: *If Your Parents Break Up* (videocassette).

Session 1
Topic: Sharing family situations

Resources
- Parent Letter handout

Beginning

INTRODUCTION

You may want to begin this way:

"Some of you may have parents who have recently separated, are divorced, or who have divorced and remarried, giving you additional parents and families. Students have found this group to be very helpful because they can share their feelings with other students who have similar experiences. You may remember times when you felt alone and thought no one else could possibly understand what you were feeling. Or you may have felt embarrassed, ashamed, guilty, angry, or hurt. These feelings are all normal, and represent the different stages we go through when we have a breakup in our family.

"At the end of these ten weeks, I hope you will have learned some new skills to help you adjust to your situation, to understand what has happened, and to improve the communication within your family."

SHARING THE CURRENT SITUATION

1. Ask students to tell their name, grade, and a brief summary of their family situation (how long their parents have been divorced or separated, whom they are living with, and what their biggest family concerns are at this time). Give them 30 seconds to think about what they want to say. The counselor may introduce himself/ herself first to get the group started.

2. After the introductions, ask the following questions:

   "What are some things you noticed we had in common with each other?"

   "Sometimes it's helpful to remember that others have problems similar to ours. How many of you have ever felt that you were the only one who had divorced parents, or felt that no one else understood?"

Middle

RULES AND HOUSEKEEPING

1. Let students come up with the rules, but be sure they include:
   - What is said in group is confidential. You own what you say and can share what you say with others if you choose. You do not own what others say and it is important to keep what others say within this group.
   - Don't put each other down.

2. Distribute and explain the parent letter. Remind students that the group meets once per week for ten weeks. They are expected to make up the work they miss while in the group. (You may want to go around and ask each person what class is being missed and how the work will be made up.)

3. Address any comments or questions.

   Ask students to think about the statement, "One thing that has improved since the divorce/separation is . . .". Give them a minute, then go around the circle and ask students to respond.

End

1. Ask students to summarize the purpose of group and the number of sessions.
2. Ask students to complete the statement, "One thing I learned today was . . .".
3. Preview next meeting.
4. Remind students to return the letter in order to attend group next time.
5. Remind students that you are available to them on an individual basis as well as in the group.

Parent Letter

Dear Parents:

We would like to acquaint you with the counseling services at our school. In addition to individual counseling, classroom guidance, and parent-teacher conferences, we offer group sessions that deal with specific concerns. Topics such as getting along with others and managing conflicts, making friends, academic support, changing family group (divorce), dealing with loss, handling peer pressure, and coping with stress and anger are offered to students.

We have invited your child to join a group that emphasizes coping with parent divorce, separation, or remarriage. Many students think of themselves as having problems that no one else has. In the group they discover that other students have similar kinds of issues and problems. For students who have been through a divorce, a separation, or a remarriage, it is frequently a comfort to learn how to accept the situation, build better communication in the family, and then go on with life.

Your son/daughter, _____, has expressed an interest
                                    (student name)
in this group. If you would like to know more about the group, please call. Also, please sign and return this letter to our office.

Sincerely yours,

Counselor

_____

Parent Signature

Session 2
Topic: Video discussion, bibliotherapy

Resources

- Video: *If Your Parents Break Up* (Sunburst)
- Library, other books on divorce

Beginning

1. Ask students to complete this statement: "My name is . . . and today I'm feeling . . ." (on a scale of 1 to 10, where 1 is rotten and 10 is the top of the world). After everyone has responded, ask who can name everyone in the group.

2. Ask students to briefly share with a partner how the past week has gone.

3. Ask volunteers to share past week with group.

4. Collect parent permission letters and discuss parent reaction to student being in group.

Middle

1. Introduce video *If Your Parents Break Up* (Sunburst). Ask students to write down any ideas that occur to them during the video—something they agree or disagree with, or something they hadn't thought of before. Ask them about those ideas when the video is over.

2. Discuss ideas from the video. "What was similar to your situation? What was different? What things did you agree with/disagree with?"

3. Show students library books on divorce. Encourage them to read one during the next ten weeks. (See the list of Recommended Resources on page 156.) You may wish to collect magazine articles on divorce. Ask your media specialist for the Book-Finder, a book that lists children/adolescent books by special topics.)

4. Discuss some positive ways that families can help each other in adjusting to divorce.

End

1. Ask students to think and write their answers to the following:

   "Today I learned . . ."

   "Today I relearned . . ."

   "Today I was surprised that . . ."

   "One thing I learned that I can use this week is . . ."

2. Ask students to share their answers with a partner first, then ask for volunteers to share what they choose with group.

3. Preview next meeting.

Session 3
Topic: Art activity

Resources
- Art supplies

Beginning
Ask students to complete the following statements with a partner:

"I wish my mother would . . ."

"I wish my father would . . ."

"This week has been . . ."

Middle

ART ACTIVITY
1. Provide students with art supplies and have them draw their family. (Long construction paper, magic markers, pieces of fabric, glitter, and glue are useful to have on hand.)
2. Some suggested directions for the family picture: Where in the house are the family members, and what are they doing?

3. When they finish, ask each student to tell group about his/her picture, and then hang the picture on the wall.
4. As the sharing progresses, ask students to comment on similarities they notice.

BOOKS
Discuss books the students have been reading.

End
1. Ask students to think and write their answers to the following:

   "Today I learned or relearned . . ."

   "Today I was surprised that . . ."

   "One thing I learned that I can use this week is . . ."

2. Ask students to share their answers with a partner first, then ask for volunteers to share what they choose with the group.
3. Preview next meeting.

Session 4
Topic: True-False Questionnaire

Resources

- True-False Questionnaire handout
- Optional: Curran, *Traits of a Healthy Family*

Beginning

Ask students, "What are three things that you will do as a parent if you have children one day? They can be things that your parents do that you like, or things you wish they would do. Write them down." Give students time, then ask them to discuss responses in pairs. Ask volunteers to share with group.

Ask students to rate on a scale of 1–10 how things are going at home this week.

Ask who has been trying something they learned in group and how it went.

Give students time to discuss their weekend visitation with a parent or problems at home.

Middle

1. Distribute the True-False Questionnaire, and ask students to fill it out. Discuss each item. Remember to be nonjudgmental!

2. You may want to discuss their future relationships and how their marriages will not necessarily end in divorce.

3. Sometimes students have already decided that they won't get married. It would be a good time to discuss what kinds of things make a good marriage. (*Traits of a Healthy Family* is an excellent book for the purposes of this discussion.)

End

1. Ask students to think and write their answers to the following:

   "Today I learned . . ."

   "Today I was surprised that . . ."

   "One thing I learned that I can use this week is . . ."

2. Ask students to share their answers with a partner first, then ask for volunteers to share what they choose with the group.

3. Preview next meeting.

Name_____ Date _____

True-False Questionnaire

Directions: Write either T for true or F for false.

1. _____ Parents who don't love each other should stay together for the sake of the children.

2. _____ Parents should tell their children why they are getting a divorce.

3. _____ If your parents are divorced, it is likely that when you grow up you will get a divorce.

4. _____ The parent that you visit should not have rules or make you do work.

5. _____ One parent should not make negative comments about the other parent.

6. _____ Your stepparent has no right to discipline you.

7. _____ Children should be included in the decision of whom the parent remarries.

8. _____ Children should not let their parents know how they feel about the divorce.

9. _____ A child should try to make up for the parent who has left by taking on extra responsibilities and being an emotional support to the parent he or she is living with.

10. _____ Children should be able to decide which parent they want to live with.

Session 5
Topic: Sentence completion

Resources
- Sentence Completion handout
- Pencils and paper

Beginning
1. Ask students to complete the following sentences with a partner. Then ask volunteers to share with group.
   "I feel lonely when . . ."
   "I am happy when . . ."
   "I wish . . ."
2. Ask students to review the previous session, anything they tried from group, and how it went.
3. Last, ask students to rate their mood and energy today, each on a 1–10 scale. Discuss briefly how exercise, social support, and fun activities can help increase mood and energy.

Middle

SENTENCE COMPLETION HANDOUT

1. Students fill out two sentences at a time and discuss with a partner. Then volunteers share answers with the group.
2. Have students change partners and answer the next two questions, share answers with partner, then share with group.
3. Continue in this way until all sentences have been completed.

FURTHER DISCUSSION
Rate how things are going at home and discuss reasons for rating.

READING
Discuss books that the students have been reading on the topic of divorce.

End
1. Have students write anonymous "Dear Abby" letters, to be turned in to you and discussed the following week. The letters should be written about a current problem that the student is experiencing because of the family situation. They can make up names to sign the letters (like "Worried and Confused") so that when they're read aloud the letters will be anonymous.
2. Ask students to think and write their answers to the following:
   "Today I learned or relearned . . ."
   "Today I was surprised that . . ."
   "One thing I learned that I can use this week is . . ."
   Ask students to share their answers with a partner first, then ask for volunteers to share what they choose with group.
3. Preview next meeting.

Name_____ Date_____

Sentence Completion

Directions: Complete the following sentences.

1. When I first found out that my parents were getting a divorce, I felt

   _____

   _____

   _____

2. Something I still don't understand about divorce is _____

   _____

   _____

3. One thing that I miss is _____

   _____

   _____

4. A way that I have changed is _____

   _____

   _____

5. I appreciate my mom for _____

   _____

   _____

   but I wish she would _____

   _____

   _____

6. I appreciate my dad for _____

   _____

   _____

   but I wish he would _____

   _____

   _____

(continued)

 Group Counseling for School Counselors: A Practical Guide

Name_____ Date_____

Sentence Completion *(continued)*

7. When my friends learn that my parents are divorced, they _____

_____

_____

8. The way I feel about divorce is _____

_____

_____

9. I can help other students whose parents are divorced by _____

_____

_____

10. If I could change one thing about myself now, it would be _____

_____

_____

11. Negative effects of the divorce are _____

_____

_____

12. Positive things that have happened because of the divorce are

_____

_____

_____

13. Marriage is _____

_____

_____

Session 6
Topic: Dear Abby, role-play

Resources

• "Dear Abby" letters from Session 5

Beginning

Ask students to share their answers to these sentence stems with a partner. Then ask volunteers to share with the group.

"One strength I have . . ."

"One way I am getting better at handling the divorce is . . ."

"One thing I am doing to take good care of myself is . . ."

REVIEW

1. Ask students to state one thing they learned in last week's session, then share something they tried that they learned from group and how it went.

2. Have a quick go-round to share where students are today, on a scale of 1–10, in terms of mood and energy.

Middle

1. Read "Dear Abby" letters and discuss solutions to problems. The students give advice to each other about what to do in each situation. These are usually significant situations and deserve time and attention.

2. After sharing situations and brainstorming solutions, ask students to pick several situations that have the most common ground and then, one at a time, role-play solutions from the group. Multiple students can play the child role in each situation to provide multiple models. The leader may also decide to role-play the student handling a situation.

Note: This session and the previous session with the open sentences provide much material to explore. These could be extended into several sessions. Decide what seems to be most helpful to the students in your group.

End

1. Ask students to think and write their responses to the statements,

"Today I learned or relearned . . ."

"Today I was surprised that . . ."

"One thing I learned that I can use this week is . . ."

2. Ask students to share their answers with a partner first, then ask for volunteers to share what they choose with group.

3. Preview next meeting.

Session 7
Topic: Communicating with body language

Resources

- Body Language in Communication handout

Beginning

1. Ask students to rate their mood and energy on a 1–10 scale and share with group in a go-round.

2. Ask students to share with partner their responses to the statements, "One thing that is going better is . . ." and "One thing I need to work on is . . .".

3. Ask for volunteers to share with group their pair-share discussion.

REVIEW

Ask students to review last meeting, then share what they tried from group this past week and how it went.

Middle

NON-LISTENING EXERCISE

1. Have students get into pairs. One student talks for one minute about any topic: favorite movies, pet, hobby, or vacation spot. The other student demonstrates not paying attention, interrupting, and any other non-listening practices.

2. Switch roles, but this time have the other person demonstrate what he or she considers to be good listening practices.

3. Have the group discuss the behaviors that they noticed with not listening and listening. Have a recorder write down the group's lists of behaviors for both.

BODY LANGUAGE IN COMMUNICATION

1. Distribute the Body Language in Communication handout and go over it with students. Stress the importance of good listening during conflicts and discussions with high emotional levels.

2. Explain the importance of nonverbal communication by using the information on the handout. As you go over each item, ask group to demonstrate do's and don'ts.

3. Use the body language and listening information to role-play some of the situations from the Dear Abby letters from last week. Have group members give feedback on listening and body language after each role-play.

End

1. Ask students to summarize the session.

2. Ask students to share with a partner their responses to the statement, "One thing I learned that I can use this week is . . .".

3. Preview next meeting.

Name_____ Date _____

Body Language in Communication

The communication process is always nonverbal as well as verbal. Behavior expresses meaning, sometimes more clearly than words. To be an effective communicator, one must tune in to body language and tone of voice. Consider the following:

70 percent of what we communicate is through body language.

23 percent of what we communicate is through tone of voice.

7 percent of what we communicate is through words.

How we say something is frequently more important than *what* we say.

	Dos	Don'ts
Eyes	good eye contact	stare, glare, jittery, no eye contact
Voice (volume)	loud enough to be heard clearly	too soft or too loud
Voice (tone)	tone communicates understanding	disinterested, gruff tone, sarcastic
Facial expressions	matches your own or other's feeling; smile	frown, yawn, sigh, scowl, blank look
Posture	leaning forward slightly, relaxed	leaning away, rigid, slouching, crossing arms
Movement	toward	away
Distance	arm's length	too close (less than two feet); too far (more than five feet)

Session 8
Topic: Communication skills

Resources

- Communication Skills handout

Beginning

1. Ask students to rate how they are feeling and their energy level today on a scale of 1–10.
2. Ask them to share with a partner something positive that's happened to them this past week and something they want to change or improve on.

REVIEW

Ask students if, during the last week, they paid attention to body language. What did they notice?

Middle

COMMUNICATION SKILLS

1. To introduce communication skills, have the group members complete the sentence stems on the Communication Skills handout.
2. Discuss with students appropriate times to talk with parents or teachers. Talk about being aware of adult moods, and how to best introduce a topic. Suggest that they make an appointment with the parent. *Example:* "Mom, after we've finished with the dishes tonight, there's some stuff going on at school that I would like to talk with you about. Would you have some time around 8:00?"
3. Have students brainstorm topics they would like to discuss with their parents.
4. Then ask volunteers to role-play the situations. Have the group give feedback on the use of good listening, body language, and communication skills.

End

1. Ask students to share with a partner their responses to the following statements, then ask for volunteers to share with group.

   "Today I learned . . ."

   "One thing I need to do when communicating with my parents is . . ."
2. Preview next week's session.

Name_____ Date_____

Communication Skills

Directions: Complete each of the following statements.

I can tell if Mom or Dad is really listening to me when _____

_____

_____

_____

When something is bothering me, I let them _____

_____

_____

_____

When they start giving advice, I feel _____

_____

_____

_____

I am willing to listen to them if _____

_____

_____

_____

The best time to talk to Mom/Dad is _____

_____

_____

_____

When the parent I am visiting makes negative comments about my other

parent, I _____

_____

_____

Session 9
Topic: I-messages

Resources

- I-Message Model handout
- "Dear Abby" letters from Session 5

Beginning

"A time someone listened to me this week was . . . and I could tell they were listening because . . ."

REVIEW

1. Ask students to recall what the group did last meeting.
2. Ask students to give examples of communication skills—body language, listening, and timing—that they used this past week.

Middle

1. Distribute the I-Message Model handout, and go over it with students.
2. Take a situation from the "Dear Abby" letters or have students describe briefly on paper a problem they are having with a parent right now. Allow 2–3 minutes. In pairs, students take turns being the person who has the problem and giving an I-message to the other person. The person receiving the message checks its accuracy using the checklist on the I-Message Model handout.
3. Save time for some participants, who you can see have the right idea, to role-play their situations in front of the group.

End

1. Ask students to complete the following statements in pairs:

   "Today I learned or relearned . . ."

   "One way I can use what I learned is . . ."
2. Preview the next and last meeting.

ASSIGNMENT

Find a time this week to use an I-message with your parent.

Name_____ Date _____

I-Message Model

When your goals, rights, or safety are being interfered with, **I-messages** are one of the most appropriate ways to communicate what the conflict is to the other person.

I-messages show your concern in a calm and respectful way.

We commonly use **you-messages** instead, which accuse and blame the other person and are usually said with anger or sarcasm.

These are the messages we send with I-messages and you-messages.

I-Messages	You-Messages
I respect you.	do not show respect
This is how I feel.	blame, cause hurt, anger
This is what I want to happen.	accuse, ridicule, criticize

A typical I-message has three parts, which can come in any order: (a) what the speaker feels, (b) the cause of the speaker's feelings, and (c) the reason the speaker feels that way.

"I feel (state feeling) when you (describe specific behavior) because (state how it affects you)."

(continued)

Name_____ Date_____

I-Message Model *(continued)*

Examples of I-Messages and You-Messages

- **I-message:** *I feel* angry *when you* tell something I told you in secret *because I* didn't want anyone else to know.
  You-message: You can't ever keep a secret. You are a pig. I'm never going to speak to you again.

- **I-message:** *I feel* irritated *when you* back out of going at the last minute *because* it leaves me stuck with no one to go with.
  You-message: You're always messing up my plans. I can never count on you. You are such a loser.

- **I-message:** *I feel* upset *when you* tell me to tell Dad stuff about the child support *because* it makes him mad and messes up my weekend.
  You-message: You're ruining my weekends because you're too weak to talk to Dad yourself.

- **I-message:** *I feel* lonely *when you* are gone all the time *because I* miss us doing things together.
  You-message: You're always leaving me here alone. You're so selfish.

I-Messages Checklist

A. Did you:

Say in one brief sentence what you were mad about, by

___ describing the specific behavior that was upsetting;

___ telling the person how you felt about the behavior;

___ stating how the behavior affected you?

B. Were you careful not to:

___ blame, put down, or criticize;

___ bring up the past, threaten, or accuse;

___ get caught up in winning rather than solving the conflict?

Session 10
Topic: Suggestions for parents, closure

Resources

- Art supplies
- Suggestions for Parents from Middle School Students handout
- Group Evaluation form (page 10)

Beginning

In a go-round ask students to complete the statement, "One way I have grown since this divorce is . . .".

REVIEW

Have students review the topics discussed in the divorce group and how these issues have affected their lives.

Middle

1. Ask students to draw a picture using symbols, colors, or real images that represent some ways they have grown in their ability to cope with the divorce or get along with their parents or take good care of themselves, or the most important thing they have learned from participating in the group. They may want to draw the picture as a before-and-after or as a then, now, and in the future.

2. Ask students to share their pictures with the group. Encourage the group to give positive feedback to students as they share about their ability to cope with difficulty, their resiliency, or some positive quality they have.

3. Have group generate a list of suggestions to parents from middle school kids of divorce.

4. Have group compare their lists with the Suggestions for Parents handout, which gives suggestions from other middle school students. Provide a copy of this list for each student who wants one.

End

Allow time for students to fill out evaluations. Then invite students to share anything from the evaluation questions or anything else they would like to say to the group.

CLOSURE

Leader wrap-up includes discussion of seeking outside help, having someone to talk to, and problems that parents may be having. Encourage students to come to you individually. You may wish to continue with a once-a-month support group during the year.

Suggestions for Parents from Middle School Students

- Don't have arguments with your ex and then take it out on your kid.

- Do more things with me.

- Spend time with me.

- When you get remarried don't forget I'm still here.

- Don't put bad ideas into my head about my dad/mom.

- Don't put me in the middle.

- Don't tell me things that you don't want my mom/dad to know.

- Don't leave me alone.

- Don't play favorites.

- Don't influence my decision about whom to live with.

- Don't put me on a guilt trip: "If you leave you can't come back!"

2.5
Handling Conflicts

Grade Level: Middle School	Time Required: 8 Sessions	Author: Greg Brigman

Purpose

This group is designed to teach self-management skills including conflict management, stress management and related social skills, and self awareness. Role-play with coaching feedback is a key strategy in this group.

Logistics

GROUP COMPOSITION

Students grades 6–8 mixed with regard to activity level and behavior control. Avoid loading group with only overactive behavior problem students. Students need multiple models of appropriate behavior. Groups with only behavior problem students usually do not show significant gains in prosocial behavior. Mixed groups are generally very effective.

GROUP SIZE

6–8 students

GROUP TIME PER SESSION

45 minutes

NUMBER OF SESSIONS

Eight, with optional booster sessions spaced approximately one month apart after regular group ends.

Recommended Resources

Full bibliographic details for these publications are included in the Bibliography at the end of this book.

Carruthers et al., 1996: "Conflict resolution as curriculum."

Cross and Rosenthal, 1999: "Three models of conflict effects on intergroup expectations and attitudes."

Elliot and Mihalic, 1997: "Blueprints for Violence Prevention and Reduction."

Goldstein and McGinnis, 1997: *Skillstreaming the Adolescent.*

Johnson et al., 1997: "The impact of conflict resolution training on middle school students."

McWhirter et al., 1998: *At Risk Youth.*

Masten and Coatsworth, 1998: "The development of competence in favorable and unfavorable environments."

Moote, Smythe, and Wodarsky, 1999: *Social Skills Training with Youth in School Settings.*

Newcomb, Bukowski, and Patee, 1993: "Children's peer relations."

Prout and Brown, 1999: *Counseling and psychotherapy with children and adolescents.*

Prout and Prout, 1998: "A meta-analysis of school-based studies of counseling and psychotherapy."

Slavin, Karweit, and Madden, 1989: "What works for students at risk."

Weisz et al., 1987: "Effectiveness of psychotherapy with children and adolescents."

Weisz et al., 1995: "Effects of psychotherapy with children and adolescents revisited."

Session 1
Topic: Thirty personal characteristics

Resources
- How I See Myself: 30 Characteristics handout
- Processing the 30 Characteristics handout
- Student journals

Beginning

INTRODUCTION

Introduce yourself and welcome the group. Give an overview of the topics covered in the group and how the skills and awareness gained can be used. This is a review of the information covered during pre-group screening with individual group members.

HOUSEKEEPING AND RULES

1. Explain the time and length of meetings and the notebook for journal writing.
2. Ask, "What kind of rules do you think we need for this group to make sure everyone feels safe to share ideas and feels respected? Limit rules to a few key ones, making sure that the following rules are included in some form:
   - Share the talk time.
   - Respect the opinions of others even if you disagree—don't put anyone down.
   - You have the right to pass.
   - What you say in the room is confidential. You can share what *you* say with whomever you choose, but you should not share what *others* say.

INTRODUCTIONS

Have the group divide into pairs and allow students five minutes to get acquainted with their partners. Partners will introduce each other to the group, telling about their interests and hobbies and information that was shared.

Middle

1. Distribute the How I See Myself: 30 Characteristics handout. Read each item and clarify terms

when necessary. Students circle their responses. Then have the students write a short paragraph that explains how they see themselves.

2. Next, divide students into pairs. Have partners share with each other how it felt to do this activity and how they see themselves.

3. Discuss these questions with the whole group: "How did you feel when you did this activity?" Students will usually say it felt awkward or embarrassing to grade or judge themselves. Give them permission to grade themselves honestly, to give themselves high scores when they feel that way. "Why does it feel different to give ourselves credit?" Usually we have been taught not to brag, and doing this activity makes you feel as if you are bragging.
   "Which ones were hardest to do?"

4. Finally, have students complete the processing of the How I See Myself sheets using the Processing the 30 Characteristics handout. Use this sheet to discuss the activity. You may want to have students share answers in pairs, then ask for volunteers to share with the whole group.

End

JOURNAL WRITING

Allow students 2–3 minutes to record their impressions of today's session, responding to these questions:
"What was it like to participate in group today?"
"What were some feelings you had?"
"What are some thoughts you have about the group?"
"What do you hope to gain from the group?"

SUMMARY

Ask volunteers to share with the group their responses to the statement, "One thing I learned today was . . .", and anything they would like from their journal.

Name_____ Date _____

How I See Myself: 30 Characteristics

Directions: Rate yourself on a scale from 1 to 5 on the following 30 characteristics. A rating of 5 means you have a lot of that characteristic. A rating of 1 means you have none, and 3 means about average.

Go with your first impression and be honest. There are no right or wrong answers or good or bad characteristics.

No one will see this list but you unless you want to show it to someone.

Characteristic	Not at All		Average		Very Much
1. Happy	1	2	3	4	5
2. Athletic	1	2	3	4	5
3. Follower	1	2	3	4	5
4. Responsible	1	2	3	4	5
5. Enthusiastic	1	2	3	4	5
6. Creative (artistically or in problem solving)	1	2	3	4	5
7. Intelligent	1	2	3	4	5
8. Good listener	1	2	3	4	5
9. Aggressive	1	2	3	4	5
10. Friendly	1	2	3	4	5
11. Optimistic	1	2	3	4	5
12. Leader	1	2	3	4	5
13. Shy	1	2	3	4	5
14. Helpful	1	2	3	4	5
15. Loner	1	2	3	4	5
16. Competitive	1	2	3	4	5
17. Clumsy	1	2	3	4	5

(continued)

         Group Counseling for School Counselors: A Practical Guide

Name_____ Date _____

How I See Myself: 30 Characteristics *(continued)*

Characteristic	Not at All		Average		Very Much
18. Sincere	1	2	3	4	5
19. Good sense of humor	1	2	3	4	5
20. Outgoing	1	2	3	4	5
21. Carefree	1	2	3	4	5
22. Open (willing to share)	1	2	3	4	5
23. Attractive	1	2	3	4	5
24. Worried	1	2	3	4	5
25. Like to be part of a group	1	2	3	4	5
26. Popular	1	2	3	4	5
27. Angry	1	2	3	4	5
28. Dependable	1	2	3	4	5
29. Bored	1	2	3	4	5
30. Confident	1	2	3	4	5

Now write a short paragraph explaining how you see yourself.

_____

_____

_____

_____

_____

_____

_____

_____

Name_____ Date_____

Processing the 30 Characteristics

1. I learned I was more _____ and
_____ than I thought. I was also less
_____, _____,
and _____ than I thought.

2. Write a summary sentence about yourself using what you learned from reviewing your ratings. You may want to begin with:

   I'm the kind of person who is _____

   _____

   _____

   _____

3. Three strengths I have are: _____,
_____ , and _____.

4. The qualities I would like to have more of are _____,
_____, and _____.

5. With a partner, share some strengths and qualities you'd like more of.

   _____

   _____

   _____

   _____

6. Each person share this with the group:

   I was surprised that _____

   _____

   _____

   _____

   _____

Session 2
Topic: Stress

Resources
- Getting a Handle on Stress handout
- Student journals

Beginning

Have each student in turn tell the group, "My name is . . . and something I do to relax after a stressful day is . . .".

REVIEW

Have each student share what he or she learned in last week's session.

Middle

1. Introduce the topic of stress with the following questions:

   "How many of you feel some stress today?"

   "How do you know when you are under stress?"

   "What are the symptoms?"

   "Name some physical symptoms."

   "Think about the things that cause you stress. Imagine tossing all those words into the center of our circle in a pile. Tell us what causes you stress and throw them on the pile." Some answers that are typically given:

grades	boys/girls
friends	relationships
teachers	school
parents	decisions
time	tests
goals	

2. As students call out different answers, have them explain how that topic causes stress. Say, "Sometimes we feel stress when we think we have to be perfect, expecting perfection of ourselves or others. We may feel disappointed or angry when we feel we have to perform and we don't have the resources for it. Let's look at some ways to handle stress."

3. Hand out the reproducible activity "Getting a Handle on Stress." Say, "As we read the 11 suggestions for dealing with stress,"
   - "Choose your favorites."
   - "Check the ones you already use."
   - "Circle the ones you would like to use more."

4. Have volunteers read each suggestion, using each one as a stimulus to generate student discussion.

5. Have students share their ratings and ask for examples. Discuss which strategies are hardest, easiest, most helpful.

End

JOURNAL WRITING

1. Allow students 1–2 minutes to record their impressions of today's session.

2. Ask students to complete, in their journals, the statements "Today I learned . . ." and "One way I can use what I learned is . . .".

SUMMARY

1. Ask students to share their answers with a partner, then ask for a few volunteers to share with the whole group.

2. Preview the next session.

Name_____ Date _____

Getting a Handle on Stress

Here are some suggestions for how to handle stress.

1. **Work off stress.** If you are angry or upset, try to blow off steam physically through activities such as running or sports. Even taking a walk can help.

2. **Talk out your worries.** It helps to share worries with someone you trust and respect. This may be a friend, family member, teacher, or counselor. Sometimes another person can help you see a new side to your problem and, thus, a new solution.

3. **Learn to accept what you cannot change.** If the problem is beyond your control at this time, try your best to accept it until you can change it. It beats spinning your wheels and getting nowhere.

4. **Get enough sleep and rest.** Lack of sleep can lessen your ability to deal with stress by making you more irritable.

5. **Balance work and recreation.** "All work and no play can make Jack a nervous wreck!" Schedule time for recreation to relax your mind.

6. **Do something for others.** Sometimes when you are distressed, you concentrate too much on yourself and your situation. When this happens, it is often wise to do something for someone else and get your mind off yourself. There is an extra bonus in this technique: It helps to make friends.

(continued)

Name_____ Date _____

Getting a Handle on Stress *(continued)*

7. **Take one thing at a time.** Many times we set ourselves up for failure by trying to do too many things at the same time. It is defeating to tackle all your tasks at once. Instead, set some aside and work on the most urgent tasks first.

8. **Give in once in a while.** If you find the source of your stress is other people, try giving in instead of fighting and insisting you are always right. You may find that others will begin to give in, too.

9. **Know your abilities and your limitations.** Many times stress is caused by asking yourself to do something you are not able to do. Before agreeing to do something you do not have to do, ask yourself if the task is within your ability to accomplish.

10. **Organize yourself and your time.** Learn ways to help yourself keep up with what you have to do. Plan how you will accomplish the necessary work. Organization can help you avoid wasting time and energy.

11. **Avoid being a perfectionist.** No one person can be perfect at everything. Do your best, but don't be afraid of making a mistake. Everyone makes mistakes, and many times we learn by our mistakes.

Adapted from "Plain Talk About Stress," DHHS Publication No. (ADM) 81-502, and Linda Worley's "The Stress Group." Cobb County Schools, Georgia.

Session 3
Topic: Things I like to do

Resources
- Things I Like to Do handout
- Student journals

Beginning
1. Have each student in turn tell the group, "My name is . . . and how I feel on a scale of 1 to 10 is . . ." (where 1 is the pits and 10 means wonderful.)
2. Also, have each student name something he or she has done for fun in the past week.

REVIEW
Ask students to tell you some things they remember from your last meeting.

Middle
Give a rationale for spending time on things we like to do. "One of the best ways to relieve stress and improve our mood is to routinely do things that we enjoy. Having a clear idea of many things we can do helps us not be bored and to live more healthily."

1. Tell students you'd like them to think about all the things they enjoy doing. Hand out the reproducible activity sheet Things I Like to Do. Let students spend about 2–3 minutes listing as many activities as they can. Lists should include at least 10 activities.
2. After students have listed the things they enjoy doing, ask them to do the following:
   - In the first column on the right, check your five favorite activities.
   - In the second column, put a **P** beside those activities you like to do with people and an **A** beside those that you like to do alone.
   - In the third column, put a **$** sign if the activity costs $5 or more each time you do that activity.
   - In the next column, indicate by a **W** or **M** whether you have done this activity in the past week or month. If you haven't done this activity in a month, leave it blank.
   - Now fill in the lines at the bottom of the activity sheet.
3. When students have finished marking their activity sheets, complete the activity as follows:
   - Go around the circle and have students share the top three things they like to do.
   - Ask how many students found that they enjoy doing more activities with people than alone, and vice versa.
   - How many students had at least five or more activities that don't cost $5 each time they do them? What were these activities?
   - How many of the activities have students done within the last week?
   - Ask students to share with the group what they wrote at the bottom of the activity sheet about being surprised and learning about themselves.

End
1. Allow students 1–2 minutes to record their impressions of today's session.
2. Ask students to complete, in their journals, the statements
   "Today I learned . . ." and "One way I can use what I learned is . . .".
3. Ask volunteers to share their statements with the group.
4. Preview next session.

Name_____ Date _____

Things I Like to Do

Directions: List as many things as you can that you really enjoy doing, that are fun, that make you happy. These can be very simple or complicated; they can be done with people or alone. List at least 10 things.

1.				
2.				
3.				
4.				
5.				
6.				
7.				
8.				
9.				
10.				
11.				
12.				
13.				
14.				
15.				

What did you find out about yourself?

I learned that _____

_____

_____

I was surprised (or pleased) that _____

_____

_____

Session 4
Topic: Managing ourselves

Resources

- Index cards prepared with role-play questions

Beginning

THE NAME GAME

Go around the circle with students saying their first name and an animal they like. After the first person, the second person says, "That's Tom, he likes gorillas; I'm Venetta and I like horses." Each person begins with the first person and says the name and animal of all persons before him or her. The last person—the group leader—names all the group members and the animals they like.

REVIEW

Ask students to tell you some things they remember from your last meeting.

Middle

1. Ask the group to brainstorm the top 10 reasons students their age get into conflicts with each other. Next ask for some real-life examples they have experienced recently.

2. Ask group members to help decide on one event for the group to role-play. Look for events with the most common ground among group members.

3. Ask the person with the chosen situation to become the director and choose 1–3 group members to help act out the story. The director plays himself/herself and shows/tells the other actors what to do/say. General guidelines for setting the scene and directing the story include answering the following questions. Give these questions on a card for the person who is the director.

QUESTIONS FOR ROLE-PLAY

- What is the setting (where and when)?
- Who are the main characters and how are they feeling at the beginning of the story?
- What is the problem?

- What happens first?
- What are the feelings and reactions of the other characters?
- What do the characters do to try and solve the problem?
- How does the story end and how are the characters feeling?

Limit role-play prep to 2–3 minutes and role-play to 2–3 minutes.

4. After the role-play, have group discuss the pros and cons of how the director handled the situation and explore alternative ways to handle the situation. Both supportive and corrective feedback/coaching are needed to help people improve. Model the sandwich approach: give supportive feedback (bread), then corrective feedback (meat), then finish with supportive feedback (bread).

5. Ask students to use a go-round to share positives about the role-play: "I liked the way you . . .". Then have another go-round for coaching feedback: "You may want to consider . . .".

6. Have group members act out alternative ways of handling the situation and get group feedback as to strengths and things that may need changing.

End

1. Allow students 1–2 minutes to record their impressions of today's session.

2. Ask students to complete, in their journals, the statements

   "Today I learned . . ." and "One way I can use what I learned is . . .".

3. Ask students to rate their energy, mood, what they've eaten, and how much sleep/rest they've gotten, each on a 1–10 scale (10 is the best).

4. Remind students that this is the halfway point of the group sessions, with just four to go.

5. Preview next session.

Session 5
Topic: Handling conflict

Resources
- Handling Conflicts handout

Beginning
1. Ask students to create a weather report that reflects how they are feeling today. They can use wind, all forms of precipitation, temperature, sun, and clouds. *Example:* "Today I am feeling sunny and clear with a slight chance of afternoon thundershowers," or "partly cloudy with a chance of rain, clearing about 3 P.M., and then warm and sunny."
2. Review last session. Ask, "What do you remember about our last meeting?"

Middle
1. Tell students, "I want to share with you some ideas about how students your age can handle conflicts when they occur. I want us to discuss these ideas and I would like your opinion of each of them. After we finish going over them I would like for us to have a chance to role-play a few situations and use some of the ideas that you find most helpful."
2. Distribute the Handling Conflicts handout. As you go over the items on the handout, ask the following questions:
   - Why is #1 important?
   - What errors in #2 do you most frequently use and which do you most often see used by others?
   - Why is it so difficult to tell someone what you are angry about?
   - Who knows what reflective listening is? Why do you think reflecting/rephrasing someone's ideas would be helpful in settling a conflict? What would an example sound like?

3. After going over the handout, ask for an example of a recent conflict. Choose one that is typical so all group members can benefit from the role-play. Select a student to direct the role-play. First have the student provide the background using the following cues:
   The setting—Where and when and who the main characters were.
   The problem—and what each character was feeling.
   The attempted solution and how each character felt afterward.
4. Now ask the director to try solving the conflict by going through the steps on the Handling Conflicts sheet.
5. Ask the other students to provide feedback—first, on what the director did that was helpful/useful/positive, then any other ideas they have for handling the conflict. Have students role-play the best alternatives, and provide them with feedback.

End
1. Ask students to record their reaction to participating today in their journals. Ask them to respond to the questions, "What did I learn or relearn today?" and "How can I use what I learned?"
2. Also ask them to rate on a 1–10 scale their mood, energy, amount of sleep, exercise, and fun for the week.
3. Ask students to share their answers with a partner.
4. Ask for volunteers to share their reflections with the whole group.
5. Preview the next session.

Name_____ Date _____

Handling Conflicts

Listed below are seven keys to handling conflicts that end in a win-win situation. Adolescents who use these keys regularly tend to have fewer conflicts and better relationships than those who handle their conflicts either more passively or more aggressively. Look over the list and decide which ideas would be most helpful to you.

1. Notice when you start to become angry and rate your anger quickly on a 1–10 scale, where 10 is volcano and 1 is relaxed and peaceful. If you are at 9 or 10, cool off to at least a 7 or 8 before you try to handle the problem with the person with whom you are in conflict.

2. Avoid these common errors in handling the conflict:

   - Interrupting

   - Bringing up the past—"You always . . ."

   - Bringing in allies—"Everybody thinks you . . ."

   - Trying to win rather than trying to solve the problem—work for a win-win solution

   - Blaming—"It's all your fault."

   - Name-calling and other put-downs—"You're so dumb," "That's a stupid idea."

   - Threatening—"If you don't shut up, I'm going to punch you."

3. Tell the person with whom you are in conflict specifically what he or she is doing that is causing you a problem. Keep this very short and to the point. Name the action that bothers you, and the way it affects you: "When you _____,

   then I _____."

(continued)

Name_____ Date _____

Handling Conflicts *(continued)*

4. Expect the other person to defend himself/herself and to want to tell his/her side of the story. Listen respectfully and reflect the other person's point of view—even if you totally disagree with it. You are trying to let her know you heard what she has to say, because you want her to hear what you have to say. The best reflective responses include a paraphrase of what the person said and your best guess as to how he is feeling.

5. Brainstorm possible solutions. Now that the other person knows what your position is and you know what his or her position is, the next step is to see if you can find a solution that will satisfy both. It may not be the perfect solution. You are looking for the best available alternative. "Best available" means both people can live with it. "OK so you want this and I want that—how can we work this out so we both get what we need?"

6. Weigh the pros and cons of each alternative. You are looking for the alternative with the most pros and the fewest cons.

7. Decide on the best alternative and commit to putting it to work. Set a time to check with each other to see how the new plan is working. You may need to alter the new plan when you actually put it into action. Be careful not to throw it out too soon just because it is not perfect. Most new plans take some fine-tuning.

Session 6
Topic: Managing ourselves

Resources
- Chart paper

Beginning

Have students complete the following open-ended sentences in their journals and share them with the group.
"I like being with people who . . ."
"I trust people who . . ."
"I'm a good friend because . . ."

REVIEW

Ask students to tell you some things they remember from your last meeting. If you didn't get a chance to finish the do's and don'ts of handling conflicts, now is the time.

Middle

HANDLING CONFLICTS

1. Ask students to write down typical problems either that they have had with other students at school or that they notice lots of other students have at school. Ask them not to put their names on the lists. Tell them you will collect everyone's ideas in a moment and the group will discuss: (a) if they agree that each problem is typical and (b) some possible solutions.

2. Collect the lists of problems. Read each one and ask if it is a typical problem for this age group. List on a flip chart all the agreed upon typical problems. Ask group members to rank the top three problems in terms of interest to them for discussing possible solutions.

3. Lead a discussion on possible solutions for the selected top three problems. Use a brainstorming

technique. List all offered solutions first. Then go back and have the group code each one as "H," helpful, or "HA," harmful to self or others. *Note:* Some will be rated as both. Have group decide if the helpful side outweighs the harmful side.

4. Ask group to divide into pairs and plan a role-play for one of the three problems. The role-play should include one of the helpful solutions. Ask students to use some of the ideas from last week's Handling Conflicts sheet. Allow approximately five minutes for planning.

5. Ask pairs to present their role-plays. Ask the rest of the group to discuss how realistically each problem and solution were portrayed, and to demonstrate additional suggestions for handling the problem. You can also demonstrate various positive alternative ways to handle the situation or coach students in different ways to act. *Note:* It is the role-play and coaching that make this a powerful learning activity.

End

1. Allow students five minutes to record their impressions of today's session.

2. Ask them to rate their energy, mood, what they've eaten, and how much sleep/rest they've gotten, each on a 1–10 scale (where 10 is the best).

3. Ask students to complete, in their journals, the statements "One thing I learned or relearned today was . . ." and "One way I can use what I learned is . . .", then share them with the group.

4. Preview the next session.

Session 7
Topic: More practice in handling conflicts

Resources
- Optional: video camera, TV, VCR

Beginning
1. Ask students to respond to the sentence: "One way I am getting better at handling conflicts is . . ."
2. Review last meeting:

   "What do you remember about what we did last week?"

   "Who tried some of the strategies we practiced? How did it go?"

Middle
1. Say, "Today is our next-to-last meeting and I wanted you to have a chance to put everything you have learned together. I have planned to videotape some of our role-plays and we will get a chance to watch the tape when we finish." (*Note:* You should cover the videotaping during pre-group screening and get parent permission). Taping is not essential but recommended. Students' learning increases when they can see and hear how they act when trying to handle a conflict. The use of videotape speeds up learning and is a great teaching tool.
2. Ask students to think of some typical conflicts that would be good for role-play. With a go-round, hear possible situations for the role-play. Have the group select one that has a lot of common ground.
3. The student whose situation is chosen is the director. Use cues to get the background:

Setting—when, where, and who the main characters are

Problem—in one brief sentence, and how each character is feeling about problem

4. Next have director and other characters role-play their best shot at handling the conflict skillfully and respectfully. When they finish, ask other students if they have any changes they would like to model.
5. Stop the tape, rewind, and show it to group, stopping at spots for group feedback. If you are not taping, then use the normal feedback system. Either way be sure to point out both positive behavior and share ideas for improving.
6. If time permits, repeat the process.

End
1. Allow students five minutes to record their impressions of today's session.
2. Ask them to rate their energy, mood, what they've eaten, and how much sleep/rest they've gotten, each on a 1–10 scale (where 10 is the best).
3. Ask students to complete, in their journals, the statements "One thing I learned or relearned today was . . ." and "One way I can use what I learned is . . ." and then share them with the group.
4. Remind the group that the next meeting is the last weekly meeting for the group.

Session 8
Topic: Wrap-up and evaluation

Resources

- Index cards or sheets of paper
- Group Evaluation form (page 10)

Beginning

REVIEW

1. Students review last meeting. Briefly go over each topic you've covered since the group began, asking for what they remember.

2. Go around the circle, asking students to finish this sentence: "The most important thing I have learned in this group is . . ."

Middle

ACCEPTING AND GIVING COMPLIMENTS

1. Hand out index cards or sheets of paper. Each person is to write down at least one thing they like or appreciate about each other group member. Specific qualities and behaviors are the goal here, not general terms like "you're nice," but what makes that person nice, e.g., "you are friendly, kind, thoughtful, funny."

2. Spotlight: Each group member will say directly to the "spotlighted" person, with eye contact: "[person's name], one thing I like or appreciate about you is . . .".

   After each comment the spotlighted person simply says "thank you," nothing else. (Be sure you get in on this. It feels good.)

3. Process the spotlighting activity. How did it feel receiving compliments? Giving compliments?

End

1. Students complete anonymous evaluation.

2. Concluding remarks: Invite students to make individual appointments if they want.

3. A follow-up meeting in a month is very helpful in maintaining gains. Many counselors set monthly follow-up meetings when their regular weekly meetings end.

Part 3:
Elementary School Group Plans

3.1
Academic and Social Support: Student Success Skills

| Grade Level: 3–5 | Time Required: 10 Sessions | Author: Greg Brigman |

Purpose

To develop academic and social skills with school success. Goal setting, progress monitoring, taking responsibility, social problem solving, and friendship skills and stress management are the focus of the group.

Logistics

GROUP COMPOSITION

Students in grades 3–5, mixed with regard to activity level and behavior control. Avoid loading group with only overactive behavior problem students. Students need multiple models of appropriate behavior. Groups with only behavior problem students usually do not show significant gains in prosocial behavior. Mixed groups are generally very effective.

GROUP SIZE

4–6 students

GROUP TIME PER SESSION

30 minutes

NUMBER OF SESSIONS

Ten, with booster sessions spaced approximately one month apart after regular group ends.

Recommended Resources

Full bibliographic details for these publications are included in the Bibliography at the end of this book.

Brigman, Lane, and Lane, 1994: *Ready to Learn.*

Goldstein and McGinnis, 1997: *Skillstreaming the Adolescent.*

Hattie, Biggs, and Purdie, 1996: "Effects of learning skills interventions on student learning."

Masten and Coatsworth, 1998: "The development of competence in favorable and unfavorable environments."

Prout and Prout, 1998: "A meta-analysis of school-based studies of counseling and psychotherapy."

Prout and Brown, 1999: *Counseling and Psychotherapy with Children and Adolescents.*

Slavin, Karweit, and Madden, 1989: "What works for students at risk."

Wang, Haertel, and Walberg, 1994: "What helps students learn?"

Weisz et al., 1987: "Effectiveness of psychotherapy with children and adolescents."

Weisz et al., 1995: "Effects of psychotherapy with children and adolescents revisited."

Zimmerman and Arunkumar, 1994: "Resiliency research."

Session 1
Topic: Get acquainted, self-evaluation

Resources

- This Is Me handout
- Student Success Skills Self-Evaluation handout

Beginning

INTRODUCTION

Review the purpose of the group (this has been covered individually during the screening): to have fun exploring interests, abilities, strengths, and areas you want to improve. Emphasize that each person is special and unique, and the group will give each person an opportunity to learn more about himself or herself. It will also give each person a chance to understand how to use his/her strengths to be successful in school. We'll play, draw, and talk about topics like friends, stress, and doing well in school.

Go over number of meetings, time, and place.

GROUP RULES

Ask: "What rules do we need to work together, feel safe, and enjoy ourselves?" Be sure to include:

- Confidentiality (You own what you say and can share that with anyone, but what others say stays in the group.)
- Respect others' opinions (no put-downs).
- The right to pass

Secure group consensus on each group rule.

Middle

SKILL-BUILDING OR AWARENESS ACTIVITY 1

1. Distribute the "This Is Me" handout. Students break into pairs. Partners interview one another using the handout, and then each student introduces his or her partner to the group.
2. Discuss similarities and differences. This activity usually works better if you take two items at a time to discuss in pairs, then share with a large group, then discuss next two items in pairs, etc.
3. Get the students involved in looking for what group members have in common.

SKILL-BUILDING OR AWARENESS ACTIVITY 2

1. Introduce the Student Success Skills Self-Evaluation handout. Let the group know that each week they will go over these items and learn how to use problem solving to improve in any area they are not doing as well as they would like.
2. As you go over the form use each item as a discussion starter. These are the behaviors that successful students are able to do well and that struggling students have not yet mastered. Repeated exposure to concrete examples of how to perform these essential skills is the core of this group. If deficits in reading and/or math are present it is advisable to also involve the student with tutoring.

End

1. Ask students the purpose of the group, how many meetings, and so forth.
2. Ask them to share one thing they are looking forward to about the group.
3. Preview the second meeting.

Name_____ Date_____

This Is Me

Name _____

Birthday _____

Favorite TV show _____

Favorite movie _____

Favorite thing to eat _____

Things I like to do (hobbies, sports, etc.) _____

_____

- -

Name_____ Date_____

This Is Me

Name _____

Birthday _____

Favorite TV show _____

Favorite movie _____

Favorite thing to eat _____

Things I like to do (hobbies, sports, etc.) _____

_____

196

Name_____ Date_____

Student Success Skills Self-Evaluation

Directions: The following skills are all important for doing well in school. Rate yourself on each item. Use a 1–5 scale, in which 5 is the highest/best and 1 is the lowest/worst.

1. I go to class with the materials I need.	1	2	3	4	5
2. I read and understand all assignments.	1	2	3	4	5
3. I have a folder or notebook for each class to help me stay organized.	1	2	3	4	5
4. I turn in all work on time— no zeros.	1	2	3	4	5
5. I keep track of my grades. I know how my teacher decides the final grade.	1	2	3	4	5
6. I listen and focus during class. I usually understand what is being taught.	1	2	3	4	5
7. I ask questions when I do not understand what is being taught. I know when and how to ask questions.	1	2	3	4	5
8. I know what to study for tests and what is expected for reports. I plan ahead for both to avoid last-minute cramming.	1	2	3	4	5
9. I have at least one study buddy in each class.	1	2	3	4	5
10. I work well in pairs or small groups with others in class.	1	2	3	4	5

(continued)

Name_____ Date_____

Student Success Skills Self-Evaluation *(continued)*

My top three strengths from the list on the other page are:

1. _____

    _____

2. _____

    _____

3. _____

    _____

The areas I most want to improve are:

1. _____

    _____

2. _____

    _____

     Group Counseling for School Counselors: A Practical Guide

Session 2
Topic: Process self-evaluation handout

Resources

- Student Success Skills Self-Evaluation handout (page 197)

Beginning

MOVEMENT AND GROUP NORMS

1. Build movement into each group session: a few stretches, follow the leader, Simon Says, and a few slow deep breaths. Suggestions for stretches and breathing: stand and stretch (picking grapes or "head, shoulders, knees and toes" song), shoulder rolls, neck rolls, hand clasped behind back. For breathing—inhale slowly to count of three. Hold to count of three. Exhale slowly to count of three. Hold to count of three. Repeat three times.

2. After modeling these, ask students to take turns leading the others in each one. These can be used at the beginning of each session or during the session when a change of pace is needed.

REINFORCING POSITIVE GROUP NORMS

In a go-round ask students for a five-second response to each of the following stems. Summarize the results at the end.

"When people talk to me, I like for them to . . ."

"A person who talks all the time makes me feel . . ."

"A 'put-down' makes me feel . . ."

"I am willing to listen if . . ."

"When I am not listened to, I feel . . ."

Middle

STUDENT SUCCESS SKILLS SELF-EVALUATION

1. Go through each item, reading it aloud and asking students to rate how they did during the last week. Ask, "Who rated that item 'Good,' who rated it 'OK,' who rated it 'Needs to improve?'"

2. Use the items to stimulate discussion and to clarify problem areas that need to be addressed.

3. Introduce problem solving by asking students to brainstorm solutions to problems raised as you move down the list. Role-playing solutions to problems is a valuable way to help students learn alternative strategies for handling difficult situations. The problem solving can also include how to handle the social problems that come up as the group meets.

End

1. Ask students to write an ending to the following two statements. Ask them to share their answers with a partner. Then ask for volunteers to share what they wrote.

   "One thing I learned today was . . ."

   "One way I can use what I learned today is . . ."

2. Preview next session.

Session 3
Topic: Drawing and storytelling

Resources

- Paper and markers
- Student Success Skills Self-Evaluation handout (page 197)

Beginning

MOVEMENT, CHECKING GROUP TEMPERATURE, GOAL REPORTING

Stretches, movement, and breathing (student-led), used to balance active and passive activities.

THE NAME GAME

1. Go around the circle asking students to say their first name and an animal they like. After the first person, the second person says, "That's Tom, he likes gorillas, and I'm Mary and I like horses," and so on. Each person begins with the first person and gives the names and animals of all persons coming before. (Pay attention. The leader says all of the names and animals at the end.) It is important to have everyone know and use all the names.

2. In a go-round ask students to rate how they are feeling on the "great, pretty good, not so wonderful, really bad" scale. Be sure to check with any "not so good" or "really bad" to determine if follow-up is needed.

3. Ask, "Who used something we talked about last week during the week? How did it go?"

Middle

DRAWING AND STORYTELLING ABOUT A FRIEND

1. Hand out a blank sheet of paper with markers. Say, "Draw a picture of you and a friend (now or in the past—or the friend you'd like to have) doing something fun." Model by drawing a primitive picture and stressing that the quality of the drawing is not the focus.

2. Ask the students to put the fun event into a story. Put the four Ws and an H questions—who, what, when, where, how—on a chart and go over these questions with the students. Ask them to include the answers in their story.

3. Ask the students to pair up and take turns telling their stories. As the first person finishes the listener summarizes the story by going through the four

Ws and an H questions. Then the listener becomes the storyteller and the process is repeated.

Note: Model storytelling first by listening to a story. Demonstrate eye contact, leaning forward, looking interested, and avoiding distractions. Then summarize by using the four Ws and an H questions—the who, what, when, where, how of the story:

- **who** story was about
- **what** story was about
- **when** story happened, e.g., day, night, spring, summer
- **where** story happened, e.g., inside, outside
- **how** story made storyteller feel, and **how** the story ended

4. Next have pairs tell story (approximately one minute), then lead the group in answering each of the four Ws and an H questions. The storytelling and listening provide practice for key learning skills.

STUDENT SUCCESS SKILLS SELF-EVALUATION

1. Go through each of the items, reading them aloud and asking students to rate how they did that week. Ask "Who rated that item 'Good,' who rated it 'OK,' who rated it 'Needs to improve?'"

2. Use the items to stimulate discussion and to clarify problem areas that need to be addressed.

3. Use group problem solving by asking students to brainstorm solutions to problems students bring up as you move down the list. Role-playing solutions to problems is a valuable way to help students learn alternative strategies for handling difficult situations. The problem solving can also include how to handle the social problems that come up during the group meetings.

End

1. Ask students to write an ending to the following two sentences. Ask them share their answers with a partner. Then ask for volunteers to share what they wrote.

   "One thing I learned today was . . ."

   "One way I can use what I learned today is . . ."

2. Preview next session.

Session 4
Topic: Problem solving

Resources

- Student Success Skills Self-Evaluation handout (page 197)

Beginning

1. Stretches, movement, and breathing (student-led), used to balance active and passive activities.

2. In a go-round ask students to rate how they are feeling on the "great, pretty good, not so good, really bad" scale. Be sure to check with any "not so good" or "really bad" to determine if follow-up is needed.

3. Ask students to tell you some things they remember from last meeting.

4. Ask, "Who used something we talked about last week during the week? How did it go?"

Middle

SOCIAL PROBLEM SOLVING

1. Ask students about problems either that they have had with other students/teachers at school or that they notice lots of other students have with each other at school. Make a list.

2. Ask the group members to rank the top three problems in terms of interest to them for having the group discuss possible solutions.

3. Lead a discussion on possible solutions for the selected top three problems. Use a brainstorming technique. List all offered solutions first. Then go back and have group code each one as "H," helpful, or "HA," harmful to self or others. *Note:* Some will be rated as both. Have group decide if the helpful side outweighs the harmful side.

4. Ask group to divide into pairs and plan a role-play for one of the three problems. The role-play should

include one of the helpful solutions. Allow approximately five minutes for planning.

5. Ask pairs to present their role-plays. Ask the rest of the group to discuss how realistically the problem and solution were portrayed, and to demonstrate additional suggestions for handling the problem. The leader can also demonstrate various positive alternative ways to handle the situation or coach students in different ways to act. *Note:* It is the role-play and coaching that make this a powerful learning activity.

STUDENT SUCCESS SKILLS SELF-EVALUATION

1. Go through each item, reading it aloud and asking students to rate how they did that week. Ask, "Who rated that item 'Good,' who rated it 'OK,' who rated it 'Needs to improve?'"

2. Use the items to stimulate discussion and to clarify problem areas that need to be addressed.

3. Use group problem solving by asking students to brainstorm solutions to problems raised as you move down the list. Role-playing solutions to problems is a valuable way to help students learn alternative strategies for handling difficult situations. The problem solving can also include how to handle the social problems that come up during the group meetings.

End

1. Ask students to write responses to the following two sentences. Ask them share their answers with a partner. Then ask for volunteers to share what they wrote.

   "One thing I learned today was . . ."

   "One way I can use what I learned today is . . ."

2. Preview next session.

Session 5
Topic: Problem-solving role-play

Resources

- Friendship Problems handout
- Student Success Skills Self-Evaluation handout (page 197)

Beginning

1. Stretches, movement, and breathing (student-led), used to balance active and passive activities.

2. In a go-round ask students to rate how they are feeling on the "great, pretty good, not so good, really bad" scale. Be sure to check with any "not so good" or "really bad" to determine if follow-up is needed.

3. Ask students to tell you some things they remember from last meeting.

4. Ask, "Who used something we talked about last week during the week? How did it go?"

5. Have students complete the following statements and share their responses with the group.

   "I like being with people who . . ."

   "I trust people who . . ."

   "I'm a good friend because . . ."

Middle

SOCIAL PROBLEM SOLVING

1. Use the three typical friendship problems on the Friendship Problems handout to stimulate discussion, problem solving, and role-playing of solutions. Divide the group into pairs and ask them to develop a specific solution to the typical problems presented on the handout. The problems are presented as if students had written to a newspaper counselor similar to Dear Abby for advice.

2. After coming up with a solution for each problem, each pair plans a role-play of one of the three problems and the solution. Both role-plays last a maximum of one minute.

3. Each pair presents their role-plays of the problem and their solution. After each problem and solution is role-played the group discusses their reaction to the problem and to the solution as well as to other possible alternatives. Three helpful tips for using role-play:

   - It is important to point out positive reactions and feelings to prosocial solutions and negative reactions and feelings to antisocial solutions.

   - If the original student-generated alternatives are not prosocial, look for students who can model appropriate alternatives. The group leader and other students are important models for appropriate prosocial solutions to typical problems. Students learn best from multiple positive models.

   - The group leader can use the sandwich approach of feedback to respond to each role-play, pointing out all positive aspects and adding alternatives to any inappropriate ideas, followed by a positive summary of the pair's efforts.

4. After all role-plays, the group can generate a list of other typical problems for future problem solving and role-play.

5. To wrap up, the group leader can ask students to discuss what it was like to work together to find solutions:

   - Did any of the pairs have trouble coming to an agreement on any of the solutions or how they would role-play them?

   - How did they work it out?

   - How did they feel about how the disagreement was settled?

   - What suggestions do they have for next time they work in groups to solve problems and present role-plays?

STUDENT SUCCESS SKILLS SELF-EVALUATION

1. Go through each item, reading it aloud and asking students to rate how they did that week. Ask, "Who rated that item 'Good,' who rated it 'OK,' who rated it 'Needs to improve?'"

2. Use the items to stimulate discussion and to clarify problem areas that need to be addressed.

3. Use group problem solving by asking students to brainstorm solutions to problems raised as you move down the list. Role-playing solutions to problems is a valuable way to help students learn alternative strategies for handling difficult situations. The problem solving can also include how to handle the social problems that come up during the group meetings.

End

1. Ask students to write an ending to the following two sentences. Ask them to share their answers with a partner. Then ask for volunteers to share what they wrote.

   "One thing I learned today was . . ."

   "One way I can use what I learned today is . . ."

2. Preview next session.

Friendship Problems

Typical Problem 1

Dear Mary Jo,

My problem is the big J—jealousy:

My friend tries to control whom I spend time with. She threatens to not be my friend if I hang out with certain people. It feels like she wants to keep me all to herself. I really like her but I also want to be friends with other people. What should I do?

Signed,

Confused

Typical Problem 2

Dear Mary Jo,

There are these two kids in my class who are very pushy. Every time we play it has to be by their rules. They always have to go first. When we work in teams they have to be the leader. It's really frustrating. Don't they know how rude they are? I am sick and tired of it. They are smart and could be good friends but they really need to learn to share the lead. What can I do to make them see how bossy they are?

Signed,

Frustrated

Typical Problem 3

Dear Mary Jo,

A couple of my friends have to be the center of attention all the time. It gets boring to be around them because they always have to be the focus. I don't think they know how irritating it is when they won't let me or anyone else have any of the attention. How can I get them to look past themselves and notice how other people feel?

Signed,

Irritated

Session 6
Topic: Dos and don'ts of being a friend

Resources

- Dos and Don'ts of Being a Friend handout
- Chart paper
- My Friendly Environment handout
- Student Success Skills Self-Evaluation handout (page 197)

Beginning

1. Stretches, movement, and breathing (student-led), used to balance active and passive activities.
2. In a go-round, ask students to rate how they are feeling on the "great, pretty good, not so good, really bad" scale. Be sure to check with any "not so good" or "really bad" to determine if follow-up is needed.
3. Ask students to tell you some things they remember from last meeting.
4. Ask, "Who used something we talked about last week during the week? How did it go?"

Middle

DOS AND DON'TS OF BEING A FRIEND

1. Explain to the students that you need their help as consultants. Your friend, Mary Jo, writes a column for a school newspaper about typical problems for elementary school students. You would like their advice on a problem recently sent in to Mary Jo. Give each student a copy of the Dos and Don'ts of Being a Friend handout.
2. In pairs, students brainstorm things to do and things not to do to for keeping friends.
3. Pairs share their lists and a composite list is made on a flip chart. Items are then coded by consensus agreement as "DH," definitely helpful, or "PNH,"

probably not helpful. Discuss the fact that our behaviors toward others create an environment around us. If we want to attract and keep friends we have to maintain an environment that is inviting and friendly so that others will enjoy being around us.

4. Ask students to complete the My Friendly Environment handout.
5. Ask them to share what they wish to from their goal sheets with the group.

STUDENT SUCCESS SKILLS SELF-EVALUATION

1. Go through each item, reading it aloud and asking students to rate how they did that week. Ask "Who rated that item 'Good,' who rated it 'OK,' who rated it 'Needs to improve?'"
2. Use the items to stimulate discussion and to clarify problem areas that need to be addressed.
3. Use group problem solving by asking students to brainstorm solutions to problems raised as you move down the list. Role-playing solutions to problems is a valuable way to help students learn alternative strategies for handling difficult situations. The problem solving can also include how to handle the social problems that come up during the group meetings.

End

1. Ask students to write an ending to the following two sentences. Ask them to share their answers with a partner. Then ask for volunteers to share what they wrote.

   "One thing I learned today was . . ."

   "One way I can use what I learned today is . . ."
2. Preview next session.

Name_____ Date _____

Dos and Don'ts of Being a Friend

Dear Mary Jo,

I am a third grader and things are not going well for me at my school. I am having trouble keeping friends and it is really bothering me a lot. Do you have a list of things that I could do to be accepted more with my friends? Also a list of what not to do would help.

Thanks,
Worried About Friends

Dear Worried About Friends,

I checked with my experts on third-grade friendship and this is what they suggested to help you create the kind of friendly environment that attracts and keeps good friends:

Be sure to do these things:	Be sure not to do these things:
_____	_____
_____	_____
_____	_____
_____	_____
_____	_____
_____	_____
_____	_____
_____	_____

Name_____ Date _____

My Friendly Environment

Directions: Complete the three areas below and share with a partner. Give this goal sheet to your teacher. You will have a chance next week to share specific examples of things you did to reach your goal.

Three things I already do that create a friendly environment and help me to be a good friend:

1. _____

2. _____

3. _____

Two things I will do more of in the next week to create a friendly environment:

1. _____

2. _____

One thing I will do less of this week to create a friendly environment:

1. _____

A picture of me and my friends in my friendly environment:

Session 7
Topic: Handling stress

Resources

- Chart paper
- Student Success Skills Self-Evaluation handout (page 197)

Beginning

1. Stretches, movement, and breathing (student-led), used to balance active and passive activities.

2. In a go-round ask students to rate how they are feeling on the "great, pretty good, not so good, really bad" scale. Be sure to check with any "not so good" or "really bad" to determine if follow-up is needed.

3. Ask students to tell you some things they remember from last meeting.

4. Ask, "Who used something we talked about last week during the week? How did it go?"

Middle

STRESS

1. Introduce the topic of stress with the following: "What does 'stress' mean? How do you know when you are under stress? What does it feel like? Name some physical symptoms. How many of you feel some stress today?"

2. Storytelling in pairs—a time I felt stressed out. "Think about the things that cause you stress. Tell your partner a story with a beginning, middle, and end about a time when you felt stressed out."

3. Discuss the stressors contained in the stories: "We need a list of things that cause students your age the most stress. Share with the group things from your stories that cause stress. Imagine tossing all those words into the center of our circle in a pile. Tell us what causes you stress and throw them on the pile. We need at least twelve."

Some answers that are typically given:

grades	boys/girls
friends	relationships
teachers	school
parents	decisions
time	tests
goals	performing

As students call out different answers, have them explain how that topic causes stress.

4. Ask, "What are some ways you handle stress?" List group's answers on a flip chart. After listing all their strategies go back through and have them rate each one as "H" for healthy or "HA" for harmful to self or others. Preview next meeting, when they can compare their list with seven other strategies for handling stress that other students their age find helpful.

STUDENT SUCCESS SKILLS SELF-EVALUATION

1. Go through each item, reading it aloud and asking students to rate how they did that week. Ask "Who rated that item 'Good,' who rated it 'OK,' who rated it 'Needs to improve?'"

2. Use the items to stimulate discussion and to clarify problem areas that need to be addressed.

3. Use group problem solving by asking students to brainstorm solutions to problems raised as you move down the list. Role-playing solutions to problems is a valuable way to help students learn alternative strategies for handling difficult situations. The problem solving can also include how to handle the social problems that come up during the group meetings.

End

1. Ask students to write an ending to the following two sentences. Ask them to share their answers with a partner. Then ask for volunteers to share what they wrote.

   "One thing I learned today was . . ."

   "One way I can use what I learned today is . . ."

2. Preview next session.

Session 8
Topic: Ways of handling stress

Resources

- Seven Ways to Handle Stress handout
- Student Success Skills Self-Evaluation handout (page 197)

Beginning

1. Stretches, movement, and breathing (student-led), used to balance active and passive activities.

2. In a go-round ask students to rate how they are feeling on the "great, pretty good, not so good, really bad" scale. Be sure to check with any "not so good" or "really bad" to determine if follow-up is needed.

3. Ask students to tell you some things they remember from last meeting.

4. Ask, "Who used something we talked about last week during the week? How did it go?"

Middle

GETTING A HANDLE ON STRESS

1. Say, "Last meeting we talked about what stress was, some causes of stress, and some strategies you use for handling stress. Let's look at some other ways students your age find helpful to handle stress. How many matches do you see between your list from last meeting and the first six ideas on this list?"

2. Distribute the handout Seven Ways to Handle Stress.

3. Say, "As I read the suggestions for dealing with stress, do the following:
   - Choose your three favorites—put an asterisk (*) by these.
   - Mark the ones you already use with a check (√).
   - Circle (O) the ones you would like to use more."

4. Read each suggestion, using each one as a stimulus to generate student discussion.

5. Have students share their ratings and ask for examples.

STUDENT SUCCESS SKILLS SELF-EVALUATION

1. Go through each item, reading it aloud and asking students to rate how they did that week. Ask "Who rated that item 'Good,' who rated it 'OK,' who rated it 'Needs to improve?'"

2. Use the items to stimulate discussion and to clarify problem areas that need to be addressed.

3. Use group problem solving by asking students to brainstorm solutions to problems raised as you move down the list. Role-playing solutions to problems is a valuable way to help students learn alternative strategies for handling difficult situations. The problem solving can also include how to handle the social problems that come up during the group meetings.

End

1. Ask students to write an ending to the following two sentences. Ask them to share their answers with a partner. Then ask for volunteers to share what they wrote.
   "One thing I learned today was . . ."
   "One way I can use what I learned today is . . ."

2. Preview next session.

Name_____ Date _____

Seven Ways to Handle Stress

Here are seven ideas children your age have used to handle stress. As you look at each idea, decide if it may be useful for you. Then do the following:

A. Choose your top three ideas from the list. Put a * by each of these.

B. Mark the ones you already use with a **check mark (√)**.

C. **Circle** the ones you would like to use more.

_____ 1. **Work it off** by being active—running, playing hard, doing soccer, dance, gymnastics.

_____ 2. **Talk it out** with someone you trust—a parent, teacher, friend, school counselor.

_____ 3. **Get plenty of rest.** You should be getting 9–10 hours of sleep each night.

_____ 4. **Make time for fun**, like playing games with friends or family.

_____ 5. **Expect yourself to make mistakes.** Nobody always does everything perfectly or never makes a mistake. Don't expect that you can always be perfect, either.

_____ 6. **Do something nice for someone**—such as helping around the house, or sending a nice note to a friend.

_____ 7. **Give in once in a while.** Let your friend go first or decide where to go.

Session 9
Topic: Self-evaluation, problem solving

Resources

- Student Success Skills Self-Evaluation handout (page 197)

Beginning

1. Stretches, movement, and breathing (student-led), used to balance active and passive activities.

2. In a go-round ask students to rate how they are feeling on the "great, pretty good, not so good, really bad" scale. Be sure to check with any "not so good" or "really bad" to determine if follow-up is needed.

3. Ask, "Who has been using something we talked about in the group? How did it go?"

Middle

STUDENT SELF-EVALUATION FORM

1. Go through each item, reading it aloud and asking students to rate how they did that week. Ask, "Who rated that item 'Good,' who rated it 'OK,' who rated it 'Needs to improve?'"

2. Use the items to stimulate discussion and to clarify problem areas that need to be addressed.

3. Use group problem solving by asking students to brainstorm solutions to problems raised as you move down the list. Role-playing solutions to problems is a valuable way to help students learn alternative strategies for handling difficult situations. The problem solving can also include how to handle the social problems that come up during the group meetings.

SOCIAL PROBLEM SOLVING

1. Ask students about problems either that they have had with other students/teachers at school or that they notice lots of other children have with each other at school. Make a list.

2. Ask group members to rank the top three problems in terms of interest to them for group to discuss possible solutions.

3. Lead a discussion on possible solutions for the selected top three problems. Use a brainstorming technique. List all offered solutions first. Then go back and have group code each one as "H," helpful, or "HA," harmful to self or others. *Note:* Some will be rated as both. Have group decide if the helpful side outweighs the harmful side.

4. Ask group to divide into pairs and plan a role-play for one of the three problems. The role-play should include one of the helpful solutions. Allow approximately five minutes for planning.

5. Ask each pair to present their role-play. Ask the rest of the group to discuss how realistically the problem and solution were portrayed, and any additional suggestions for handling the problem. The leader can also demonstrate various positive alternative ways to handle the situation or coach students in different ways to act. *Note:* It is the role-play and coaching that make this a powerful learning activity.

End

1. Ask students to write an ending to the following two sentences. Ask them to share their answers with a partner. Then ask for volunteers to share what they wrote.

   "One thing I learned today was . . ."

   "One way I can use what I learned today is . . ."

2. Preview next session.

Session 10
Topic: Review, spotlight, evaluation

Resources

- Index cards or sheets of paper
- Group Evaluation form (page 10)

Beginning

1. Stretches, movement, and breathing (student-led), used to balance active and passive activities.

2. In a go-round ask students to rate how they are feeling on the "great, pretty good, not so good, really bad" scale. Be sure to check with any "not so good" or "really bad" to determine if follow-up is needed.

3. Ask students to tell you some things they remember from last meeting.

4. Ask, "Who used something we talked about last week during the week? How did it go?"

Middle

REVIEW THE LIFE OF THE GROUP

1. Briefly go over each topic you've covered during the last nine weeks, asking for what they remember.

2. Then ask the following questions:

   - What are some the most important things you have learned about yourself?

   - What has been the most helpful part of this group for you?

   - What is a goal you have set for yourself?

ACCEPTING AND GIVING COMPLIMENTS

1. Hand out index cards or sheets of paper. Each person is to write down at least one thing he or she likes or appreciates about each of the other group members.

2. Spotlight: Ask each group member to say directly to the "spotlighted" person, with eye contact: "[person's name], one thing I like or appreciate about you is . . .". Explain and give examples of the types of qualities you are asking the students to think of and how to say and receive them. Ask students not to use things such as "I like your shirt, shoes, hair," etc., but rather qualities or actions.

3. After each comment, the spotlighted person says "thank you," nothing else. (Be sure you get in on this—it feels good.)

End

1. Process the spotlighting activity. How did it feel receiving compliments? Giving compliments?

2. Students complete anonymous evaluation.

3. Concluding remarks. Invite students to make individual appointments if they want. Remind them of the monthly follow-up sessions.

3.2
Building Math Confidence

| Grade Level: 3–5 | Time Required: 9 Sessions | Author: Chari Campbell |

Purpose

Math proficiency is increasingly important to students in our highly technological society. However, many American students are not performing as well as they might. Although there are many reasons for low performance, math anxiety has been found to play a critical role in mathematics learning. In fact, some researchers in math education have established that a student's attitudes and feelings toward math may, in some cases, play a more important role in math success than any innate aptitude for math.

In addition, school counselors recognize that many of the career-related choices that students make are influenced by their feelings and attitudes toward math. Therefore it is important for school counselors to help students learn strategies that will help them cope with math anxiety.

The following nine-session small group counseling plan is designed to help students manage anxious feelings related to math. In a small group setting, students learn that they are not alone with their math anxiety. They are given a chance to vent their frustration and anger at people and situations that caused them embarrassment and shame related to their math performance. They are taught coping skills and techniques such as deep breathing, deep muscle relaxation, positive self-talk, positive imaging, and journaling to cope with math anxiety. In the beginning stages of the group, negative feelings toward math are recognized and acknowledged. Gradually the focus of the group activities shifts to the positive, with an emphasis on encouraging success.

It is suggested that the counselor hold monthly booster sessions, after the completion of the nine sessions, to reinforce the use of the coping skills. Also, parents and teachers can help children maintain their newly acquired coping skills so that they become well-established habits, which will lead to long-term increased learning and success with math.

Logistics

GROUP COMPOSITION

Students in grades 3–5 who seem to be struggling with math.

GROUP SIZE

4–6 students

GROUP TIME PER SESSION

30 minutes

NUMBER OF SESSIONS

Nine, with booster sessions spaced approximately one month apart after regular group ends.

Recommended Resources

Full bibliographic details for these publications are included in the Bibliography at the end of this book.

Arem, 1993: *Conquering Math Anxiety.*

Campbell, 1991: "Group guidance for academically under-motivated children."

Davidson and Levitov, 2000: *Overcoming Math Anxiety.*

Hebert and Furner, 1997: "Helping high-ability students overcome math anxiety through bibliotherapy."

Tobias, 1995: *Overcoming Math Anxiety.*

Session 1
Topic: Drawing, goal setting

Resources
- Drawing supplies
- Chart paper

Beginning

INTRODUCTION

1. Say, "Today we are going to learn more about each other and the purpose of our group. Let's start with a go-round. Tell us your name, your favorite food, and your least favorite food." Allow a volunteer(s) to repeat everyone's name and their chosen food.

2. "This time when we go around, tell us your favorite subject in school and your least favorite subject." Ask, "Who can remember someone's favorite subject?" until everyone has been remembered. Then ask: "Who can remember someone's least favorite subject?" Point out commonalities. (Since the children in the group were self-referred or referred by teachers because they feared or disliked math, many children will have identified math as their least favorite subject. Help them see that they are not alone.)

3. Explain that in this group we are going to learn ways to enjoy math.

CONFIDENTIALITY, GROUP NAME

Discuss confidentiality.

Say to group, "Let's think of a good name for our group." Let the children brainstorm and vote on a name. (*Examples:* Math Warriors, Math Busters, Rawlings Raiders)

Middle

FEELINGS MURAL

1. Put a sheet of chart paper on the floor or on a table and label it "Feelings Mural." Explain that each child will have her/his own space on the paper to draw.

2. Say, "Draw a picture or just use shapes and colors to describe how you feel when it's time to do math in school or for homework."

3. When the drawings are completed, each child shares his or her feelings while you write the feeling words on a second piece of chart paper.

4. Ask the group to examine the list for commonalities. Point out the ratio of negative to positive feelings listed. Identify the opposite feelings for each of the negative offered (e.g., calm vs. nervous, anticipation vs. dread). Explain that in this group we will learn how to get rid of the unpleasant feelings we have associated with math and replace them with pleasant feelings.

5. Since young children do not have an expansive feelings vocabulary, this activity allows you the opportunity to teach children words they can use to express their feelings. Introduce new words or synonyms for feeling words or phrases that children understand, such as "to anticipate" means "to look forward to."

GOALS

1. Talk about goals, asking "What is a goal?"

2. Discuss general goals for the group: to develop positive feelings about the ability to do math, to get a good grade in math, to like to do math, etc.

3. Ask for student commitment. "Who wants to learn how to relax and love math?"

4. In pairs, have students share their goals for the group. Then ask for volunteers to share.

5. List the group's goals on chart paper to hang on the wall.

WRAP-UP

"What did you learn from today's group?" Lead a discussion group and summarize the session.

HOMEWORK

"Notice how you feel when you are doing your math assignments this week. We will share your feelings at our next meeting."

Session 2
Topic: Math feelings

Resources

- Chart paper or poster board
- Scratch paper cut into small (6" × 8") rectangles
- Markers
- Colored pencils or crayons
- Tape
- Paper or notebook for Math Feelings Journal

Beginning

REVIEW

1. Ask, "Who can remember someone's name and their favorite food?" "Who can remember everyone's name?"

2. "Does anyone want to share your thoughts about our last session?" "At our last session, I asked you to pay attention to your feelings while you were doing math this week. What did you notice?" Lead the discussion and summarize.

Middle

THROW OUT NEGATIVE FEELINGS

1. Put a stack of scratch paper in the center of the group. Ask each member to write as many feeling words as they have to describe the feelings associated with math of which they became aware last week. Write one word per sheet of paper.

2. Ask students to put the positive words in a stack to save.

3. Explain that we are going to get rid of the unpleasant feelings. Students have the option of wadding up, tearing, shredding, or stomping on each of the unpleasant feeling words before throwing them into a trashcan.

4. Ask, "How did that feel?"

MATH POSTER

1. Have students tape any positive feeling words to a large poster paper. Label the poster "Math can be fun" and hang it on the wall, explaining that students can add positive feelings to it each week. "Our group goal will be to cover it with pleasant feelings over time."

2. Children tape pleasant feeling words from the Throwing Out Negative Feelings activity onto the poster chart.

MATH FEELINGS JOURNAL

1. Introduce the Math Feelings Journal.* Fold a piece of paper horizontally, or use the chalkboard to draw a rectangle representing a piece of paper. Draw a line down the middle of it. Label the left side "My Feelings" and the right side "My Work."

2. Tell the children to use words, phrases, or symbols to represent feelings and/or physical symptoms they experience while working on math.

3. Use the chalkboard to brainstorm symbols that might be appropriate, such as happy, sad, or worried faces.

4. Ask students to record their feelings as they move through their work.

5. Ask how the students would feel about sharing their feelings with their teachers. Explain that their teachers are very interested in knowing how students feel because it will make it easier to help them learn.

6. Ask students to keep the Math Feelings Journal daily and to bring it to group next session.

(*Note: The Math Feelings Journal is adapted from Bonnie Donnady's original work at the Wesleyan Math Clinic.)

End

DEAR ABBY

1. Tell the students to pretend that they are going to write an anonymous letter to Dear Abby about their problems with math. Explain that after you collect the letters, you are going to read them all to the group but that we are not going to try to guess who wrote which letter.

2. As you read each letter, ask the students to share how they would feel if the problem were theirs and what they might try to do. This is a chance for each child to receive a large dose of empathy and perhaps some helpful advice.

WRAP-UP

In pairs, ask students to share what they learned from today's session. Then ask for volunteers to share with the group the most important thing they learned today.

HOMEWORK

Remind students to notice their feelings as they work on math and to record them in their Math Feelings Journal (MFJ). *Note:* You should work with the elementary teacher on the best way to use the MFJ. If the teacher requires a special notebook for all math work, then it may be possible to have students use this format for journaling feelings on whatever type of paper or notebook the teacher requires. At the elementary level, the teacher may need to remind students, as they make daily assignments, to use the MFJ. Younger children may need to use a happy, worried, sad face format. Older children should be encouraged to use words to describe their feelings and physical symptoms in their journals.

Session 3
Topic: Learning to relax

Resources

- Optional: tape recorder and blank cassette tape

Beginning

1. Check in with the group. Ask, "How was your week? (Show me on your fingers. Five fingers means it was a great week, one finger means it's been a bummer.)" Ask for volunteers who want to share more about their week.

2. Say, "Share with the person seated next to you some of the feelings you are writing about in your Math Feelings Journal."

3. Next, ask for volunteers to share. Then lead a discussion to help students learn how the journal can help them become more aware of their feelings and how their feelings are related to their thoughts and behavior.

Middle

1. Ask students to identify any physical symptoms of stress they might experience while taking a test or being called on to answer a problem in class. Help students make a common list (such as weak knees, sick stomach, dizziness, blanking out).

2. Introduce the concept of two-word poetry. Ask students to write poems that describe their math anxiety.

   Example:

Rubber Knees	Blanked Out
Shaky hands	Sick Stomach
Cloudy Mind	Achy Head

3. Say, "Today we are going to learn to use our lungs and all of our muscles to train our bodies to relax." Invite the children to close their eyes if they wish, then lead the students through deep breathing exercises. Next lead them through deep muscle relaxation exercises, using the Relaxation Script below.

Relaxation Script

You may wish to make a tape of the relaxation script to play during each succeeding session rather than reading or speaking it each time. Also, copies of the tape may be made for children to take home to practice relaxation. A tape may also be used in the classroom at a learning center where children can practice in their free time.

Say, "Get into the most comfortable position you can in your chair. Uncross your legs and rest your feet flat on the floor. Let your arms rest comfortably in your lap. Now close your eyes and relax. Take several deep, relaxing breaths. I will count while you breathe. Inhale, one, two; hold, three, four; exhale, five, six. (Repeat this three times.)

Now say, "While you're breathing deeply, listen to all the sounds you hear, the noises outside, the noises in the room, the sounds from the person next to you and the noises from yourself. (Pause for 20 seconds) Now just listen to the sounds in the room. (Pause for 20 seconds) Now just listen to your own sounds as you become more and more relaxed until you are completely at peace."

"Focus on your right foot. Notice your toes. Scrunch them as tight as you can, and release. Now arch your foot, tighten, and release. Now, notice your calf. Tighten your calf muscle. Tighter. Now release. Now, be aware of your thigh. Make it as hard and tight as you can. Now release."

Ask the children what that felt like. Let them talk about the experience. Then suggest that they close their eyes again and move to the left foot. Repeat the above paragraph for the left foot. Continue by tightening and relaxing all the muscles in the leg.

Then move up the body to the abdomen (children may refer to it as their stomach) and on to the arms, beginning with the fingers, and on to the shoulders and head. Include the forehead, eyebrows, cheeks, nose, lips, and jaw.

During the deep muscle relaxation, remind children to periodically pay attention to their breathing, telling them to take deep relaxing breaths.

Process the activity. Ask students how they felt while doing the relaxation exercise. Tell students they can use this relaxation technique whenever they feel tense or ill at ease—for example, before starting on their math homework.

Ask students to practice this technique during the week.

End

1. In pairs, have students share what they learned from today's session. Lead the discussion and summarize.

2. For homework remind students to continue with the Math Feelings Journal and to practice relaxing all their muscles for ten minutes in the afternoon before doing their homework.

Session 4
Topic: Using clay to vent anger

Resources

- Clay
- Relaxation script or tape from Session 3
- Poster board or chart paper

Beginning

1. Check in with the group. Ask students to share what they have learned from keeping a Math Feelings Journal thus far.
2. Ask who remembered to practice the relaxation exercises. Ask how it felt.
3. Practice the relaxation exercises with the group.

Middle

VENTING ANGER WITH CLAY

1. Give each student a piece of natural clay (about the size of a baseball). Let them make shapes and squeeze and roll the clay for a few minutes, but ask them not to make an object.
2. After they have enjoyed the clay, show them how they can use the clay to vent anger. Ask the students to stand and throw the clay (onto a safe surface—the table, a wall, wash table, etc.). Ask them to think of something that makes them mad and say: "I feel so angry when . . ." and wham, have them throw the clay as hard as they can.
3. Now ask students, "Can you think of a time you felt 'put down' by someone when you were trying to do math? Don't use their name, but tell us what happened."
4. Then say: "You made me mad when you . . ." And have them slam their clay. Have them say: "I'm really mad at you for doing . . .". Students can all yell their angry phrases and slam the clay for a few minutes. The resulting laughter will feel good and takes some sting from the memory.

5. Next, show students how they can pound (flatten) their clay by beating it with the palms of their hands, their fists, etc. Also they can poke holes in the clay, jab it with pencils or rulers, and pinch it into pieces while expressing anger at someone who they believe made them feel dumb, embarrassed them, or made them angry regarding their attempts at math.

IDEAL MATH TEACHER

1. In pairs, have the students describe an ideal math teacher. What would he or she be like? What kinds of things would the ideal math teacher say and do to make you like math, help you learn math, help you feel confident about your ability to do math?
2. Have the pairs share with the group and collect the descriptions on a poster titled "Wanted—Ideal Math Teacher."

IDEAL MATH CLASSROOM

1. In groups of three, have students describe the ideal math classroom. What would it look like? What activities, games, books, work, etc. would there be for students? Would it be quiet or noisy? Would there be music? Would students work on their own or in groups or pairs?
2. Have the groups report back to the group. Lead a discussion and summarize.

End

Ask: "What did you learn in today's session that you can use to help you feel better about math?" Have the students share with a partner and report back to the group. Summarize student reports.

HOMEWORK

Say, "Practice the relaxation exercises for at least ten minutes every night and we'll talk about it next session."

Session 5
Topic: Self-talk

Resources

- Self-Talk handout
- Chalkboard or chart paper
- 4" × 12" pieces of colored poster board
- Relaxation script or tape from Session 3

Beginning

1. Check in with the group. "How was your week? (Show me on your fingers. Five fingers means it was a great week, one finger means it's been a bummer.)" Ask for volunteers who want to share more about their week.

2. Share the Math Feelings Journals. Say, "Share with the person seated next to you what feelings you are writing about in your Math Feelings Journal." Ask for volunteers to share; then lead a discussion to help students learn how the journal can help them become more aware of their feelings and how their feelings are related to their thoughts and behavior.

3. Practice deep breathing exercise. Ask, "Who practiced?" Then say, "Let's do it together." Play the tape or read the script and go through the exercises with the children.

Middle

SELF-TALK

1. Say, "Today we are going to learn how to recognize some of the negative things we are saying to ourselves about math or our ability to do math that are keeping us from doing our best and feeling good about math. Then we are going to replace those negative thoughts with positive ones and begin to practice thinking positively about ourselves and math."

2. Pass out the Self-Talk handout and ask students to remember some of their math goals. These can be shared aloud to help students select the goals on which they want to work. Sample goals are included on the handout.

3. Next, lead a discussion about negative self-talk. Examples of negative self-talk are provided on the handout.

4. In pairs, have students share some of the negative thoughts that are preventing them from meeting their math goals.

5. When all pairs have finished sharing, have them share all their negative thoughts with the group; record this on the chalkboard or chart paper.

6. Have the group brainstorm positive self-statements to replace each of the negative statements generated by the group. As they generate positive statements, record them on chart paper. (*Note:* Hang this list on the wall and save it for future use.) Students then complete their self-talk handout.

BUMPER STICKER ART

1. Ask each student to select his or her three favorite positive thoughts. Give students pieces of colored poster board on which to design their bumper stickers. They can take these home to hang on the wall above their desk or over their bed.

2. In a go-round, have each student select one of his or her positive thoughts and say it out loud ten times. Encourage students to say the thought in a strong voice and to sound very sure of themselves.

3. If time allows, students can make extra bumper stickers for the classroom, and small ones to use as bookmarks.

End

1. Ask, "What did you learn from today's session that you might be able be able to use tonight when you do your homework, or tomorrow when you take your test?" Summarize the discussion.

2. Ask students to practice saying each positive thought ten times throughout the day.

Name_____ Date_____

Self-Talk

1. My math goals are:

    1. _____

    2. _____

    3. _____

    4. _____

Examples: to get a good grade in math, to do well on my math test, to learn my multiplication tables.

2. But, my negative thoughts are:

    1. _____

    2. _____

    3. _____

    4. _____

Examples: "I'm going to fail the test," "I'll never figure out this problem," "I must be a dummy," "I might as well give up."

(continued)

Name_____ Date_____

Self-Talk

3. Change each negative thought to a positive thought.

"I'm going to fail the test."	becomes	"I'm going to pass the test!"
"I never get it right."	becomes	"I'll keep working until I get it right."
"I'm a dummy."	becomes	"I'm smart. I can learn this!"
"I might as well give up."	becomes	"I'll never give up. I'll call a friend for help."

My new, positive thoughts will be:

1. _____

_____

2. _____

_____

3. _____

_____

4. _____

_____

221   *Group Counseling for School Counselors: A Practical Guide*

Session 6
Topic: Success imaging

Resources

- Relaxation script or tape from Session 3

Beginning

1. Check in with the group. "How was your week? (Show me on your fingers. Five fingers means it was a great week, one finger means it's been a bummer.)" Ask for volunteers who want to share more about their week.

2. Ask students to share where they put their math "bumper stickers."

3. Ask who remembered to recite each of their positive statements at least ten times. Ask how it felt to do that.

4. Have each student turn to the student seated next to him and share two or three of his favorite positive statements.

5. Next, in a go-round, have each student select one of his or her positive statements and say it aloud to the group three times. Instruct: "Use a strong voice . . . show excitement . . . show your confidence!"

6. Ask: "Who practiced the relaxation exercises?" Then say, "Let's practice together." Play the tape or read the script and go through the exercises with the children, but this time, at the close of the relaxation exercises, ask the children to select one of their positive self-statements and repeat it ten times. Say, "Think your positive self-talk silently to yourself. Say the self-talk slowly. Really believe what you are saying and think about it as you are saying it."

Middle

SUCCESS IMAGES

1. Say, "Today we are going to learn another technique to prepare our minds for success. We are going to use our imaginations to picture ourselves being successful with math. What you are doing is training your mind to have the successful experiences that you want."

2. Say, "Let's practice creating mental pictures. First, get into a comfortable position. Closing your eyes may help you use your imagination while you listen to my voice. I'm going to describe a place and I want you to picture being there."

"It is a glorious morning. The weekend is here and you are going to go biking with your friend. Where is your bike? You've found it. Now you are riding down the road, away from your home. You feel the wind in your face and in your hair. It smells sweet, like freshly mowed grass. You hear birds chirping. They sound as happy and free as you feel. You notice the warmth of the sun on the top of your head and shoulders. You feel like you could ride forever. Take a ride with your friend for a few more minutes. Where will you go? What will you see?" (Give them one or two minutes to mentally ride their bikes. Then say: "In a few more seconds I'm going to ask you to return to this room and then we'll talk about your bike trip.")

3. Ask for volunteers to describe their experiences. What did they see, hear, smell, feel? Did they picture themselves on the bike as though they were looking at a TV screen, or did they seem to be looking out at the scenery through their own eyes? Was it pleasant? Was anything unpleasant? Explain to students that they are completely in control of their own mental pictures, so it can always be a pleasant experience.

4. "Now, let's try using success images to help us obtain our math goals. For example, one of our goals was to remain calm during math exams. Close your eyes while I talk you through the steps. You are smiling and feeling confident. You are practicing your relaxation exercises. You are repeating your favorite positive self-statements. Now the teacher passes out the exam. You continue to use deep relaxing breaths as you work through the problems. When you feel stuck, you repeat your positive self-talk, and guess what? It works! You figure out how to solve the problem and move on to the next one. You complete the test and turn it in. You feel great. You know that you did your best work. You flash your teacher a big smile and leave feeling proud of yourself."

5. Now you are ready to create your own success images. In a go-round, ask each student to share one of her math-related goals for which she wants to create a success image. Ask students to work in pairs to write down the details of their success image. Then each student shares with the group.

6. Say, "Now we are ready to combine relaxation, self-talk, and visualization. We will take a shortcut to relaxation this time. Just get into a comfortable position and stretch and relax your muscles. Now take three relaxation breaths." (The counselor counts: "Inhale 1, 2; — hold 3, 4; — exhale 5, 6, —.") "Good. You are feeling very relaxed. Now practice your positive self-talk." (Allow one minute.) "Now use your imagination and see your success image. Include your positive self-talk where it fits. When you have finished, open your eyes and wait quietly until we are all ready to speak." Ask students to describe what the experience was like.

End

Ask, "What did you learn from today's session that you might be able be able to use tonight when you do your homework, or tomorrow in class?" Summarize the discussion.

HOMEWORK

Say, "Practice, practice, practice! Combine all three techniques and use them each night and in class. Continue to use your Math Feelings Journal."

Session 7

Topic: Creating a math rap song

Resources

- Blank tapes
- Tape recorder
- Relaxation script or tape from Session 3
- Optional: tapes of rap songs, musical instruments

Beginning

1. Check in with the group. "How was your week? (Show me on your fingers. Five fingers means it was a great week, one finger means it's been a bummer.)" Ask for volunteers who want to share more about their week.

2. Ask, "How did your practice go?" Facilitate a discussion, encouraging children to make the practice a routine in their daily lives. Help them find the best time of day to practice. Suggest doing the exercises right before or after taking a shower or brushing their teeth so that they are less likely to forget.

3. Say, "Think of one thing you like about math, or a time you enjoyed doing math. Share that with the person sitting next to you." After the pairs have shared, ask the students to share in a go-round.

4. Practice the entire relaxation exercise; include the positive self-talk and success images. Then process the experience with the children.

5. Inquire about the Math Feelings Journals. What kinds of feelings are they experiencing in class while doing math or taking tests? Suggest that when they notice that they are anxious or feel "stuck," that would be the best time to use the relaxation or success exercises. Ask them to record in their journals what happened when they used the exercises to relax or to get "un-stuck." Tell them to remember so that we can talk about them next time.

Middle

RAP SONGS

1. Ask, "How many of you like rap music? Can anyone teach us how to do it?" Allow volunteers to demonstrate how to set words to the beat.

2. Ask the group to write a math rap song using their positive self-talk in the lyrics. You might ask each student for one line and write them all on the board, or you might start them off with a line and ask for more lines that rhyme. Encourage students to use scenes from their success images in the rap song. Also, they can include positive memories of doing and enjoying math. Encourage them to include positive feeling words and phrases such as proud, trying harder and harder, and motivated.

3. Then add movement to the rap (kicks, jumps, hand-jive, etc.). Say: "You may set it to music if you want." (You may have tapes of rap music that could be used, or borrow basic musical instruments from the music teacher to add to the fun.)

4. Have the group practice the rap song, then record it. Play back the rap song and say/sing along with it. Ask students to picture themselves doing and feeling what the lyrics in the song say.

5. Process the experience. Ask, "How did creating and singing/saying the rap song make you feel? How did creating and singing/saying the song affect your feelings toward math? What new positive affirmations did you hear today? How could you use this song to motivate you to keep trying when you are feeling discouraged?"

End

Remind students that we have two sessions left. Remind them to use the Math Feelings Journal and to practice, practice, practice!

Session 8
Topic: Math is fun mural

Resources

- Tapes/CDs with relaxing music
- Relaxation script or tape from Session 3
- The rap song made by the group
- The chart of positive self-talk made in Session 5
- Paint
- Large sheet of paper

Beginning

1. Check in with the group. "How was your week? (Show me on your fingers. Five fingers means it was a great week, one finger means it's been a bummer.)" Ask for volunteers who want to share more about their week.
2. Ask, "How did your practice go?" Facilitate a discussion.
3. Practice the entire relaxation exercise; include the positive self-talk and success images. Then process the experience with the children.

Middle

A MATH IS FUN MURAL

1. Give students a large sheet of art paper and paint. Tell the students, "Today we are going to make another math mural, but this one will focus on our positive experiences, thoughts, and feelings about math. (Refer to the list of positive self-statements made in Session 3.) Ask students to think of a time that they enjoyed doing math, a time they felt proud, capable, in control. Ask if anyone has experienced feeling successful using the self-talk while doing class work, doing homework, or taking a test. Label the mural "Math is Fun" and allow students to creatively express positive emotions related to math.

2. Before the students begin to paint, play the rap music for inspiration, then play the relaxing music while they are painting.
3. When students have cleaned up, give each child a chance to share what he or she painted.
4. Hang the mural on the wall.
5. Lead a short discussion about recent successes with math, successes they have had at calming themselves when they felt uptight, and experiences of getting "unstuck" when they relaxed while doing their math.
6. Encourage each child by reflecting feelings of growing confidence, even if it is unspoken. Repeat to each child words to the effect of, "You did that on your own! You gained control of your anxious feelings. You must be so proud!"

End

1. Remind students that the next session is the last session of the math confidence-building group and that they may bring party snacks to share.
2. Ask them to continue their relaxation and success exercises and to continue using the Math Feelings Journal. Explain that now that they know how to use these tools to help them conquer math anxiety, they will be able to continue to build their math confidence on their own.
3. Tell students that after the next session we will no longer be able to meet once a week, but that we will meet once a month for a "booster session." Tell them you will want to see their Math Feelings Journals and hear about any new self-talk or success images they are using. Maybe someone will make up a new rap song to share.

Session 9
Topic: Confidence cards, closure

Resources

- Snacks, drinks, and party food for kids
- Colored poster board (4" × 8" or 4" × 12" pieces)
- Markers
- Relaxation script or tape from Session 3

Beginning

1. Check in with the group. "How was your week? (Show me on your fingers. Five fingers means it was a great week, one finger means it's been a bummer.)" Ask for volunteers who want to share more about their week.
2. Ask: "How did your practice go?" Facilitate a discussion.
3. Practice the entire relaxation exercise; include the positive self-talk and success images. Then process the experience with the children. Point out to them that they seem to be able to relax more completely. Explain that if they continue to practice on their own they will be able to achieve complete relaxation in shorter periods of time, so that they can just take three long, relaxing breaths and feel refreshed. Ask students which of the self-statements seem to be the most helpful in getting them "unstuck," to encourage them to work harder, to give them confidence in math.

Middle

1. Ask the children to count with you the number of party foods. Say, "Let's have fun doing math together." Ask, "How many cookies are there? How many snacks are there? So how do we figure out how many of each we get to eat?" Discuss how math played a role in the making of candy, chips, etc. For example, as you are passing out the snacks, ask them to name the jobs of the people who made them (e.g., farmers, cooks, delivery persons, salespeople, accountants). Ask them to describe how those individuals use math on their jobs.
2. While students are enjoying the snacks, lead a group discussion about what it was like to participate in a math confidence group and what students learned as a result of being in the group. Some questions you may ask include: "What have you learned from these sessions that will help you learn math and enjoy the learning process?" "What changes have you noticed in your attitude toward math and taking math tests?" "How did you feel about math at the start of the sessions?" "How do

you feel now?" "How has participating in a math confidence group affected your feelings about math? About yourself? About others?"

End

CONFIDENCE CARDS

1. Have each student write his or her name as decoratively as possible, using colored markers, in the middle of one of the poster board rectangles. Explain that they can decorate each letter, but that they need to leave room for people to write around the edges of the name.
2. Then have the students silently pass the cards to the right and direct them to write a word or phrase that describes a personal strength they have observed about the person whose name is written on the card. If the students have not participated in this type of activity before, take a few minutes to talk about the kinds of personal strengths people have, and give concrete examples, such as: He is kind; she has a good sense of humor; he thinks of others' feelings; she is a good listener; he is creative; she is brave; he is friendly; you can count on her to do what she says. Ask them to be as specific as possible in their feedback to each other.
3. After everyone has his or her card back, ask each student to tell the group (a) the strength of which they are most proud, (b) the strength they were most surprised to see, and (c) a strength of theirs that the group did not mention, if they would like to share it.

CLOSURE

1. Set a date a month from now for a booster session.
2. Tell the students that you would like to stop by their desks periodically to see their Math Feelings Journals. Explain again how the Math Feelings Journal will encourage them to keep working and manage anxious feelings when they crop up.
3. Remind them that everyone sometimes feels uptight about math, even mathematicians. It is how you cope with your anxious feelings that counts.
4. Suggest that if everyone in the group continues to use the Math Feelings Journal to record his successes using relaxation and success exercises, the group can celebrate with a popcorn party at the booster session.
5. Say goodbye.

3.3
Social Problem Solving, K–2

Grade Level: K–2	Time Required: 8 Sessions	Author: Donna Steinberg

Purpose

To develop social problem solving skills and thinking skills. Students use a problem-solving model to apply to typical social problems. Role-play provides practice in applying the new skills.

Logistics

GROUP COMPOSITION

Students grades K–2 mixed with regard to activity level and behavior control. Avoid loading group with only overactive behavior problem students. Students need multiple models of appropriate behavior. Groups with only behavior problem students usually do not show significant gains in prosocial behavior. Mixed groups are generally very effective.

GROUP SIZE

4–6 students

GROUP TIME PER SESSION

30 minutes

NUMBER OF SESSIONS

Eight, with booster sessions spaced approximately one month apart after regular group ends.

Recommended Resources

Full bibliographic details for these publications are included in the Bibliography at the end of this book.

Dinkmeyer and Dinkmeyer, 1982: *Developing Understanding of Self and Others.*

McGinnis and Goldstein, 1997: *Skillstreaming the Elementary School Child.*

Shure, 1992: *I Can Problem-Solve: An Interpersonal Cognitive Problem-Solving Program.*

St. Germain, 1990: *The Terrible Fight.*

Vernon, 1989: *Thinking, Feeling, Behaving: An Emotional Education Curriculum for Children.*

Vernon, 1998: *The Passport Program.*

Session 1

Topic: Getting to know each other

Resources

- Chart paper
- Enough sets of Matching Game Cards for each student to have two cards

Beginning

Before the group begins, have teachers complete a pre-group evaluation.

1. Welcome children to the group. Have them tell the person next to them their name, what they like to be called (could be a nickname), and one thing they like to do for fun. Then children introduce each other.

2. Talk about the purpose of the group. Ask children,
   - "Have you ever had a problem with another person?"
   - "How did you feel when . . . (for example, someone was mean to you)?"

   Say, "In this group, you can learn about solving these kinds of problems. When you make a problem better you are 'solving' the problem."
   - "How do you think this will help you?"

3. Provide a summary of what to expect—sharing, games, stories, role-play, drawing, and puppets.

4. Tell students that today you will talk about rules "that will make our group a happy and safe place to learn. Then we can play a game that will help us think of feeling words and will help us tell the difference between same and different. This can help us with things we will be doing in our group. Does this sound like a good idea?"

Middle

GROUP RULES

1. Discuss rules for the group. Encourage rules that are established by the children.

2. Write the rules on chart paper, making sure to include no put-downs, one person talks at a time, and not talking about what other members say. Children like to sign the rule chart. Talk about confidentiality and limits in concrete terms.

MATCHING FACES GAME

1. Practice with identifying feeling words and understanding same/different are prerequisite skills for upcoming activities. Pass out doubles of picture cards so each member has two pictures. Children hold pictures face down.

2. One child turns a picture for all to see, then chooses a child to show one of his/her pictures. Ask children to name the feeling of the first child's card. Then ask if the second child's picture shows the same or a different feeling. If it is the same, collect the pair of cards. If it is different, turn both cards face down.

3. The last child to show a picture chooses another child. The game continues until all matches are made.

End

Process with members, "What was it like for you to be in group today?" "Who else feels that way?" "What did you learn?" "How do you think our group will help you?"

Name_____ Date _____

Matching Game Cards

Session 2
Topic: Feelings

Resources

- The Swing illustration

Beginning

1. Review names by greeting each child, for example, "Hi Jamie, I'm glad you are here."

2. Ask children to partner with another and tell how they feel about being in group today. Have them choose a different partner from the last session. Emphasize commonalities in feelings.

3. Ask members what they remember about the last session. Review the rationale for the group, the meaning of "solving a problem," and rules.

4. Provide a rationale for today's activity: "Sometimes pictures are a good way to think about problems people have and their feelings. I have a picture we can look at and talk about. Then we can pretend to be actors and act out a real problem one of you may have had. How do you think this might help us?"

Middle

1. Show the illustration or pass it around for all to see. Ask,
   - "What is the problem in this picture?"
   - "What do you think is happening?"
   - "How do you think this person feels?"
   - "How do you think that person feels?"

2. Ask members, "What kinds of problems have you had where you felt like that?" Using a problem from a member, explain how to role-play. "We can act out Megan's problem. Someone can pretend to be the other person and Megan can play herself. Megan, you tell Lisa what to do."

3. Help children to role-play the incident. Model role-playing the other person if needed. Ask:
   - "What is the problem?"
   - "How does Megan feel?"
   - "How does Lisa feel?"

4. Have players reverse roles. Ask questions like, "How was Lisa thinking about Megan's feelings?"

5. Process the role-play by asking, "What was it like to role-play a problem? What was it like to role-play the other person? How can it help to think about your feelings? How can it help to think about the other person's feelings? What do you think about people having different feelings about the same thing?"

End

Ask children what it was like for them to be in group today. Ask, "What did you learn? How is it going to help you think about how others feel? How can you use what you learned today?"

The Swing

       Group Counseling for School Counselors: A Practical Guide

Session 3
Topic: What's the problem

Resources

- Story with problem; recommended: *The Terrible Fight*, by Sharon St. Germain
- Drawing paper

Beginning

1. Ask children how they used what they learned in the last session.

2. Have children tell about a time when they thought about how someone else was feeling. For example, "Who would like to share how they were able to think about the feelings of someone else?"

3. Tell children, "Today I have a story I will read to you. We can learn about solving problems with stories. Some kids have found out that when they know what the problem is, they can understand better. I think this story will help us practice. Does that sound good?"

Middle

1. Use a story with a problem, for example, *The Terrible Fight*, St. Germain (1990).

2. Read the story aloud, stopping at appropriate times to ask:

- "What is the problem?"
- "How do you think ___ feels?"
- "How can you tell?"
- "How did they solve the problem?"
- "What else could they do?"
- "How did it work out?"

3. Focus on who feels the same and who feels different about the same thing. Also elicit responses for ways to find out how someone else feels. Encourage children for listening.

End

1. Ask children, "What have you learned today? What have you learned about getting along with others? How do you feel about our group today? How are you going to use what you learned?"

2. Talk to members about how it can help if they draw a picture of a problem they have for the next time. Talk about examples: "It could be with your teacher, parents, brothers, sisters, or friends." Ask if they think this is a good idea. Distribute drawing paper for students to take with them.

Session 4
Topic: There's more than one way

Beginning

1. Ask children to share their drawings from the last meeting and tell what the problem was.

2. Discuss, "How have you been thinking about how other people feel? Who would like to tell us?"

3. Tell children, "Today we can role-play different ways to solve a problem. Who remembers what role-play is? How will doing this help you when you have a problem with another person?"

Middle

1. Have a member recount the problem picture he or she brought to group; these are best for learning. Or use the following scenario: Samantha is in (grade that applies). She always wants to have her own way. Sometimes she fights with other children or takes things from them. In this problem she cuts in line while she is waiting for lunch. The person she cuts is Andrew. Andrew says, "Hey, that's not fair, you cut." Discuss:

- What is the problem?
- How is Andrew feeling?
- How can you tell?
- How is Samantha feeling?
- How can you tell?

2. Ask for volunteers to role-play. Ask children, "What can Andrew do? Think of as many different things to do as you can and then we can role-play."

3. Have each member role-play his or her solution. Emphasize, "So, it looks like you were able to think about lots of things to do about this problem. How do you think it would help you if you were able to think of different things to do when you are having the problem?"

End

Ask students, "What did you learn today? How can you use what you learned? How do you feel about being in our group? What was it like for you to share in group today?"

Session 5
Topic: What will happen?

Resources

- Two hand puppets
- Small ball

Beginning

1. Ask members to complete the sentence, "I am getting better at getting along with others because . . .".

2. Ask children how they have used what they have learned. "Who would like to tell us about a time when you tried thinking of different things you can do when you have a problem? How did it help you? How do you feel about that?"

3. Tell children, "Today I have some puppets that can show us in a fun way how sometimes people do things that are by accident and what can happen. This can help us to learn and practice solving problems. How do you think getting all the information about your problem will help you?"

Middle

1. You will need two (any kind) of hand puppets. Ask for a volunteer to play a puppet throwing a ball with your puppet. Begin throwing the ball back and forth. Allow the ball to hit your puppet. Then your puppet says angrily, "You hit me in the eye!" Ask group members, "What is the problem?"

2. Give puppets to two children to role-play what might happen next. Talk about feelings and how to find out more information about a problem (asking questions, listening). Refer to examples children presented in their own problems where relevant.

3. Using a child's example problem, have two children role-play the scene with the puppets. "Lisa, would you like to act out the problem you told us about?" Ask questions:

   - What is the problem?
   - How do you know?
   - Do you have all the information?
   - How can you find out?
   - How do you feel?
   - How do you think the other person feels?
   - What can you do about it?
   - What will happen if you do that?
   - What else can you do?
   - Then what will happen?

End

1. Ask, "What did you learn today? How will you use what you learned? What was it like to be in our group today?"

2. Tell children that the group will meet three more times.

Session 6
Topic: The waiting problem

Resources

- Paper
- Drawing materials
- The Swing illustration from Session 2

Beginning

1. Ask members to complete the sentence, "Sometimes when I have to wait I feel . . ."
2. Ask members how they have used what they are learning.
   - Who has had a problem with another person?
   - What can you share with us about the problem?
   - Did you have all the information?
   - What did you do?
3. Ask children, "Have you ever had a problem with another person because she didn't want to wait her turn to talk or to play? Or maybe you can remember a problem when you had a hard time waiting and it got you in trouble. We can draw pictures of those kinds of problems and it can help us figure out what we can do. Does this sound like something that will help?"

Middle

1. Distribute drawing paper. Tell children they will have a few minutes to draw the problem about waiting.
2. Give a two-minute notice when drawing time is over. Have children share their pictures. Problems children have personally experienced are most valuable, but if necessary use the swing illustration as an example of waiting your turn.
3. After hearing a description of the problem, ask children:
   - What is the problem?
   - Do you have all the information?
   - How do you feel?
   - How does the other person feel?
   - What did you do?
   - What happened when you did that?
   - How did you feel when that happened?
   - What else could you do?
   - What will happen then?
4. Discuss as many drawings as time allows. Choose problems that involve taking turns, sharing, and interrupting. Elicit responses where children determine solutions for themselves and acknowledge that their actions can cause responses. Elicit responses that indicate a need to calm down first. Role-play solutions when opportunity is apparent.

End

1. Process, "What did you learn today? How will you use what you learned? What will you do? How do you feel about today's group? For next time, think about problems you may have with other students that happen in your classroom. We can use them in our next group. Does that sound like a good idea?"
2. Remind children that the group will meet two more times.

Session 7
Topic: In the classroom

Resources
- Puppets

Beginning
1. Children complete the sentence, "I am getting better and better at . . ."
2. Ask members how they have used what they are learning about problem solving.
3. Ask children to share problems they have had or have seen in the classroom. Tell members, "So, it sounds like these kinds of problems can get people in trouble and they feel bad about that. We can practice what to do when this happens. What do you think about using the puppets to role-play this kind of problem?"

Middle
1. Have any kind of puppets available. Using a member's experience if possible, role-play a distraction in class with the puppets. Or use the following situation: You are working on your seat-work and the student sitting next to you shows you a toy he has in his backpack. He starts to tell you all about it.
2. Ask for volunteers to role-play this scene with the puppets. Help them with the role-play, "You be the other student, his name is _____. And you be _____. First, pretend you are working on seatwork, then . . ."

3. Ask members:
   - What is the problem?
   - How do you feel?
   - How does the other person feel?
   - What can you do about it?
   - What will happen if you do that?
   - How will you feel about that?
   - What else can you do?
   - Then what will happen?
   - And then how would you feel?
4. Tell children, "I have something for you to think about that has worked for other students. When someone is keeping you from getting your work done or listening to your teacher you can talk to yourself. You can say to yourself: I won't answer, I'm going to do my work. Then when she stops bothering you, you can smile, and say to yourself, I can do it. Who would like to practice this with the puppets?" Allow all group members to role-play this solution with puppets.

End
1. Process, "What did you learn today? How are you going to use what you learned? How do you feel about today's group?"
2. Talk about the group's last meeting and how members would like to say good-bye.

Session 8
Topic: Saying goodbye

Resources

- Refreshments
- Teachers' post-group evaluation form
- Group Evaluation handout (page 239)

Beginning

1. Children share, "When I have a problem with someone, something I do now that I didn't do before this group is . . ."
2. Celebrate success. Ask students to share a time when they used their problem solving. Model complimenting each child and invite members to join in the congratulating.
3. Tell children how you feel about having them in a group. Tell them, "It would help me to know about how you feel and how you think the group has helped you. It will help me with other groups of children who also want to learn about problem solving. And it will help me to know what you learned. I have a few questions that you can answer that will tell me that."

Middle

1. Share snacks. Share, "How do you feel about the group ending?"
2. Ask and record answers to evaluation questions for kindergarten and first grade. Second graders can usually complete the simple form included.

End

1. Children share, "The best part of being in our group was . . .".
2. Tell children that although the group has ended you are there to help with a problem.
3. Have teachers complete post-group evaluation.

Teacher Pre/Post Evaluation

Student _____ Date _____

Teacher _____

Please rate student on a scale of 1–5. Your time is appreciated.

1—Almost Never   5—Almost Always

_____ Behaves positively with classmates

_____ Takes turns/shares

_____ Works well in classroom

_____ Shows understanding of feelings of another person

_____ Is distracted in class

_____ Overreacts frequently

_____ Is involved in fights

_____ Bothers other children

Name_____ Date_____

Social Problem-Solving
Group Evaluation

 Always   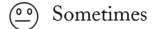 Sometimes   Never

1. I get along with other students.

2. I think about how other people feel.

3. When I have a problem, I think of
different things to do.

4. I think about what will happen
before I do something about a
problem.

5. I think the group has helped me.

       Group Counseling for School Counselors: A Practical Guide

Booster Session

Resources

- Chart paper

Beginning

1. Tell students that after a group ends, it is a good idea to check with members to see how they are doing.
2. Remind students that although the group has ended, there are the same rules for this meeting. Ask, "Who would like to remind us of the rules?"

Middle

1. Ask, "How are you using what you learned in the group? What questions do you have? What can we talk about that would help you?"
2. Review briefly, "When you have a problem with another person, what do you do?" Use chart paper to list responses from students. Elicit responses that include: Find out what the problem is. How do you feel? How does the other person feel? What can you do? What will happen if you do that? How will you feel? What else can you do? Then how will you feel? What do you choose to do? How did it work?
3. Ask students to tell about a time when they worked hard to solve a problem. Model a compliment to the speaker and then ask other members, "Who would like to say something to _____ about how he/she did?"

End

1. How did this meeting help you? What did you learn? What was it like to get together again?
2. Remind children they can see you if they need help.

3.4
Social Problem Solving, 3–5

| Grade Level: 3–5 | Time Required: 8 Sessions | Author: Donna Steinberg |

Purpose

To develop social problem-solving skills and thinking skills. Students use a problem-solving model to apply to typical social problems. Role-play provides practice in applying the new skills.

Logistics

GROUP COMPOSITION

Students grades 3–5 mixed with regard to activity level and behavior control. Avoid loading group with only overactive behavior problem students. Students need multiple models of appropriate behavior. Groups with only behavior problem students usually do not show significant gains in prosocial behavior. Mixed groups are generally very effective.

GROUP SIZE

4–6 students

GROUP TIME PER SESSION

30 minutes

NUMBER OF SESSIONS

Eight, with booster sessions spaced approximately one month apart after regular group ends.

Session 1
Topic: Getting started

Resources

- "Think First" Self-Evaluation form (student)
- "Think First" Teacher Pre/Post Evaluation form
- Chart paper

Beginning

1. Students and teachers complete the pre-group evaluations before the group begins. A good time may be after the student has accepted the invitation to the group at the screening interview.

2. Welcome children and let them know you are happy they have chosen to participate. Have them tell a partner their name and something they like to do. Then, members introduce each other.

3. Talk about the purpose of the group. Ask children:
   - "How do you feel when you are having a problem with another person?"
   - "What kinds of problems have you had?"
   - "How do you think a problem-solving group will help you?"

4. Provide a summary of what to expect. "In this group we can learn how to find solutions to problems, how things we do can affect others, how to choose a solution, how to use self-control, and steps for making a decision. Does this sound like something that will help you?"

5. Ask students to "think about what kinds of rules will make our group a happy and safe place to learn."

Middle

1. Discuss rules for the group. Encourage rules that are established by the children. Write the rules on chart paper, making sure to include no put-downs, one person talks at a time, and not talking about what other members say. Talk about confidentiality and limits in concrete terms. Signing the rule chart indicates agreement and adds to cohesion.

2. Tell members, "When we talk about problem-solving, it will help to have real problems you have had or seen. For the next time we meet it would be helpful for each of you to bring an example with you. You can draw a picture of the problem or you can write about it. It can be a problem with a friend, someone at school, or at home."

End

Process with members,
"What was it like for you to be in group today?"
"Who else feels that way?"
"What did you learn?"
"How do you think our group will help you?"

"Think First" Self-Evaluation

Student _____ Date _____

Teacher _____

Rate yourself on the scale indicated. Help yourself by being honest.

1—Almost Never   2—Sometimes   3—Almost Always

_____ I get along well with classmates.

_____ I think about how others are feeling.

_____ I say no in a friendly way when I don't want to do something that will get me in trouble.

_____ When I have a problem I think first before I do anything about it.

_____ I think of other ways to solve a problem instead of fighting.

_____ When I do something I shouldn't have, I admit I did it and I accept what happens.

_____ I can calm down when I am angry.

_____ I do not pay attention to others when I am doing my classwork.

_____ When I have a problem I think about how I feel.

_____ When I have a problem I think of different things to do about it.

_____ When I have a problem I think of what will happen if I do something about it.

"Think First" Teacher Pre/Post Evaluation

Student _____ Date _____

Teacher _____

Please rate student on the scale indicated. Your time is appreciated.

1—Almost Never   2—Sometimes   3—Almost Always

_____ Behaves positively with classmates

_____ Shows understanding of how other people feel

_____ Avoids trouble

_____ Acts without thinking

_____ Gets involved in fights

_____ Blames others

_____ Has angry outbursts

_____ Is distracted in class

     244   *Group Counseling for School Counselors: A Practical Guide*

Session 2
Topic: Solutions

Beginning

1. Members complete the sentence, "I can tell when someone is happy when . . ."
2. Explain to members, "Today we will use the problems we have brought with us to learn about identifying a problem, gathering information about a problem, and thinking about solutions for a problem. How do you think this will help us?" Elicit responses that indicate these steps can help to solve the problem.

Middle

1. Have children present their problem: "Who would like to start by telling us about the problem you brought? Tell us what happened without telling us what you did about it." Model telling about a problem without telling the solution. Immediately after the problem is presented, ask, "What is the problem?"
2. Very quickly, ask, "What should _____ do about it?"
3. Tell children, "I asked you to identify the problem and think of a solution very quickly. Now I will give you some time to think about it and answer again." Have children work in pairs. Ask:
   - "What was different about answering without thinking, then having a chance to think about it?"
   - "How is thinking about it better?"
4. Have another child present a problem without telling the solution. Tell members, "This time you can ask (the child presenting the problem) questions

to learn more about the problem." Model asking questions: "How do you feel? How does the other person feel? How can you tell?" After members have asked questions, ask, "What is the problem? What should _____ do about it?"

5. Discuss:
   - How does it help to get all the information about a problem?
   - How does it help to think about how you feel?
   - How does it help to think about how the other person feels?
   - How can you tell how another person feels? (watch, listen, ask)
   - What are some other ways you can know the whole story of a problem? (ask questions)
6. Process remaining problems using questions:
   - How can you get the facts about this problem?
   - What is the problem?
   - How do the people feel?
   - How do you know?
   - What can be done about it?
7. Discuss: What did you notice about the solutions you thought of? Was there more than one solution for a problem? What do you think about that?

End

Ask, "What was it like for you to be in group today?"
"What did you learn?"
"How will you use what you learned?"

Session 3
Topic: Consequences

Resources
- Andrew's Problem narrative

Beginning
1. Members complete the sentence, "The best thing about last session was . . .".
2. Members share how they have used what they have learned about problem solving.
3. Ask children, "How does it help to think of more than one solution? So it sounds like you are thinking about which one will work best; how do you choose? Today I brought a problem we can use to think about consequences, what will happen if we choose a solution, and to think about how we take responsibility for a problem we have caused. Role-play can be very helpful because it gives us a chance to practice what we are learning. Does this sound like a good idea?"

Middle
1. Read "Andrew's Problem." Discuss:
   - Do you have all the information?
   - What is the problem?
   - How do the people feel?
   - What can Andrew do?
   - What will happen if he does that?
   - What else can he do?
   - What will happen then?
2. Continue to consider solutions and consequences.
3. Choose a solution.
4. Model role-playing if necessary. Ask for volunteers to pretend to be Andrew and his brother to role-play the chosen solution.
5. Ask children, "What if I told you Andrew told Sam it wasn't his fault? What do you think about that?" Elicit responses that indicate owning the problem, taking responsibility, and accepting consequences.
6. Continue discussion about responsibility. Ask, "Who chooses how you behave?"
7. Ask children, "Do you think all problems have good solutions? What can you do when this happens?" Elicit responses that indicate doing your best to choose a solution.
8. Ask children, "What if Andrew's brother called him a name? What would you do?" Ask for volunteers to role-play this problem using what they have learned.

End
Ask, "How do you feel about being in group today?"
"Who else feels that way?"
"What did you learn?"
"How are you going to use what you learned?"

Andrew's Problem

Andrew really admired his brother's trading cards. He told his friends at school about the wonderful collection his brother Sam had worked hard to assemble. But his friends said, "You are always bragging about your brother. Nobody has all those cards." This made Andrew feel upset and frustrated because he was telling the truth.

That afternoon after school Andrew asked Sam if he could take his cards to school to show his friends. Sam said, "No way do I let you take my cards anywhere. If your friends want to see my cards, they can come here and I will show them." Andrew felt angry. He felt that Sam was mean to him and didn't trust him with his cards.

The next morning Andrew took Sam's cards from his room and put them in his backpack. He couldn't wait until lunch so he could show everyone the wonderful collection and they would know he was telling the truth. Lunchtime finally came and as everyone at the lunch table was looking at the cards a crowd formed. One person fell into another person. Before Andrew knew what was happening, a pile of gooey beefaroni was all over Sam's cards.

Session 4
Topic: Making a choice

Resources
- Drawing materials

Beginning
1. "Something I am getting better at is . . ."
2. Children share how they are using problem solving.
3. Ask, "Who has ever gotten into a fight with someone? How did you feel? How do you think it will help you to think of different things to do to solve a problem like this without fighting? We can do something different today. I will tell you a problem and you can draw a picture of what you think you could do about it. Then you can tell about your solution. That way we can get ideas. How does that sound?"

Middle
1. Read to children: You are working on your math in class when rubberbands begin to fly by your head from the back of the room. You are trying hard to ignore the distraction and concentrate on the math. Then you feel a strike on the back of your head. You turn around and tell the kid to stop fooling around. You try to get back to your math and you feel a sting on your ear.
2. Discuss, "How do you feel?" Distribute drawing paper. Have members draw, "What you will do to solve this problem." For each solution, question the consequences. Emphasize consequences for "hurting back."
3. Members share their solutions. Elicit responses or offer "suggestions to think about" that include:
   - Asking permission to leave the classroom for a short time to calm down and think about what to do
   - Telling the person how you feel without an attitude
   - Talk to yourself—for example, "I am going to keep working. I'm not going to let this kid get to me."
   - Asking the person why they are shooting rubberbands at you—maybe you are not the target
   - Asking for help—deciding who can help best
4. Discuss: "How does it help you to think first in a problem like this?"

End
Ask, "What have you learned?"

"How do you feel about your experience in group today?"

"How is the group helping you?"

"How are you going to use your problem-solving skills?"

Session 5
Topic: Saying no

Beginning

1. Members complete the sentence, "When a friend asks me to do something I don't want to do, I . . .".

2. Members share how they have used problem solving.

3. Ask children, "Who has ever had a problem with someone who wanted you to do something and you didn't want to do it? How is it going to help you to learn about some things you can do? We can role-play your problems and that will help you to practice what you can do the next time it happens."

Middle

1. Suggest that you role-play a problem first to get started and maybe give some ideas to think about. The problem is your friend wants to copy the answers from your homework. Model the problem-solving steps. "OK, first I am thinking about what this problem is. I don't like saying no to my friend. I am pretty sure I have all the information. I am feeling guilty to say no to her. I think she is feeling worried that her homework is not done. Thinking about a solution for this kind of problem, I am going to:
   - Make a decision if I want to do it.
   - Think about why I will or will not do it.
   - Think about consequences.
   - Then I will tell the person no in a way that is friendly.
   - Maybe I will tell the person why I won't do it so they will understand.

2. Ask for a volunteer to play the friend asking to copy homework. Model saying no in an amiable tone: "No, I don't want to do that because the teacher will know you copied when we both hand it in late and we have the same answers. She may even think I copied. And besides, it's kind of like cheating."

3. Role-play the students' problems, allowing everyone the opportunity to practice saying no in a way that is not threatening.

4. Discuss, "Can anyone make you do something? Who chooses how you behave?"

End

1. Process with children, "What was it like to role-play today? How do you feel about group today? What did you learn? How will you use the skills you are learning?"

2. This can be a good time to remind the students they will meet three more times.

Session 6
Topic: Chill out

Resources

- Problem-Solving Steps handout

Beginning

1. Members complete the sentence, "When I get angry I can calm down by . . ."
2. Discuss how members are using problem-solving skills.
3. Ask children, "Who has had a problem with another person that made you so angry that you did something that got you in trouble? Knowing how to calm down can be helpful for these kinds of problems. Today we can practice ways to calm down and chill out. How does that sound?"

Middle

1. Refer to the students' ideas in completing the icebreaker sentence as ways that are successful for them. Suggest other ideas for calming down before dealing with a problem:
   - Count to ten.
   - Recognize how your body feels.
   - Think of things you can do:
     - Leave the area.
     - Use a relaxation activity.
     - Write how you feel in a journal.
     - Talk to someone.
     - Talk to yourself.
     - Choose what you will do to calm down.
2. Discuss ideas with students, and then invite them to try a relaxation exercise. Progressively move from the head to the toes, telling children to tighten muscles and release as they take a breath and let it out. For example: "Scrunch up the muscles in your forehead really tight, take a deep breath. Now let out your breath and relax your forehead. Think about how your head feels now. Now squeeze the muscles all around your eyes and take a deep breath. Let out your breath and relax your eyes. Think about how your eyes feel." Continue with shoulders, arms, etc.
3. Suggest to students that there are ways to relax just by tightening and releasing your fists in your pockets or your arms on your chair if you cannot leave the situation right away. Allow students to practice.
4. Cut the Problem-Solving Steps handout into strips, separating each step. Cut off the numbers. Encourage children to name the ways they have used their skills. Ask, "What have you noticed about the skills you have learned? What do you do when you have a problem?" As members name each step, present the strip indicating the step. Have them put the steps in order.
5. Tell students it would be helpful to the group if they take a problem-solving form with them and complete it with a problem they have or they see happening. Ask students to bring it to the next meeting.

End

1. Ask, "What was it like for you today?"
   "How do you feel about the group?"
   "What did you learn?"
   "How will you use what you learned?"
2. Remind students that two sessions remain.

Name_____ Date _____

Problem-Solving Steps

1. **Calm down.**

   I calmed down by _____

   I feel _____

   I think the other person feels _____

2. **Identify the problem.**

   The problem is _____

   _____

3. **Think about different ways to solve the problem.**

   Solution _____

4. **Consequence**—If I do this, then what might happen?

   _____

5. **What are other things I can do?**

   Solution _____

   Consequence _____

   Solution _____

   Consequence _____

6. **Choose a solution.**

   I think this is the best thing to do because _____

   _____

7. Is the problem solved? How did this work? _____

   _____

8. What would you do differently next time? _____

   _____

Session 7
Topic: Problem solving

Resources

- Problem-Solving Steps handout from Session 6
- "Think First" Self-Evaluation form (page 243)

Beginning

1. Students complete the sentence, "The best part about what I have learned in our group is . . .".

2. Discuss how children have used their skills by sharing the problem-solving forms. Encourage members to give each other feedback.

3. Ask students, "Who has ever had to make a hard decision? How did you feel when you had to decide? Maybe it was a decision about being invited to two places at the same time. Maybe it was a decision about what to buy with your birthday money. How do you think knowing how to solve a problem can help you make a decision? Today we can practice using what you already know in a different way. Does this sound like a good idea? There is something else I would like to do today that will tell me what you have learned in our group and how I can help others like you. It is a form that will take a few minutes. You may recognize it as the form ("Think First" Self-Evaluation) you completed when I talked to you about joining the group."

Middle

1. Use decisions from members or use those previously stated. Divide the group in half. Have each group use the problem-solving steps to make a decision. Then, discuss:
   - How was making a decision similar to solving a problem?
   - How was it different?
   - How does it help you to look at the steps on paper?

2. Distribute problem-solving handouts. Ask, "Where can you keep this in case you want to look at the steps?"

3. Distribute the "Think First" Self-Evaluation form. Ask students to complete; give directions if necessary.

End

1. How do you feel about the group today? What have you learned? How are you going to use what you learned?

2. Discuss the last session and ask members how they would like to end their group.

Session 8
Topic: Saying goodbye

Resources

- Refreshments
- Group Evaluation form (page 10)
- "Think First" Teacher Pre/Post Evaluation (page 244)

Beginning

1. Members share, "How do you feel about the group ending?" Include yourself in the go-round and validate feelings.

2. Tell members, "We will celebrate as you planned. Then I have a paper (the Group Evaluation) that will take a few minutes for you to complete. It is different from the form you completed last session. Your ideas will help me to know about how you feel and how you think the group has helped you."

Middle

1. Serve snacks. Suggest telling "success stories" using problem-solving skills. Model and encourage children to tell each other what they are doing well, what they liked, what was a good idea, etc.

2. Ask members to complete a Group Evaluation form. "Please be honest about your feelings. You do not have to put your name on it if you don't want to."

End

1. Tell children that although the group is over they can see you if they have a problem.

2. Have teachers complete post-group evaluations.

Booster Session for Problem-Solving Groups

Resources

- Chart paper

Beginning

1. Tell students that after a group ends, it is a good idea to check with members to see how they are doing.
2. Remind students that although the group has ended, there are the same rules for this meeting. Ask, "Who would like to remind us of the rules?"

Middle

1. Ask, "How are you using what you learned in the group? What questions do you have? What can we talk about that would help you?"
2. Review briefly, "When you have a problem with another person, what do you do?" Use chart paper to list responses from students. Elicit responses by inquiring:
    - What is the problem?
    - How do you feel?
    - How does the other person feel?
    - What can you do?
    - What will happen if you do that? How will you feel?
    - What else can you do? Then how will you feel?
    - What do you choose to do?
    - How did it work?
3. Ask students to tell about a time when they worked hard to solve a problem. Encourage feedback. Model a compliment to the speaker and then ask other members, "Who would like to say something to _____ about how he/she did?"

End

1. How did this meeting help you? What did you learn? What was it like to get together again?
2. Remind children that they can see you if they need help.

3.5
Social and Academic Skills Through Storytelling

Grade Level: K–2	Time Required: 8 Sessions	Author: Lori Bednarek

Purpose

To develop the learning skills and social skills that are critical to long-term school success. The skills include attending, listening, asking questions for clarification, and the social skills of encouragement, sharing, empathy, and team work.

Logistics

GROUP COMPOSITION

K–2 students mixed with regard to activity level and behavior control. Avoid loading group with only over-active behavior problem students. Students need multiple models of appropriate behavior. Groups with only behavior problem students usually do not show significant gains in prosocial behavior. Mixed groups are generally very effective.

GROUP SIZE

4–6 students

GROUP TIME PER SESSION

30 minutes

NUMBER OF SESSIONS

Eight, with booster sessions spaced approximately one month apart after regular group ends.

Recommended Resources

Full bibliographic details for these publications are included in the Bibliography at the end of this book.

Brigman, Lane, and Lane, 1994: *Ready to Learn.*
Hutchins, 1993: *My Best Friend.*
Silverstein, 1964: *The Giving Tree.*
Waber, 1988: *Ira Says Goodbye.*

BOOKS ON STORYTELLING

Duke, 1992: *Aunt Isabel Tells a Good One.*
Haley, 1988: *A Story, a Story: An African Tale.*
Long, 1978: *Albert's Story.*
Ziegler, 1993: *Mr. Knocky.*

BOOKS ON FRIENDSHIP

Auch, 1993: *Bird Dogs Can't Fly.*
Carlson, 1992: *Arnie and the New Kid.*
Delton, 1986: *Two Good Friends.*
DePaolo, 1992: *Rosie and the Yellow Ribbon.*
Engel, 1993: *Fishing.*
Henkes, 1990: *Jessica.*
Komaiko, 1988: *Earl's Too Cool for Me.*
Pfister, 1992: *The Rainbow Fish.*
Russo, 1992: *Alex Is My Friend.*
Waber, 1972: *Ira Sleeps Over.*
Wolkstein, 1994: *Step by Step.*

BOOKS ON LISTENING AND PAYING ATTENTION

Gray, 1994: *Small Green Snake.*
Mosel, 1989: *Tikki Tikki Tembo.*
Showers, 1991: *The Listening Walk.*
Vollmer, 1988: *Joshua Disobeys.*

BAD DAY BOOKS

Bourgeois, 1997: *Franklin's Bad Day.*
Hall, 1995: *A Bad, Bad Day.*
Hood, 1999: *Bad Hair Day.*
Mayer, 1995: *Just a Bad Day.*
Michaels, 2000: *Bulbasaur's Bad Day.*
Pellowski, 1986: *Benny's Bad Day.*
Simon, 1998: *The Good Bad Day.*
Viorst, 1972: *Alexander and the Terrible, Horrible, No Good, Very Bad Day.*

WORDLESS PICTURE BOOKS

Asch, 1986: *Goodbye House.*

Goffin, 1991: *Oh!*

McCully, 1988: *The Christmas Gift.*

McCully, 1984: *Picnic.*

Mariotti, 1989: *Hanimations.*

Rohmann, 1994: *Time Flies.*

Turkle, 1976: *Deep in the Forest.*

Ueno, 1973: *Elephant Buttons.*

Ward, 1973: *The Silver Pony: A Story in Pictures.*

Wiesner, 1991: *Tuesday.*

Session 1
Topic: Getting to know you

Resources

- Chart paper
- We Listen with Our Ears handout
- Book with positive theme (recommended: *The Giving Tree*, by Shel Silverstein)

Beginning

1. Introduce yourself and have all the group members say their names.

2. Tell about the purpose of the group. "We are going to be meeting together for eight weeks. In this group we are going to learn about a lot of different things. We are going to learn about making friends, listening to one another, saying positive things to each other, and asking questions. We are also going to learn all about stories. We are even going to be making up our own stories and acting them out!"

Middle

1. "Before we get started we need to talk about some group rules. Who knows what a rule is?" List group members' ideas on chart paper.

2. "Let's come up with some rules together that we can use in our group." With the group brainstorm some general rules. Try to make the list no longer than five rules. Some sample rules are:

   - We listen to each other.
   - No put-downs.
   - Be on time.
   - Respect others.
   - Work cooperatively.

3. Focus on a rule that has to do with listening and introduce the handout "We Listen with Our Ears."

As a group read the poem and talk about what it means to listen with your whole body. Give examples of people who might be listening with their ears, but not with their bodies. Students can practice being active listeners.

4. Next go over the confidentiality rule and its limits. You might say, "We are going to be working together for the next eight weeks. When you leave this group you may talk to your friends or family about anything that **you** say or do in this group. However, you may not talk about anything that **another person** said or did in the group. I will not tell anyone about anything that any of you say in this group except if you are being hurt, or if you could hurt someone else. Whatever we say in our group is confidential. That means private."

5. Share a book with the group that has a positive theme, such as *The Giving Tree* by Shel Silverstein. This story has many positive themes to expand on with the group. During the reading of the story encourage the group members to "listen with their whole bodies."

6. After reading the story check for understanding of the main idea.

End

1. Each student should share what he or she learned about the group rules and confidentiality.

2. Have each group member state what time and day your next meeting will be.

3. Each group member should share one way that he or she is going to use active listening throughout the week.

Name_____ Date_____

We Listen with Our Ears

We listen with our ears of course!

But did you know it's true,

That eyes, and lips, and hands, and feet

Can help us listen too!

Session 2
Topic: Practicing listening and paying attention

Resource

- Book on listening (recommended: *Miss Nelson Is Missing* by H. Allard)
- Four Ws and an H handout
- Feeling Faces sheet (page 9) *or* a poster with similar faces

Beginning

1. Check in with students. Begin by showing the Feeling Faces sheet. Go around the table and ask each student to point to a feeling that he or she is having today. Each student should explain why he or she is feeling that way.

2. Review group rules from the first session.

3. Review listening with the whole body. Have students recite the poem "We listen with our ears."

4. Introduce today's topic. "Today we are going to read a story about a class that is having trouble listening to their teacher. This story will remind us how important listening and paying attention are."

Middle

1. Before reading the story, have students predict what will happen by looking at the pictures.

2. Read the story *Miss Nelson Is Missing* (alternative books on listening/paying attention are listed on page 254).

3. Discuss the story. Explore questions about the book that deal with the social skill of paying attention and listening.

4. Introduce retelling the story. "Pretend that you are telling a friend about this story. This friend has never heard this story before. Let's practice retelling the story so that he or she would know everything that happened in the story."

5. Make three boxes on the chalkboard for the beginning, middle, and end of the story.

Beginning	Middle	End

6. Have students tell what happened in the beginning, middle, and end of the story.

7. Introduce the 4 Ws and an H Questions handout. As a group make sure that the retelling of the beginning, middle, and end contains answers to all the questions on the 4 Ws and an H chart.

End

1. Have students share what they learned about listening and paying attention.

2. Have students share what they learned about the way stories are organized (beginning, middle, and end).

3. Students state one way that they can be good listeners during the next week.

Name_____ Date_____

The 4 Ws and an H Questions

| WHO | Who was the story about? |

| WHAT | What happened in the story? |
| | What was the story about? |

| WHEN | When did the story happen? |
| | Daytime, nighttime, morning, afternoon, spring, summer, winter, fall? |

| WHERE | Where did the story happen? |
| | Inside, outside, city, farm? |

HOW	How was the person feeling at the beginning of the story? At the end?
	How did the story begin?
	How did the story end?

Session 3
Topic: Showing encouragement to friends

Resources

- Feeling Faces sheet (page 9) or poster
- *My Best Friend*, by Pat Hutchins
- Four Ws and an H handout

Beginning

1. Check in with students. Begin by showing the Feeling Faces. Go around the table and ask each student to point to a feeling that he or she is having today. Each student should explain why he or she is feeling that way.

2. Review group rules from the first session.

3. Review listening with the whole body. Have students recite the poem "We listen with our ears."

4. Introduce today's topic. "Today we are going to read a story about two girls who are friends." We are going to talk about how to make friends and why friends are important.

Middle

1. Look at the cover of the book *My Best Friend*, by Pat Hutchins. (Alternative books on friendship are listed on the overview page, p. 254.)

2. Have students predict what will happen in the story by looking at the pictures.

3. Read the story to the group.

4. Discuss the story. Explore questions about the book that deal with the social skill of making and keeping friends.

5. Work through the 4 Ws and an H handout with the group, pointing out the questions (who, what, when, where, how).

6. Explain to the students that all stories contain information about **who** (characters), **what** (plot), **when** (setting), **where** (setting), and **how** (plot). Some students will be familiar with the terms **character** and **setting**.

End

1. Students share what they learned about making friends and why friends are important.

2. Students share what they learned about the way stories are organized.

3. Students state one way that they can be good friends throughout the week.

Session 4
Topic: Making up and telling stories

Resources

- "Feelings" poster or Feeling Faces handout (page 9)
- 4 Ws and an H handout
- Paper and crayons
- We Listen with Our Ears handout (from Session 1)
- Story Beginners handout
- Chart paper

Beginning

1. Check in with students. Begin by showing the Feeling Faces. Go around the table and ask each student to point to a feeling that he or she is having today. Each student should explain why he or she is feeling that way.

2. Goal reporting: Students share one way in which they tried to be good listeners throughout the week.

3. Say, "Today we are going to practice telling stories. Last week we learned that all stories have a beginning, a middle, and an end. We also learned that most stories answer 4 Ws and an H questions. We are going to try to tell stories that answer those questions today."

4. Review the 4 Ws and an H handout with the group.

Middle

1. Model telling a 1–2 minute story. Use one of the story starters below.

STORY STARTERS
One of my favorite things to do at home (outside)
One of my favorite things to do at home (inside)
One of my favorite things to do at school (outside)
One of my favorite things to do at school (inside)
A time I helped someone feel better
A time I made a new friend
A time I invited someone I didn't know well to play or asked to join someone in play
A time I helped someone with schoolwork or working through a problem
A time I started a healthy habit
A time I learned to do something that I thought was too hard or scary

2. The story that you tell should model the 4 Ws and an H story structure. In addition, make sure that your story has a clear beginning, middle, and end.

3. After telling the story, ask the group to answer the who, what, when, where, and how questions, and to identify the beginning, middle, and end of the story.

4. Review the skill of using encouragement. Ask group members how they could show you encouragement as you told your story. Make a list on chart paper of the encouraging things to say and do while listening to a partner's story. Label the list "Encouraging Things to Say and Do."

5. Tell the students that they are now going to get a chance to make up a story on their own. Give the students the following story starter.

> **STORY STARTER:** *A time I made a new friend*

6. Have students use crayons and paper to write/draw their story. Allow 4–5 minutes for this activity. Remind students that their story should contain answers to the 4 Ws and an H questions.

7. Tell students that sometimes starting to tell their stories can be difficult and sometimes it helps to use story-beginning words. Show students the handout Story Beginners. Encourage them to choose one to begin their story.

8. Pair the students up. Have students take turns telling their stories to their partners. Make sure that the listeners pay attention to the storyteller using their active listening skills. (You may want to review the poem "We Listen with Our Ears." Remind the storyteller to include answers to the 4 Ws and an H questions in their story. Allow 1–2 minutes for each student to retell his or her story.

9. To check active listening, have partners report the answers to the 4 Ws and an H questions as they take turns.

10. If time permits, have one or two group members share their stories with the whole group. During this time model encouragement by making two positive compliments about the group member's story.

End

1. Students share what they learned about listening, paying attention, and encouragement.

2. Students share what they learned about the way stories are organized (beginning, middle, and end).

3. Students state one way that they can use encouragement during the week.

Name_____ Date_____

Story Beginners

 Once upon a time . . .

 One day . . .

 One night . . .

 Long, long ago . . .

 Once there was . . .

 Far, far away . . .

   Group Counseling for School Counselors: A Practical Guide

Session 5
Topic: Stories with positive and negative social outcomes

Resources

- Feeling Faces handout (page 9) or poster
- Stories with Two Endings handout
- Paper and crayons
- Chart paper

Beginning

1. Check in with students. Begin by showing the Feeling Faces. Go around the table and ask each student to point to a feeling that he or she is having today. Each student should explain why he or she is feeling that way.

2. Goal reporting: Students share one way in which they tried to use encouragement.

3. Tell students, "Today we are going to practice telling stories. Last week we learned how to tell a story. We practiced using encouragement and active listening to help our partners tell their stories. Today we are going to make up some more stories and practice asking questions about those stories."

Middle

1. Introduce the skill of asking questions. Ask group members, "Why is it important to ask questions?" Record their answers on chart paper. Explore this skill by asking them if they ask questions in class and how asking questions can help them learn.

2. Model telling a 1–2 minute story about being mad at your friend *excluding* the ending. Stop your story before you get to resolving the problem. Use the story starter below.

STORY STARTER: *A time that I was mad at my friend*

3. Use the Stories with Two Endings handout to chart the beginning and middle of the story that you have told. Ask the students to come up with two different endings to your story. One should be a positive outcome and one should be a negative outcome.

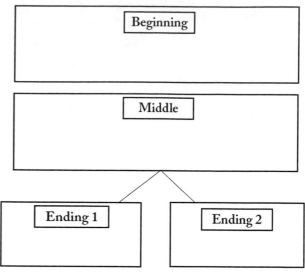

4. Discuss the negative and positive outcomes of your story.

5. Ask the students to choose one of the following story starters.

STORY STARTERS:
A time that I got mad at school
A time that I had a problem with a friend

6. Each student should use paper and crayons to draw out his or her story. Allow 1–2 minutes for this activity.

7. Put students in pairs. Review how to use active listening and encouragement while listening to a partner's story. (Review the poster of encouraging things to say and do that the group made last week). Give each student a chance to tell his or her story to a partner. Encourage them to tell their stories in two different ways. One way should include a positive ending, one should include an ending that was not positive.

8. Check the partners' active listening skills by having them retell the story using the 4 Ws and an H questions.

9. When both partners have had a chance to share, choose one group member to share his or her story out loud. Use the Beginning, Middle, and Two Endings handout to summarize the story.

10. Model good question asking by asking the group member about his or her story. Some good questions to ask might be:

    - Why did you choose the story starter that you did?

    - Is this a real story or make believe?

    - Which ending do you think is the one you would like most to happen?

    - How did the character in this story use encouragement and active listening?

11. Go around the group and have each student ask a question about the story.

End

1. Students share what they learned about listening, paying attention, encouragement, and asking questions.

2. Students share what they learned about making up stories with multiple endings.

3. Students state one way that they can learn more by asking questions during the next week.

Name_____ Date_____

Stories with Two Endings

Beginning

Middle

Ending 1

Ending 2

Session 6
Topic: Dealing with a bad day

Resources
- Feeling Faces handout (page 9) or poster
- Paper and crayons
- Optional: props, puppets

Beginning
1. Check in with students. Begin by showing the Feeling Faces. Go around the table and ask each student to point to a feeling that he or she is having today. Each student should explain why he or she is feeling that way.

2. Goal reporting: Students share one way in which they tried to use asking questions.

3. Say to students, "Today we are going to practice telling stories and then acting those stories out. Last week we practiced telling a story with two different endings. We practiced using encouragement and active listening to help our partners tell their stories. We also learned how to ask questions about those stories. Today we are going to make up some more stories and act those stories out."

Middle
1. Model telling a 1–2 minute story. Use the story starter below.

> **STORY STARTER:**
> *One of my favorite things to do at school*

2. The story should model the 4 Ws and an H story structure. In addition, make sure that your story has a clear beginning, middle, and end.

3. After telling the story, ask the group to answer the who, what, when, where, and how questions, and to identify the beginning, middle, and end of the story.

4. Review the skill of using encouragement. Ask the group members how they could show you encouragement as you told your story.

5. Tell students that they are now going to get a chance to make up a story on their own. Give the students the following story starter.

> **STORY STARTER:**   *A very bad day*

6. Tell the students that they are going to make up this story with a partner. Put the students in pairs.

7. Give the students 1–2 minutes to plan their stories using paper and crayons. Remind the students that their stories should have a beginning, middle, and end. In addition they should answer all of the 4 Ws and an H questions. The stories that they make up can have just one ending; we will be adding another ending later.

8. Partners are now going to share their stories with the entire group. Have each pair of students decide who is going to be the storyteller.

9. Remind the group that they need to practice active listening and encouragement during the storytelling process. If necessary, review the poem "We Listen with Our Ears" and the poster of encouraging things to say and do made in Session 4.

10. Go around the group and let each pair tell its story. After each group has told its story, brainstorm with the group alternate endings to each story. Try to guide the group to identify actions of the characters that lead to both positive and negative endings. During this process model using encouragement. In addition, ask questions of each pair and encourage the group members to do the same.

11. After each pair has told its story, tell students that they will now act their stories out. Model this process by using the same story that you told at the beginning of the group. Stand up and enlist volunteers to be characters in your story. Dramatize your story for the group.

12. Give each group time to plan how they will act out their story for the group. You may want to provide props and/or puppets for the group.

13. Let each pair present its dramatization to the group. Again, model using active listening and encouragement during the retelling process.

End
1. Students share what they learned about listening, paying attention, encouragement, and asking questions.

2. Students share what they learned about dramatizing their stories.

3. Students state one way that they can practice using encouragement, active listening, and asking questions throughout the week.

Session 7
Topic: Stories with social themes

Resources

- Feeling Faces handout (page 9) or poster
- Paper and crayons
- Stories with Two Endings handout from Session 5

Beginning

1. Check in with students. Begin by showing the Feeling Faces. Go around the table and ask each student to point to a feeling that he or she is having today. Each student should explain why he or she is feeling that way.

2. Goal reporting: Students share one way in which they tried to use asking questions, encouragement, or active listening during the week.

3. Say to students, "Today we are going to practice making up more stories and acting them out. Last week we had fun making up different endings to stories that your group members made up."

Middle

1. Begin this session by making sure that every group member got a chance to share his or her story during the last session.

2. Tell students that today one partner will be making up the beginning and middle of a story and the other partner will help to make up two different endings to the story.

3. Give students the following prompt.

> **STORY STARTER:**
> *The day my friend made me mad*

4. Give students a chance to plan their stories using paper and crayons. At this point remind them that their story needs to include a beginning and a middle. They should have some ideas for the ending; however, their partners will help them with that later on. Remind the group members of the 4 Ws and an H questions that they need to consider when making up their story.

5. Put the group members in pairs. Remind the pairs of the importance of using active listening and encouragement when their partner is telling a story. After the first partner has told his or her story, the pair of students should chart the story on the Stories with Two Endings handout. The pairs can work together to come up with two different endings to each story.

6. After each pair has shared, have the students work together to act out one of their stories. Allow ten minutes for the students to plan for their presentation. The students should choose one ending to present to the group.

7. Give each pair a chance to act out their story for the group. Model encouragement by giving positive comments for each group. Ask the group to give encouragement to the pair that is sharing.

8. Allow time for group members to ask questions about the performance. Some good questions to include might be:

- Why did you choose that ending?
- Did the ending to the story resolve the character's problem? If not, how could a different ending resolve the problem?

End

1. Students share what they learned about listening, paying attention, encouragement, and asking questions.

2. Students share what they learned about getting along with friends.

3. Students state one way that they can practice using encouragement, active listening, and asking questions throughout the week.

4. Students state one way that they can be a good friend.

5. Remind the students that next week is the last session.

Session 8
Topic: Saying good-bye

Resources

- Feeling Faces handout (page 9) or poster
- Story with theme of saying good-bye (recommended: *Ira Says Goodbye* by Bernard Waber)
- Paper and crayons
- End of the Group Assessment handout

Beginning

1. Check in with students. Begin by showing the Feeling Faces. Go around the table and ask each student to point to a feeling that he or she is having today. Each student should explain why he or she is feeling that way.

2. Goal reporting: Students share one way in which they tried to use active listening, encouragement, or asking questions throughout the week.

3. Say to students, "Today is our last session. We are going to read a story about saying good-bye. Then we are going to talk about our favorite parts of this group."

Middle

1. Read the story *Ira Says Goodbye* by Bernard Waber (or another story on good-byes).

2. Discuss the theme of saying good-bye with the group. Have students talk about good-byes that they have said to different people.

3. Tell the group that as a group we are going to make up a story about saying good-bye. Here is our prompt:

> **STORY STARTER:**
> *A time that I had to say good-bye*

4. As a group brainstorm the beginning, middle, and end of the story. Remind the group members to include all the 4 Ws and an H questions.

5. As a group practice telling the good-bye story. If time permits group members can act it out.

6. After the telling of the story, hand out paper and crayons to each group member. Instruct them that they are to draw or write about their favorite part of the group. Allow ten minutes for this activity.

7. After all students are done, have each student share what his or her favorite part of the group was.

End

1. Hand out the End of the Group Assessment. Read each part to the students and have them circle the appropriate face.

2. Ask the students to share one way that they will use what they have learned in the group.

Name_____ Date_____

End of the Group Assessment

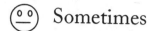 Always  Sometimes  Never

I know how to make friends.

I can listen with my whole body.

I can tell a story with different endings.

I can use encouragement and positive words to help a friend feel better.

I know how to ask good questions.

Saying good-bye is important.

3.6 Loss/Bereavement

Grade Level: K–5	Time Required: 8 Sessions	Author: Michelle Feldman

Purpose

To help students cope with the death of a loved one. Students are taught about the different types of loss, the stages of grief, feelings associated with loss, ways to say good-bye, and coping skills. Bibliotherapy is used to stimulate sharing thoughts, feelings, and ideas for healing the hurt that the death of a loved one brings.

Children usually do not know how to express their feelings and cope with the stress associated with the death of a loved one. Consequently, school work and participation in school activities are often affected. Therefore, the primary goals of the support group are identifying and validating these feelings and encouraging expression in constructive ways.

Before beginning a support group, the facilitator should be comfortable with his or her own death issues. Any self-disclosure should be limited to promoting group rapport and group cohesion. Be aware that a variety of feelings may arise for the facilitator throughout the sessions; the facilitator's knowledge of his or her own limits, and his or her perception that sharing must be for the betterment of the group, are critical. Creating a safe and loving atmosphere is paramount. Consultation with other professional counselors, along with continued education, is always encouraged.

Encouraging grieving children to externalize their grief is vital. It is crucial that professionals working with these groups are cognizant of the very specific and complex needs of grieving children. Therefore, it is recommended that the facilitator of these groups have grief training, counseling experience, and group skills training.

Logistics

GROUP COMPOSITION

Students in grades K–5 who have recently experienced the death of a loved one

GROUP SIZE

4–6 students

GROUP TIME PER SESSION

30 minutes

NUMBER OF SESSIONS

Eight

Recommended Resources

Full bibliographic details for these publications are included in the Bibliography at the end of this book.

Bernstein and Gullo, 1977: *When People Die.*

Brigman and Earley, 1991: *Group Counseling for School Counselors.*

Brown, 1988: *When Dinosaurs Die.*

Buscaglia, 1982: *The Fall of Freddie the Leaf.*

Cohen, 1987: *I Had a Friend Named Peter.*

Dolbrin, 1971: *Scat!*

Geisel (Dr. Seuss), 1998: *My Many-Colored Days.*

Johnson and Johnson, 1998: *Children Who Grieve Too.*

Loretta and Keating, 1995: *After the Funeral.*

Mellonie and Ingpen, 1987: *Lifetimes, the Beautiful Way to Explain Death to Children.*

Morganette, 1994: *Skills for Living.*

Mudy, 1998: *Sad Isn't Bad.*

O'Rourke and Worzybt, 1996: *Support Groups for Children.*

Palmer and Bourke, 1994: *I Wish I Could Hold Your Hand.*

Silverman, 1999: *Help Me Say Goodbye.*

Skivington and Care, 1998: *Balloons for Trevor.*

Steinberg, 1999: *Grief Group.*

Varley, 1992: *Badger's Parting Gifts.*

Viorst, 1988: *The Tenth Good Thing About Barney.*

Session 1
Topic: Introduction and overview

Resources

- Chart paper
- A poster showing feelings (or use Feeling Faces on page 9)

Beginning

1. Introduce yourself and then say, "This is a group for kids who have had someone special in their life die. We will be coming to my office once a week on _____ (day of the week) at _____ (time of day) for eight weeks to talk a little, play a little, maybe read or color a little bit about how you are feeling."

2. "First, I would like to go around the circle and ask everybody what their name is, the name of the special person that died, and either a thumbs-up (if you're feeling really happy), thumbs to the middle (if you are feeling so-so, not too happy, not too sad), or a thumbs-down (if you are feeling really sad or mad)."

3. "Who has ever been in a group before?" (Some examples you may want to give are Scouts, Brownies, dance class, etc.) "Did you have any rules in that group? Why do you think you have to have rules in groups? In the classroom?" Try to incorporate the idea that rules foster a safe environment and allow everyone a fair share to talk and participate in the group. Say, "Today we are going to have to make up a name for our group and a few rules for our group just to make sure that this is a safe place to talk and play together."

Middle

1. Say, "First, let's come up with some rules." (Have a chalkboard, whiteboard, chart paper, etc., to write answers as they are offered.) "Who can raise their hand and tell me one important rule they think we should have in this group?" Continue to generate answers. Make sure to include the right to pass

(only answer voluntarily), and the idea of confidentiality. ("What you say in here belongs to you and you can tell anyone you want what you say. What other students say in here belongs to them. You should not tell anyone what another student says.")

2. "OK, great, now the fun part. I want everyone to close their eyes and think really hard about a name for our group." (Offer suggestions such as the superstars, whiz kids, second grade sundaes.) "Then I am going to give you three minutes. If you would like to share your answer, you can either come and stand right next to me and tell it to the group, whisper it in my ear, or you can just stay at your seat and share, whichever one you'd like to do." Chart answers and then have students put their heads down on the desk and vote anonymously (by raised hand) to pick their favorite name.

End

1. Display handout or poster of feeling faces and say to the kids, "Well, our time is almost up. For our last activity, I would like to go around the group again and ask you one thing you learned today and how you felt being here today and talking with everyone in group. When I call your name, I would like you to come up and say one thing you learned today" (could be the name of the group, a rule, or even another kid's name) "and then look at the poster and point out which feeling you had today in group." When they point out their feeling, make sure to label that feeling for them if they are not able to: "Oh, John felt mad today in group." If there is time, process that and ask, "What made you so mad today?"

2. Remind kids about when you will see them next. (Day and time) ("Bye everyone, remember, see you next Tuesday, my office at 1:00 sharp!")

Session 2

Topic: *The Fall of Freddie the Leaf*

Resource

- *The Fall of Freddie the Leaf* by Leo Buscaglia

Beginning

1. Welcome everyone back to the group. Remind kids that this is our second meeting and we still have six meetings left. Remind the children of last week's meeting and the name of the group and rules. Have the students do a go-round and say a color that describes how they are doing today (blue = sad, red = mad, yellow = cheerful, etc.).

2. Say, "Many times when someone or something dies, no one really tells us what that means. We know it means they got sick, or hurt, or too old to live, but what does that really mean? Today we are going to read a story and talk a little so we can get a better understanding of death."

Middle

1. Read the story *The Fall of Freddie the Leaf.* Discuss afterwards.

2. As a group, brainstorm what happens when an animal or plant is alive. (It moves around, breathes, barks, grows, etc.) Chart answers.

3. As a group, brainstorm what happens when an animal or plant dies. (Its leaves turn brown, it stops breathing, doesn't move any longer, trees and flowers may rot, etc.) Chart answers.

4. Have the same discussion regarding people.

5. If you have access, take a mini hike and observe leaves, flowers, and trees (both dead and alive). As a group interact with the flowers, leaves, and trees to determine (using the characteristics discussed earlier) whether they are dead or alive.

End

1. Ask students, "How was it to be part of today's group?" "What is one thing you learned today?"

2. Remind kids to be on time and that you will see them next _____ at _____.

Session 3
Topic: Sharing feelings

Resources

- *My Many-Colored Days* by Dr. Seuss (Theodore Geisel)
- Chart paper
- Crayons
- Paper

Beginning

1. Welcome everyone back to the group. Remind kids that this is our third meeting and we still have five meetings left. Have the students do a go-round and say their names and if they are having sunny (happy) feelings today or if they are having cloudy (sad, mad) feelings today. If kids do not understand this idea, explain it to them.

2. Say, "I just want to remind everyone why we are here in this group together. That is because we all have had someone special in our life die. A few things that we would like to learn by being in our group are about feelings, and how to talk about our feelings, learn that we are not the only ones who are going through this tough time, and many other things."

3. "Who here has ever been very sad before? Who here has ever gotten really angry before? Who here has ever been very happy before? Today, we are going to learn all about feelings and how our feelings can really never be wrong."

Middle

1. Read the book *My Many-Colored Days*.

2. Ask for volunteers to raise their hands and share one feeling that they felt when their special person died. (Link and connect answers between students: "Oh, you felt mad just like Marisa did.") Chart answers. Discuss the responses afterward. Point out that everyone will have different feelings and they are all OK to have—even if someone said happy. (Try to process the answers if they seem out of the ordinary, like excited or happy, just to make sure they understand the meaning of those words.)

3. Pass out crayons and paper and instruct the children to draw a picture of how they feel today. Afterwards allow the children to voluntarily share their art and discuss with the group how many of the kids' feelings have changed between the time the person died and today. (This will be encouraging to kids who don't think they will ever feel better.)

End

1. End with a go-round and ask the kids to share one thing that they learned today and their favorite part of group today.

2. Remind kids to be on time and that you will see them next _____ at _____.

Session 4
Topic: Stages of grieving

Resources

- *When People Die* by J.E. Bernstein and S.V. Gullo
- Chart paper
- Crayons or markers
- Paper

Beginning

1. Welcome everyone back to the group. Remind kids that this is our fourth meeting and we are halfway through with group. Review last week's session. Ask the kids to do the thumbs-up check-in (up, middle, down) and then share something really fun that they have done since the last time we were together.

2. Say, "Who here ever felt so sad or mad that they thought they might just feel that way forever?" Since many kids feel that way, it is important to learn that it is normal to feel that way in the beginning but that they will begin to feel better over time.

Middle

1. Brainstorm as a group some of the other losses the children may have experienced—death of a pet, having an item stolen from them, losing a favorite toy. Have the kids discuss their specific situation and what they were feeling during that time. Go further to discuss how they felt when it first happened, then after a little while (days, weeks, months), then after a year or more.

2. Read the book *When People Die* by J. E. Bernstein and S. V. Gullo.

3. According to Dr. Elisabeth Kübler-Ross, in her book *On Death and Dying*, the stages of grief are: **denial, anger, bargaining, depression, acceptance.** On chart paper, list these in a child-friendly manner and explain them:

   (a) **Denial**—You don't believe it has happened— "Nope, she/he is just on vacation," or "It isn't true!"

   (b) **Anger/mad**—"I hate that person for leaving me—she/he said he/she would always take care of me."

   (c) **Bargaining**—Make a trade—"I promise I will never be bad again if she/he comes back" or "I will keep my room clean every day and get all good grades if I can have him/her back."

   (d) **Sadness**—"I don't want to play, I want to be by myself."

   (e) **Acceptance**—Thinking "It's OK, I can smile and remember the person. I am sad about it but I can deal with it."

4. Distribute crayons or markers and paper. Have the students use the paint and paper to show what stage they think they may be in right now.

5. Discuss the completed pictures. Ask the kids what they think a person who has reached the last stage might be thinking or feeling.

End

1. Have students complete the statements, "I learned . . .", "I was surprised that . . .".

2. Remind kids to be on time and that you will see them next _____ at _____.

Session 5
Topic: Ways to say "good-bye"

Resources

- *Scat* by A. Dolbrin
- Chart paper
- Balloons, bubbles, or paper and markers

Beginning

1. Welcome everyone back to the group. Remind kids that this is our fifth meeting and we still have three meetings left. Review last week's session. Ask if there are any questions regarding the stages discussed. Ask the kids to do the thumbs-up check-in (up, middle, down).

2. Say, "Sometimes, when somebody dies suddenly, we don't get the chance to say good-bye, or to tell them certain things that we wanted them to know. Although we can't bring them back, we can still think about all of the things that we would have wanted to tell them and say them out loud, in our minds, or write them down. This activity helps us to say our final thoughts and good-byes.

Middle

1. Read the book *Scat*. Discuss how Scat said good-bye and how it helped him. Also, discuss other ways of saying good-bye. Chart on paper. Do a go-round and process: "What would you say if you had that chance? What else?"

2. Provide balloons, paper and markers, or bubbles as a choice for the children to use to say good-bye to their loved one. They can say their words either aloud or in silence and blow the bubbles, release the balloons, or create a picture or letter to then be "mailed" in a box that you provide.

3. Convene as a group to process the activity: "How did it feel when you blew those bubbles, or released that balloon?"

End

1. Ask students, "How does saying good-bye help someone feel better?"

2. Have them complete the statement, "I can see that I need to . . .".

3. Remind kids to be on time and that you will see them next _____ at _____.

Session 6
Topic: Sharing favorite memories

Resources
- *The Tenth Good Thing About Barney* by J. Viorst
- Paper, prefolded into four sections
- Drawing materials

Beginning
1. Welcome children to group. Remind them that this is the sixth session and we have two sessions left. Briefly review last week's session. Ask if there are any unanswered questions regarding saying good-bye.
2. Have children stand by their seats (or stay seated if they prefer) and state the "weather" of their feelings today (sunny, cloudy, rainy, etc.). Process if need be.
3. Ask the children to raise their hands if they can remember a favorite time that they spent with the person who died. Explain that it is important to think about those good times and to know that it is OK to remember happy/fun things about their special person. So many times when a person dies, there is so much sadness in everyone's heart that it helps to think of fun times that have been shared.

Middle
1. Read the story *The Tenth Good Thing About Barney*. Discuss any thoughts or comments the children may have after reading.
2. Distribute a piece of paper that has been folded into four sections. Have the children draw a picture of a happy memory with their loved one in each section. When the kids complete their picture, allow each child to share memories and to identify one person in their life (preferably home life) with whom they can share these memories. Encourage the importance of thinking and talking about happy memories with self and other people.

End
1. Ask students, "How did it feel today to talk about your happy memories?"
   "What can you do so that you don't forget your memories?"
2. Remind kids to be on time and that you will see them next _____ at _____.

Session 7
Topic: Collage of memories

Resources

- Collage materials—magazines, scissors, glue sticks, construction paper

Beginning

1. Welcome kids to group. Remind them that this is the seventh session and that next week will be the last meeting. Review last week's session and attempt to answer any unanswered questions.

2. Do a go-round and have the kids give a thumbs-up check-up. Have the students also say one fun time that they have had since the last group meeting.

3. Say, "Remember in our last meeting we had a chance to discuss happy memories? We also got a chance to come up with ways to remember our happy memories. One fun thing that I have heard works great for kids who have had someone close to them die is to make a collage of memories. Today, we will make our very own personal collage (collection)."

Middle

1. Provide ample amounts of magazines; be sensitive to race, socioeconomic levels, gender, etc. Explain to the kids that they are to find any pictures in the magazines that remind them of their loved ones— it could be food the person liked, colors they liked, clothes they wore, flowers they enjoyed, makeup or perfume they wore, etc. If they need help cutting, provide assistance.

2. Provide construction paper and glue so that they can paste on their pictures.

3. Have the children share the collages.

End

1. Ask students, "What did you learn about other people's memories? Were they similar to yours? Different?"

2. Have students complete the statement, "I was surprised that . . .".

3. Remind kids to be on time and that you will see them next _____ at _____.

4. Lastly, remind them once again that next week is the last session and that you will celebrate with some snacks and surprises.

Session 8
Topic: Saying good-bye

Resources
- Chart paper
- Refreshments

Beginning
1. Welcome kids back to the last group session. Briefly discuss last week's activity and see if there are any unanswered questions.
2. Go-round—do a color check on students' feelings today (red, blue, yellow?). Have them state one feeling they have about today being the last group.
3. Say, "We have been meeting now for eight weeks and we have covered a lot of information. Today we are going to take a little time to review all of the stuff we have learned and also have the chance to ask any questions we may have about death."

Middle
1. Ask students, "What kinds of things did you learn in group? How did it feel to be in a group? (Beginning, middle, end?)" List on chart paper. "Let me see how you rate this group—thumbs up for really good, closed fist for OK, or thumbs down for not too good." (Use this as an informal evaluation of sorts.)
2. Have the collages posted around the room for all to view (with permission). In the circle, have all of the kids close their eyes and ask them these questions: "When you are in _____ grade (next year's grade), how do you think you will feel then about your special person's death? If you are still sad, what can you do to feel better?" (Talk to someone, look at memory collage, remember those happy memories we talked about in Session 6.) "Whom can you talk to?" (The person identified in Session 6)
3. Enjoy snack with the group and casually discuss how the group ending is similar to losing someone special in your life because we won't be meeting anymore. Also discuss how it is different because we will all see each other around school and will be able to touch base every now and again.

End
Have students complete the statements, "Something I learned from being in this group is . . ." and "My favorite session of all was . . .".

3.7
Divorce/Changing Families

| Grade Level: K–5 | Time Required: 8 Sessions | Author: Michelle Feldman |

Purpose

To help students cope with the stress of parent divorce. Students are taught coping skills and learn how to constructively deal with typical issues associated with divorce. Bibliotherapy is used to stimulate sharing of thoughts, feelings, and positive coping strategies.

Parent divorce is a significant and growing issue affecting children's social and academic development. Parent divorce is one of the most stressful events that can happen to a child. Support groups have been found to be effective in helping students to deal constructively with parent divorce and to return their attention to academic performance and positive peer relations.

The group leader should be comfortable with his or her own issues about divorce. Self-disclosure should be limited to promoting group rapport and cohesion.

Logistics

GROUP COMPOSITION

Students in grades K–5 who have recently experienced the divorce of their parents. Students who are within 1–2 grade levels may be grouped.

GROUP SIZE

4–6 students

GROUP TIME PER SESSION

30 minutes

NUMBER OF SESSIONS

Eight

Recommended Resources

Full bibliographic details for these publications are included in the Bibliography at the end of this book.

Apodaca and Nightingale, 1997: *My Parents Still Love Me Even Though They're Getting Divorced.*

Bienfeld, 1987: *Helping Your Child Succeed after Divorce.*

Blitzer and Shore, 1994: *My Life Turned Upside Down but I Turned It Right Side Up.*

Boulden and Boulden, 1991: *Let's Talk!*

Boulden and Boulden, 1992: *All Together.*

Brigman and Earley, 1991: *Group Counseling for School Counselors.*

Brown, 1988: *Dinosaurs Divorce.*

Friedman and Girard, 1991: *At Daddy's on Saturday.*

Hoctor, 1999: *Changes: My Family and Me.*

Ives, Fassler, and Lash, 1985: *The Divorce Workbook.*

Margolin, 1996: *Complete Group Counseling Program for Children of Divorce.*

Marks, 1995: *Good-bye, Daddy!*

Monroe and Ackelmire, 1998: *Why Don't We Live Together Any More?*

Monroe and Barnet, 1998: *I Have a New Family Now.*

Morganette, 1994: *Skills for Living.*

O'Rourke and Worzybt, 1996: *Support Groups for Children.*

Parkinson and Spelman, 1998: *Mama and Daddy Bears Divorce.*

Poleski, 1983: *The Hurt.*

Robins and Mayle, 1988: *Why Are We Getting a Divorce?*

Rogers and Judkis, 1998: *Let's Talk About It: Divorce.*

Stinson, 1988: *Mom and Dad Don't Live Together Anymore.*

Watson, Switzer, and Hirschberg, 1988: *Sometimes a Family Has to Split Up.*

Session 1
Topic: Introduction and overview

Resources

- Feelings poster (or use Feeling Faces handout on page 9)
- Chalkboard, white board, or chart paper

Beginning

1. Introduce yourself, then say, "This is a group for kids who have had some family changes (give examples of divorce situations, separation situations, as well as stepparent or sibling changes, etc.). We will be coming to my office once a week on _____(day of the week) at _____ (time of day) for eight weeks to talk a little, play a little, maybe read or color a little bit about how you are feeling."

2. "First I would like to go around the circle and ask everybody what their name is, what kind of changes are happening in their family, and either a thumbs-up (if you're feeling really happy), thumbs to the middle (if you are feeling so-so, not too happy, not too sad) or a thumbs-down (if you are feeling really sad or mad).

3. Ask students, "Who has ever been in a group before?" (Some examples you may want to give are Scouts, Brownies, dance class, etc.) "Did you have any rules in that group? Why do you think you have to have rules in groups? In the classroom?" Try to incorporate the idea that rules foster a safe environment and allow everyone a fair share to talk and participate in the group. Say, "Today we are going to have to make up a name for our group and a few rules for our group just to make sure that this is a safe place to talk and play together."

Middle

1. "First let's come up with some rules." (Have a chalkboard, whiteboard, chart paper, etc., on which to write answers as they are offered.) "Who can raise their hand and tell me one important rule they think we should have in this group?" Continue to generate answers, recording suggestions as they are made. Make sure to include the idea of confidentiality, the right to pass (only answer voluntarily), as well as attendance and tardiness.

2. "OK, great, now the fun part. I want everyone to close their eyes and think really hard about a name for our group." (Offer suggestions such as the superstars, whiz kids, second grade sundaes.) "Then I am going to give you three minutes. If you would like to share your answer, you can come and stand right next to me and tell it to the group, whisper it in my ear, or you can just stay at your seat and share, whichever one you'd like to do." Chart answers and then have students put their heads down on the desk and vote anonymously (by raised hand) to pick their favorite name.

End

1. Display poster of feeling faces and say to the kids, "Well, our time is almost up. For our last activity, I would like to go around the group again and ask you one thing you learned today and how you felt being here today and talking with everyone in group. When I call your name, I would like you to come up and say one thing you learned today" (could be the name of the group, a rule, or even another kid's name) "and then look at the poster and point out which feeling you had today in group." When they point out their feelings, make sure to label that feeling for them if they are not able to: "Oh, Paula felt mad today in group." If there is time, process that and ask, "What made you so mad today?"

2. Remind kids about when you will see them next. (Day and time) ("Bye everyone, remember, see you next Tuesday, my office at 1:00 sharp!")

Session 2
Topic: Family pictures

Resource

- Art materials

Beginning

1. Welcome everyone back to the group. Remind kids, "This is our second meeting and we still have six meetings left." Remind the children of last week's meeting and the name of the group and rules. Have students rate on a scale of 1–10 how they are feeling today (1 being low, 10 being high).

2. Say, "Sometimes it's hard when you have more than one place you call home. Today we are going to talk about different family members that may live in different homes. It's important to understand that even thought they may live in a different home, they are still our family."

Middle

1. Begin a discussion on what each member thinks the word "family" means. Most likely you will get many different spectra of family such as immediate family, extended family, and friends who are so close they are considered family. Place emphasis on family that may not live in the same home as you. Even though many members may live in other homes, cities, countries, etc., they are still your family.

2. Provide children with art materials and allow them to make pictures that show their families and the many different homes they may have.

3. When the pictures are finished, give each child an opportunity to talk about his/her picture and tell more about his/her family.

End

1. Ask students, "How was it to be part of today's group?"
   "What is one thing you learned today?"

2. Point out similarities of group member's situations.

3. Remind kids to be on time and that you will see them next _____ at _____.

Session 3
Topic: Picture album

Resources
- 5 pieces of paper for each student
- Drawing materials

Beginning
1. Welcome everyone back to the group. Remind kids, "This is our third meeting and we still have five meetings left." Have the students do a go-round and say their names and if they are having sunny (happy) feelings today or if they are having cloudy (sad, mad) feelings today. If kids are not familiar with this idea, explain it to them.

2. Say, "I just want to remind everyone why we are here in this group together. That is because we all have had some family changes. One important thing that we would like to learn by being in our group is why people divorce. We can also learn more about our feelings about the situation."

3. "How many people here really understand why there has been a divorce/separation in your family? Many times kids think they are the reason, or really don't know the reason at all why their family has changed. Today we will look at some of the reasons why people divorce."

Middle
1. "Today, we are going to create our very own mini picture album to understand what brought our parents together, and some of the reasons they have had to separate." Pass out five blank pieces of drawing paper so that kids may illustrate. Either prelabel (depending on the children's writing levels) or have the children label each piece of paper with the following headings:

- Why my parents got married
- Why my parents got divorced
- What does the future hold?
- Best time with my family
- Worst time with my family

2. Have children work on each sheet as a group. Read out the first title page and then give them time to illustrate.

3. When all students have completed the first sheet, allow share time to go over what they drew and why. Then continue to the second one.

4. Continue until finished with all five.

5. Make sure to point out and discuss why parents divorce or families have to change. Have the group brainstorm reasons. Some answers you may get are:
   - Fighting
   - Job situations
   - Don't love each other any more
   - Want to be married to someone else

   Don't forget to explain and make it clear that children are not the cause of divorce.

6. Discuss the following questions: "Have you ever hoped or wished that your parents would get back together? Have you tried anything to do this? How much control do you really have over this situation? What would it be better to do than worry?"

End
1. End with a go-round and ask the kids to share one thing that they learned about their family situation today.

2. Remind kids to be on time and that you will see them next _____ at _____.

Session 4
Topic: Dealing with feelings

Resources
- Chart paper
- *The Hurt* by T. Poleski

Beginning
1. Welcome everyone back to the group. Remind kids, "This is our fourth meeting and we are half-way through with group." Review last week's session. Ask the kids to do the thumbs-up check-in (up, middle, down) and then share something really fun that they have done since the last time we were together.
2. Say, "Kids often have many different feelings when their families go through changes such as separation or divorce. It is important to understand and discuss these feelings, especially with others who are experiencing the same thing."

Middle
1. Ask the children to think about some of the feelings they remember having when they found out their family was about to go through some changes (divorce, separation). Chart the responses. Note similarities (common feelings may include relief, shame, sadness, anger, guilt).
2. Talk about how the children deal or don't deal with their feelings. Read the book *The Hurt*. This book tells the story of a boy who held in a bad feeling and how that affected him. Then it continues to explain how he felt after he talked to someone about his feelings.
3. Discuss things that kids can do to release the bad feelings they may experience (i.e., call a friend, read a favorite story, play a game, write a letter and then throw it out). Then have kids create a Loyal Listener List. This is a list of trustworthy people they can talk to if they need to get something off their chest.

End
1. Do a go-round and have the kids identify one thing they will try in the coming week to release a bad feeling they may get relating to the separation.
2. Remind kids to be on time and that you will see them next _____ at _____.

Session 5
Topic: Stages of dealing with divorce

Resources
- Chart showing stages of divorce

Beginning
1. Welcome everyone back to the group. Remind kids, "This is our fifth meeting and we still have three meetings left." Review last week's session. Ask the kids to rate how they are feeling on a scale of 1–10.

2. Say, "In the last session we discussed feelings about divorce and how important it is to express them instead of keeping them inside. Today, we are going to further discuss feelings and get a better understanding of the stages that most people go through when experiencing a divorce or changing family."

Middle
1. Display a chart that shows the stages of dealing with divorce, based on Bienfeld (1987).

Stages of Dealing with Divorce
1. Disbelief
2. Anxiety
3. Anger
4. Sadness
5. Acceptance

2. Explain what the idea of going through stages means. You may want to give an example such as the stages of learning to ride a bike (tricycle, training wheels, two-wheeler, ten-speed). Or how you feel when you get into a fight with someone (steaming mad, less angry, then sad and missing the friendship, then sometimes even forgetting what the fight was about). Two different stage theories will be explained today; it's best to display both on one poster to allow for comparison and contrast.

3. Go through the chart and explain the meanings of words in terms the children can understand. Have them identify different times when they may have experienced these different stages. Have them identify what stage they may currently be in. Explain that people do not always go through these stages in a set order, or in a certain time frame. Some people stay in stages for much longer than others, some may go back and forth between them.

End
1. Do a go-round and ask each child to share what stage he may be in six months from now and why he feels that way.

2. Ask the kids to say one thing that they think may help them move on to the next stage.

3. Remind kids to be on time and that you will see them next _____ at _____.

Session 6
Topic: Strategies in dealing with divorce

Resources

- *My Life Turned Upside Down, but I Turned It Right Side Up* by Mary Blitzer and Hennie Shore
- Paper and pencils

Beginning

1. Welcome everyone back to the group. Remind kids, "This is our sixth meeting and we still have two meetings left." Review last week's session. Ask if there are any questions regarding the stages discussed. Ask the kids to rate how they are feeling on a scale of 1–10.

2. Say, "Sometimes it's a lot easier to get advice from other people who are going through situations similar to yours. Today we are going to read a story and write letters so we can hear from kids just like us what they would do if they were in our situations."

Middle

1. Read the story *My Life Turned Upside Down, but I Turned It Right Side Up*. Discuss some of the strategies the girl in the story uses to deal with the divorce of her parents. Ask, "Which ones have you tried? Were they successful? Why or why not?"

2. Have the children write anonymous letters to the group. In these letters they will discuss a current problem they are experiencing related to the divorce and ask for advice. Keep the letters to discuss the following week.

End

1. Have students complete the statements, "Today I learned . . ."

   "It feels_____knowing I am not the only one going through a divorce/separation."

2. Remind kids to be on time and that you will see them next _____ at _____.

Session 7
Topic: Stepfamilies

Resources

- Story of Cinderella
- Chart paper

Beginning

1. Welcome children to group. Remind them, "This is our seventh session and we have one session left." Briefly review last week's session and ask if there are any unanswered questions.

2. Have each child stand by his or her seat (or stay seated if they prefer) and state the "weather" of their feelings today (sunny, cloudy, rainy, etc.). Process if need be.

3. Say, "First we must finish our activity from last week, but then we need to talk about stepfamilies. Sometimes, when parents divorce or separate, new people come into our lives. We may get a step-parent or stepsibling. Having new additions to your family can be very tough. Today we are going to talk more about stepfamilies."

Middle

1. Process the letters from last week. Have children offer advice to each other in pairs, then with the group.

2. Make sure kids understand the terminology regarding stepfamilies. Explain that this means someone who has married into your family or has married into the family and brought children along (e.g., stepmom, stepdad, stepbrother, stepsister).

3. Read the story of Cinderella. Emphasize the relationship that Cinderella had with her stepmother and stepsisters. Process the story. Ask, "Does this sound as if it could be a true story? Do you know any stepmoms or stepsisters this bad?"

4. Chart some of the tough situations stepfamilies may run into (space, sharing, jealousy regarding attention, respecting new authority, etc.). What are some ways to deal with these stressors?

End

1. Have the kids name one new thing they learned today about stepfamilies.

2. Ask, "Do you feel differently about stepfamilies than you felt before we talked today?"

3. Remind kids to be on time and that you will see them next _____ at _____.

4. Remind that next week is the last session.

Session 8
Topic: Warm-fuzzy collages

Resources
- Collage materials—magazines, scissors, paper, glue sticks

Beginning
1. Welcome kids to group. Remind them that this is our last meeting. Review last week's session and attempt to answer any unanswered questions.
2. Do a go-round and have the kids give a thumbs-up check-up. Have the students also say one fun time that they have had since the last group meeting.
3. Explain to the children that since this is the last group, it is important that we get the chance to say good-bye to each other. Since good-bye is often difficult, and, for children of divorce especially, sometimes a negative experience, we want to have a saying good-bye experience that is positive.

Middle
1. Review the content of the previous sessions.
2. Explain to group members that they are going to create warm fuzzy collages. Explain that warm fuzzys are positive, nice things that people can say to one another or show one another through pictures. Explain that because they shared so much during this eight-week group, they will now have an opportunity to create a warm fuzzy collage for someone in the group (have them draw random names) to wish them a warm good-bye.
3. Provide ample amounts of magazines; be sensitive to race, socioeconomic levels, gender, etc. Explain to the kids that they are to find any pictures in the magazine or create any kind of colorful designs that would make the person they picked feel good. It could be a picture of friends, a warm sunshine, a picture of flowers, or a game that they mentioned they liked.
4. Provide construction paper and glue so that they can paste on their pictures.
5. Have the children present and share the collages individually when they are complete.

End
1. Ask, "How did it feel to be presented with this warm fuzzy collage?"
2. Tell the children that you thank them for participating and that there might be rough times ahead. Point out that now they have a support team and, if appropriate, let them know that you will be available after the group to help them individually.

Part 4:
Group Plans for All Levels

4.1
New Student Programs

Grade Level: 3–12	Time Required: 2 small group sessions, with follow-up options	Authors: Greg Brigman and Barbara Earley Goodman

There are many ways counselors can help facilitate a new student's adjustment to moving and getting started in a new school. We have developed a four-part program that combines (a) a two-session small group model led by trained peer helpers, with follow-up using (b) a peer buddy system for monitoring academic and social progress, (c) a classroom buddy program, and (d) a mentoring system pairing seniors and freshmen, which can be modified for middle and elementary levels; see Transition—The Buddy System, in this book, for a full description of this component.

The two-session small group plan follows the explanation of the peer helper system and classroom buddy plan.

PEER HELPER SYSTEM

Trained peer helpers lead small group meetings to welcome new students. Approximately 4–6 weeks after this meeting (usually just after report cards), the peer helpers who led the group sessions meet individually with each group member. Each peer helper completes the following structured outline as he/she discusses how things are going for the new student. This system provides a means to monitor the progress of new students and to refer them appropriate support services if needed.

Introduction and Rationale

Use this approach for a follow-up individual meeting by peer helper and new student after first grade reporting period.

Hi _____, good to see you again. As we said during the new student group, I am meeting with you to check on how things are going. If it is OK with you I want to ask you to rate how things are going with grades, teachers, and peers, and getting involved in the school/community.

New Student_____ Date _____

1. How are your grades? You have received a report card by now.

Math_____ Science_____ Social Studies_____
Lang Arts_____ Elective_____ Elective _____
Rate how satisfied you are with your grades on a 1–10 scale, 1 meaning not at all satisfied and 10 meaning very satisfied_____.

If student rates satisfaction with grades at below 7, ask if he/she would like to have a peer tutor. Explain peer tutoring. Yes_____ No _____
What subject? _____

2. How are things going with you and your teachers? 1–10 _____

If not satisfactory to student, peer helper helps student explore what could be done to improve relations with the teacher. Peer asks, "Would you like to talk with a counselor about getting along with your teachers?"

Yes_____ No_____ Explain who the counselors are and how to see them.

3. How satisfied are you with making friends here? 1–10 _____

If student is not satisfied, peer helper listens, explores the student's problem, discusses what activities the student is involved in or might like to try.

4. How satisfied are you with getting involved in school and community activities? 1–10_____

If rating is high, ask about the types of activities they have found to participate in. If the rating is not high, ask about their interests and talk about other activities in and out of school that are available.

5. Peer helper summarizes meeting and tells new student about next meeting in six weeks and any follow-up before then. *Example:* "One of the counselors will get in touch with you regarding peer tutoring, or to discuss how things are going with teachers and friends."

Throughout this meeting the peer helper is using the listening and other communication skills taught in peer helper training. The goal is to have a warm, personal meeting and to give some positive life to the above structured outline.

Recommended Resources

Full bibliographic details for these publications are included in the Bibliography at the end of this book.

Combs, 1993: "A middle school transition program."

Jett, Pulling, and Ross, 1994: "Preparing high schools for eighth grade students."

Rollenhagen, 1989: "FOTP: A school transition program that works."

Roth, 1991: *Middle Level Transition: Policies, Programs, and Practices.*

Classroom Buddy Plan

The classroom buddy system is a plan to help new students feel more comfortable and become better acquainted with their new school. Each classroom teacher selects two students (one male, one female) who agree to be classroom buddies.

The following is a lesson plan for a training session for classroom buddies.

Classroom Buddy System: Introductory Meeting

1. Introduce counselors, administrator, and person in charge of registration.

2. "Congratulations on being chosen as a buddy or thank you for volunteering. Being a buddy to new students shows your care and concern about others and that you want them to feel a part of this school."

3. Questions to provide background and rationale for classroom buddy system. Divide into pairs. Ask partners to discuss the following questions.

   • How many of you remember being a new student?

   • What did you think on the first day?

   • How were you treated?

   • How long before you felt comfortable here?

   • What do we do in our classes when a new student walks in?

   • What were some things you worried about before coming to school the first day?
   Examples:
   What would students wear?
   Would I make friends?
   Would I like my teachers?
   Would I get lost?
   Would I be afraid?
   Would I be able to open my locker?

4. Discuss these items and have the partners share their answers.

5. Talk with the new classroom buddies about how new students sometimes act aloof. Why do you think they might appear that way? (Because they are frightened and are trying to look as though they're comfortable.)

Role of the Buddy

"Since this is the beginning of the school year, we have about 100 new students who have registered during the summer and the first week of school. We'll give you a list of those students so you can meet them and talk with them. As new students come in during the year, you can meet with them on the first day and help them find everything.

"You have a list of suggested activities (see next page for list) that might be helpful to a new student. Please get a partner and come up with some ideas for items 4, 7, and 8 of the suggested activities page. At the end, brainstorm other things you could do to help new students feel comfortable and welcome. I'll give you ten minutes, and at the end of that time we'll share our ideas with the whole group."

Other Services for New Students

   • Peer helpers' new-student group

   • Peer helpers talking individually with new students

   • Referral to counselors if new students are not adjusting to school

   • Counselors talk to parents and teachers of new students

   • Friendship groups by the counselors

   • Coupon book that students can redeem for items such as bookmarks from librarians or cookies from the cafeteria

"The responsibility for helping new students is not yours alone. Enlist the help of your friends, help students get involved in clubs and activities, and let them know what is offered in the community.

"You have an important job and are providing a much-needed service for new students. We'll be in touch with you throughout the year to see how things are going. If you see that a new student is having a difficult time at school or at home, we would like you to let one of the counselors know."

Name_____ Date _____

Classroom Buddy System Suggested Activities

1. Sit next to new students in class (for the first week).

2. Help with locker combinations (demonstrate).

3. Take students to class or match them with a student who is going to their class.

4. Find out their interests and introduce them to others who share the interest(s).

5. Include them with your friends at lunch.

6. Give the new students a phone call to check on how things are going (after first and second week). Ask how you can be helpful.

7. Inform the students of activities after school and in the community in which they may have an interest.

8. Tell students about who is available to help new students (e.g., peer tutors, counselors, teachers).

Classroom Buddy System

To: Homeroom Teachers

From: Counselors

Re: Classroom Buddy System

To help our new students feel more comfortable and become better acquainted with our school, we would like to begin a Classroom Buddy System.

Most of you already have a procedure for helping new students. We want to extend that program with some specific activities, phone calls, notes, and being in touch. We'll also have peer helpers working with new students in a group and then individually.

Please select a boy and a girl to be buddies for your homeroom. Please choose students who are open, caring, and who want to be a buddy.

We will meet with them and go over this list of duties. You might want to read them this list.

CLASSROOM BUDDY ROLE: (SOME SUGGESTED ACTIVITIES)

1. Sit next to new students in class (for first week).

2. Help with locker combinations.

3. Take new students to class or match them with a student who is going to their class.

4. Include them with your friends at lunch.

5. Phone once a week for the first 2–3 weeks.

6. Share some activities after school (how to join).

7. Tell students where they can get extra help (i.e., peer tutoring, counselors, teachers).

Please turn in two names to one of the counselors by _____.

We will meet with these students on _____ during period _____.

Homeroom Teacher _____

Classroom Buddy System

Name _____

Name _____

Session 1
Topic: Get acquainted, get involved

Note: These are lesson plans conducted by trained peer helpers working in pairs as described on page 290. Each new student group is lead by a pair of peer helpers. Each group has approximately six students.

Beginning

INTRODUCTION

1. Introduce self, go over purpose of group; use a go-round for group members to say names and where there are moving from.

   After go-round ask: Who came from the farthest away? Closest?

2. Students interview each other in pairs, then introduce partner to group. The following information is used for introductions:
   - brothers, sisters, and ages
   - hobbies, interests, what they do for fun
   - pets

3. After each introduction, group leader asks person introduced if anything was left out. Thank person doing introduction.

4. Discuss with group:
   - What were some things you noticed people had in common?
   - What were some things you noticed that were different?

Middle

Discuss with group:
- How many have moved more than once? Determine who has moved the most.
- What are some fun things about moving?
- What are some things about moving that you don't like?

When leader gets answers to the above, ask:
- How many of you have felt that way, or agree with that?
- When did you feel that way?
- How have you found the people here?
- How many have found at least one friend already?
- What are some ways you go about making new friends? (Spend some time on this question.)

- What are some things about this school that are like your old school? Different?
- How long do you think it usually takes to get used to a new school, to feel comfortable? What is one thing you can do to make that time shorter?
- What are some things people can do to help you feel comfortable here?
- What's one thing you like about this school? (Give them a moment to think, then go around the circle for responses.)

GETTING INVOLVED

Students who have been new in the past tell us that getting involved in activities with other students helps them feel connected and is helpful in fitting in.

- What are some activities that are available for you to join?

After group brainstorms activities and how to join, each leader shares list, pointing out any not mentioned.

KNOWLEDGE ABOUT SCHOOL

- Do you all know who the principal is?
- Do you all know the school's colors and mascot?
- How many know where the clinic is?
- If you lose something, do you know where lost-and-found is?
- Have you met any of the counselors here? Their names are _____. They can be helpful if you need to talk individually. They offer groups and come to classrooms. Peer tutoring is also available.

End

"Think about one thing you've learned about this school today, and one thing you can do to speed up the process of getting settled here. We'll go around the circle in a moment and ask each of you to share your ideas on these two areas."

"I enjoyed meeting you today and look forward to seeing you again. Each of you will have a peer helper buddy who will check with you in a couple of weeks to see how things are going."

Session 2
Topic: Making friends

Resources
• Making Friends handout

Beginning

INTRODUCTION

1. Go around the circle. Have students say their names and one positive thing that has happened to them since the last meeting.

2. Say, "Today we'll be talking about friendship. Most people moving into a new place are anxious to make new friends. How many of you feel that way?"

VOTING ACTIVITY

"Let's take a look at how you think and feel about friends. We'll start with a voting activity—raise your hand if you agree."

How many of you:

• have a best friend?

• have a good friend of the opposite sex?

• have had an argument with a good friend lately?

• have a friend that you can talk to about your problems?

• have ever had a day when you felt as if you didn't have any friends?

• think a friend is someone who will do whatever you say?

• think a friend should always agree with you?

• have a brother or sister who is also your friend?

Middle

1. Ask students to brainstorm at least ten positive ways to make new friends. After each suggestion ask group, "How many think this is a positive way to make friends? How many have used this technique before?"

2. Distribute the Making Friends handout.

"Let's compare our list to the list on this page. As we read each technique for making friends put a check by it if it is one you use and circle it if it is sometimes hard for you." Read each item and ask, "How many have used this one, and how many find this one hard to do?"

End

1. Ask, "From the all the different ways we have discussed for making friends, which 1–2 ways work best for you?"

2. Ask each group member to complete the statements "Today I learned or relearned . . ." and "One way I can use what I learned is . . .".

3. Remind group of scheduled follow-up and how they can contact counselors if needed.

Name_____ Date _____

Making Friends

1. Think about a friend you have now or used to have. Recall when, where, and how

   you met. _____

   _____

   _____

   Share your story with the group. Be sure to include what you did to help develop the friendship.

2. Check the boxes that are next to the techniques you like for meeting people, making friends, and keeping friends. Circle the boxes that are next to the techniques that are hardest for you.

   ❑ Smile. Smiling can do more to communicate that you are friendly and approachable than almost any other thing you can do.

   ❑ Listen. Being a good listener is very important. Listening says "I care" and makes the person feel important. Listening takes concentration and energy, but it's worth it.

   ❑ Introduce yourself. Usually others are just as cautious as you about starting a conversation. Most of the time they will be glad you got things started.

   ❑ Remember names and use them often.

   ❑ Spend time at places where people with some of your interests go. Spending time with people doing things you both enjoy builds friendship.

   ❑ Invite people to do things with you. Try to match what you like with people who like the same kinds of activities. Try short time periods first to find out if you enjoy spending time together.

   ❑ Be a complimenter. Give honest compliments. A phony compliment can lead to trouble. Letting people know you admire and appreciate something about them builds goodwill and shows you care.

   ❑ Share the talk time. Shoot for a 50/50 talk-listen ratio. Nobody likes the non-stop talker. Not talking isn't helpful either—people wonder if you're interested or care.

   ❑ Give parties. Invite people you think might be interesting. Ask the people you know to invite one of their friends.

   ❑ Get involved in after-school clubs or activities.

4.2
Personal Growth for Teachers

| Time Required: 8 Sessions | Authors: Barbara Earley Goodman and Greg Brigman |

How This Group Developed

Because teachers frequently experience stress and burnout, we decided to offer an after-school personal-growth group. Offering the group shows teachers your concern for their well-being, which is appreciated. Working with adults is rewarding for the counselor and gives teachers opportunities to share ideas. Serving refreshments and modeling a relaxed atmosphere is in itself therapeutic. It is certainly an excellent way to get to know each other.

Several Methods for Quick and Easy Teacher Groups

If you feel hesitant or uncertain about offering groups for teachers, your first experience could be to have speakers for each session. You might begin by offering an activity once a month or having four sessions offered weekly. There could be four speakers on one topic such as stress, or a different topic each time. Consult your local mental health agency, hospital speakers' bureau, a private therapist, or ask another school counselor. Your responsibilities would include: conducting an icebreaker with the group; discussing objectives; introducing the speaker; leading a discussion after the speaker; and concluding with a summary and written evaluation.

Another idea is to offer a series of video- or audiotapes based on a particular topic of interest to the participants.

As you begin to feel more comfortable leading groups, you could offer a staff-development course such as *Cooperative Discipline* by Linda Albert, published by American Guidance Services. If time does not allow for a 50-hour course, you could do small segments on topics such as encouragement or the democratic classroom.

An easy and ready-for-use group lesson plan is *The Encouragement Book* by Don Dinkmeyer. The activities in this book are great for motivating participants to be more loving, motivating, respectful, and encouraging to themselves and others. Cover a chapter per week. If you obtain copies for each participant, you can begin with a discussion of the reading. Next, lead the group through the chapter's activities. If participants do not have copies, summarize the key points before and/or after the activities.

A good standard format for group sessions is:

- Icebreaker
- Review of last session
- Discussion and activity
- Summary

Group Objectives

- To get to know other faculty members better
- To learn about yourself
- To develop personal growth goals and plans

TIME
Eight one-hour meetings after school

GROUP COMPOSITION
Faculty members

GROUP RULES
Rules for adult groups are similar to rules for student groups. The rules need to come from the participants and should include confidentiality, right to pass or not participate, and respect of others' opinions (no put-downs).

Recommended Resources
Griswold: *Taking Control of Your Life* (audiocassette).

Session 1
Topic: Introduction, get acquainted

Resources

- Index cards
- What Are You Doing for the Rest of Your Life handout

Beginning

INTRODUCTION AND OVERVIEW

1. Introduce the group by outlining its purpose. *Example:* "We'll be meeting for the next eight weeks from 3–4 P.M. During this time I hope you'll become more aware of your strengths and look for some areas that you may want to enhance. Our meeting together in a personal-growth group indicates that we are healthy individuals who have high expectations about the quality of life. We all have times of stress and disappointments. We also have goals that we may not pursue because of our busy lives. The group time will provide an opportunity for you to look more closely at yourself and those goals. Meeting together each week will help us get to know each other in a personal and nonthreatening manner. You will decide how open you want to be with the group. A feeling of trust will help us be more open with each other. The trust will develop as we come to feel that group members will keep what we say here confidential."

2. Establish—as a group—some group rules. Members will come up with the same rules that students do: confidentiality, respect for each other, and no put-downs. (Members should all agree on the rules.)

3. Housekeeping: Group members may take turns bringing refreshments. Encourage them to be on time.

4. Explain the purpose and advantages of keeping a journal. *Example:* "It is helpful to keep a journal while you are in the group. You will have opportunities to write down your thoughts while we are doing an activity and to write an 'I learned' statement at the end of each session. During the week, as you work on an assignment or have thought about the group, writing in the journal will help bring focus to your ideas.

NAME TAG ACTIVITY

Sample Name Tag

Place where you spent
five days of bliss:

_____

_____

Name: _____

Most serene, peaceful
place in home:

_____

_____

Something you have planned that
you are looking forward to:

_____

_____

List places you
have lived:

_____

_____

Give members a 5" × 8" index card on which to write information. (See above for a sample name tag.) The leader gives directions for each corner of the card. When the group has finished, each person joins with a partner and shares what he/she has written. Have the group spend some time with the details. For example, in the corner that asks "list places you have lived," have participants choose the one that meant most to them. Perhaps it was the place where the most growth occurred, a happy place, or a place where there was a crisis.

Back in the big group, have group members share an "I learned . . ." statement.

Middle

"WHAT ARE YOU DOING FOR THE REST OF YOUR LIFE?"

1. Group members list 20 things they would like to do in their lives that they haven't done yet. Allow 10–15 minutes for them to list the activities. In the spaces after listing the activities, have them make marks indicating:
   - one you can begin right away
   - one you would like to begin in five years
   - how many require money
   - which ones you would have chosen five years ago

   The additional spaces can be used if you have time, and might include topics such as:
   - which ones you prefer doing alone
   - which ones you prefer doing with people
   - which ones a spouse or significant other would choose
   - which ones require additional training and education

2. Ask participants to share some of the categories with a partner or with the larger group.

3. Ask the group to share aloud. Who had one that was about:
   - travel
   - profession/career
   - relationships
   - physical activity
   - spiritual life
   - intellectual pursuit

End

1. Ask participants to complete these sentences in their journals:
   "I learned . . ."
   "I was surprised that . . ."
   "One activity I want to start right away . . ."
   Ask for volunteers to share journal entries with the group.

2. Put on music (soft, instrumental) for 60 seconds. Ask participants to picture themselves doing that one thing that they want to begin right away.

ASSIGNMENT

Share your 20 things with a spouse or significant other, or spend time thinking about how to begin on this new task.

Name_____ Date_____

What Are You Doing for the Rest of Your Life?

List in the first column below 20 things that you would like to do, experience, achieve, try, or enjoy before you die.

What did you find out about yourself? I learned that _____

_____

_____

I was surprised (or pleased) that _____

_____

_____

Session 2
Topic: Connectedness network

Resources
- My Connectedness Network handout

Beginning
1. "My name is . . . and the high point of my week was . . ."
2. Volunteers share how their assignment of sharing their 20 things went.
3. Introduce main activity:

   "Alfred Adler believed that our primary goal in life was to feel a sense of belonging. Adler stated that there were three tasks in life: work, friends, and intimate relationships. Most of us have an imbalance among these three areas. Nobody is perfect. One way of checking our satisfaction with our lives is to look at these three areas. Then we need to decide which area needs the most attention right now."

Middle
A feeling of connectedness is essential for self-esteem. To be happy, we have to feel that we belong. Our connectedness network includes our family, friends, and coworkers.

1. The leader asks the following four questions, one at a time. After each question, ask participants to write a brief impression in their journals. After approximately one minute for writing, ask for volunteers to share. This sharing should not be a go-round. There should be no pressure to share.

   - How do you feel connected to your family of origin? Close your eyes and picture yourself approaching the family at a reunion. Are you welcomed with open arms and positive comments, or do you anticipate cutting remarks and disapproval?

   - How does it feel walking up to your front door at the end of the day?

   - What do your friends mean to you? Do you have friends for confidantes, for fun, and as models?

   - How do you relate to your coworkers? If you were out of work for three days, would you be missed?

2. **Connectedness handout.** Explain one category at a time and have the group list people for each area. For example:

   - *Confidantes* are those people you can really trust with your intimate feelings, and thoughts, those with whom you can share joys and sorrows.

   - *Intellectual Stretchers* are people with whom you philosophize, those who expand your knowledge and your creative thinking.

   - *Health* people are those who hand you your running shoes, who inspire and encourage your taking care of yourself.

   - *Fun and Adventure* people enjoy life, try new things, and encourage you to take part.

   - *Spiritual* has to do with those people in your life who cause you to examine and expand your beliefs and thoughts.

   - *Chicken soup* people are those who would visit you if you were sick and bring you chicken soup. These are the people who are always there to help you out.

   - *Mentors/Guides* are people whom you want to learn from. They have talents and skills that they want to share with you.

End
Ask participants to share in pairs their responses to the following three questions related to today's group meeting:

"I learned . . ."

"I relearned . . ."

"I can see that I need to . . ."

After pair share, ask for a few volunteers to share with group.

Name_____ Date _____

My Connectedness Network

Family	Friends	Coworkers and Others
Confidantes		
Intellectual Stretchers		
Health		
Fun and Adventure		
Spiritual		
Chicken Soup		
Mentors/Guides		

Session 3
Topic: Connectedness continued

Resources

- Identifying Connections handout

Beginning

1. "Today I'm a . . . on a 1–10 scale, and one thing I'm looking forward to in the next week is . . . ."
2. Review last session.

Middle

1. Connectedness handout, continued. Usually this activity requires time this session for completion (see last session).

2. Identifying Connections handout: Ask group members to take a few minutes to complete this sheet. After completing, have participants get into groups of three to share the responses to each section. Remind the group that everyone has the right to pass on any part of the handout.

End

Ask group to return to larger circle and share how it felt to complete the Connectedness sheet and the Identifying Connections sheet.

Name_____ Date _____

Identifying Connections

Four people who love you

_____   _____

_____   _____

Three people you have learned a lot from

_____

_____

_____

Three people who have learned something from you

_____

_____

_____

Four people who usually smile at you

_____   _____

_____   _____

Two people who have helped you in an important way

_____   _____

Three people who are usually kind to you

_____

_____

_____

Session 4
Topic: Relaxation training

Resources

- *Taking Control of Your Life* audiocassette by Robert Griswold
- Cassette player

Beginning

1. Ask participants to complete the following sentence stem in a go-round:

   "One quality about myself that I'm proud of is . . .".

2. Review last week's meeting.

Middle

RELAXATION TRAINING

1. Introduce the importance of learning to relax deeply. Mention regular practice, how images are helpful, and how relaxation creates your inner sanctuary.

   Many relaxation techniques are readily available. Two of the most popular are the Relaxation Response (Herbert Benson) and Progressive Relaxation (Edmund Jacobson).

There are also many useful cassette tapes that incorporate relaxation training and positive imagery—some with helpful ideas on avoiding self-defeating behavior and improving self-esteem. You may want to guide the relaxation with or without imagery.

2. Ask the participants to listen for 2–3 important ideas and to be ready to discuss their choices after the tape. After going through the tape, ask who was able to relax deeply, to clearly see the images described.

   Ask each person to identify his or her favorite image. Then, one by one, share 1–3 important ideas from the tape.

End

Ask group members to complete one of the following:

"One thing I learned or relearned today was . . .".
"Something that surprised me was . . .".

Session 5
Topic: Irrational beliefs

Resources

- Irrational Beliefs handout

Beginning

1. Ask participants to complete the following sentence stem in a go-round:

   "One (non school-related) thing I could teach someone else is . . .".

2. Review last meeting.

Middle

IRRATIONAL BELIEFS

1. Ask the participants to read the irrational beliefs by Albert Ellis and choose the 2–3 that cause them the most trouble, or that they can't see anything wrong with, or that influence their life the most.

2. In groups of 3–4, ask members to share the above. For irrational beliefs that seem appropriate to some, the other group members provide reasons that the belief is irrational or can cause problems. Designate a spokesperson to give a summary of small group to large group. Ask the small groups to give a summary of their discussion.

3. If time permits, give a brief overview of Ellis's ABC model. See any of the numerous books by Ellis on R.E.T. (Rational Emotive Therapy).

End

Ask participants to record a summary of key points and their feelings about the meeting in their journal. Ask for volunteers to share their entries with the group.

Irrational Beliefs

It is essential that one be loved or approved of by virtually everyone in the community.

One must be perfectly competent, adequate, and achieving to consider oneself worthwhile.

Some people are bad, wicked, or villainous, and therefore should be blamed and punished. It is a terrible catastrophe when things are not as one wants them to be.

Unhappiness is caused by outside circumstances, and the individual has no control over it.

Dangerous or fearsome things are causes for great concern, and their possibility must be continually dwelt upon.

It is easier to avoid certain difficulties and self-responsibilities than to face them.

One should be dependent on others and one must have someone stronger on whom to rely.

Past experiences and events are the determiners of present behavior; the influence of the past cannot be eradicated.

One should be quite upset over other people's problems and disturbances.

There is always a right or perfect solution to every problem and it must be found or the results will be catastrophic.

". . . people do not get upset but instead upset themselves by insisting that (a) they should be outstandingly loved and accomplished, (b) other people should be incredibly fair and giving, and (c) the world should be exceptionally easy and munificent."—Albert Ellis, 1973.

Session 6
Topic: Writing a five-year plan

Resources

- Enjoying Your Life script
- Picturing Your Ideal Self script

Beginning

1. Ask participants to respond to the following question in a go-round: What three things do you want for your children? for students in your class? for young people today?

2. Review Session 5 and ask:
   - Who has done something about an item on his or her list of 20 things (What Are You Doing for the Rest of Your Life handout)?
   - Who has set up some times to get together with some of their important connection people?
   - Who has tried any relaxation techniques?
   - Who has caught himself or herself holding any irrational beliefs?

Middle

1. Guided Imagery: Enjoying Your Life script (to be read to the group).

2. Read the Picturing Your Ideal Self script to the group. Tell members to write a plan for reaching their ideal selves in five years.

End

Ask each participant to complete the following and to share with the group: "One thing I learned today was . . .".

Script: Enjoying Your Life

Developing your skills in relaxation and imagery is extremely beneficial in your quest to get more joy and satisfaction from your life. Now we will go through a series of five imagery exercises, each lasting from 15 seconds to 2 minutes.

Following this series, we will use our imagination to look at our "ideal self" and develop a five-year plan for approaching our image. You will have an opportunity to share part of your plan in groups of three. Let's begin.

Take several slow, deep breaths, get into a comfortable position, and close your eyes as we practice using our imagination.

1. Picture yourself in your favorite chair. See the color, feel the texture and comfortable feelings you have when you sit there. (pause 15–20 seconds)

2. Picture an ideal place—a place where you feel tranquil, serene, and balanced. This can be a place you've been or a place you create in your imagination. (pause 30–60 seconds)

3. Picture a fun experience you've had recently. (pause 30 seconds)

4. Picture a beautiful sunrise—see the pinks and blues, the clouds—feel the wind, hear the birds. (pause 30 seconds)

5. Picture yourself on the beach alone. Watch the waves, listen to the rhythm, feel the warmth of the sand. As you inhale, imagine the incoming waves bringing you energy, peace, happiness; as you exhale, imagine the receding waves taking away your worries, concerns, stress. (pause 2–3 minutes)

Script: Picturing Your Ideal Self

Picture yourself in your ideal place, the one you created just a few moments ago. Now picture yourself as already having all the positive qualities or traits you believe are important. This is your ideal self. Don't hold back—see yourself just as you want to be. What are you doing? Who is around, if anyone?

Feel the gracefulness of your movement—the poise and balance. Feel the confidence, the courage you have to be yourself, to say and do what you feel and think even if others disapprove.

What are some of your ideal self's self-talk messages? How are these self-talk messages similar to your current self? How are they different?

Feel yourself relaxed and at ease, alert and aware, with tremendous energy. See yourself taking action on the things that are important in your life.

How is your ideal self similar to your current self? How is it different? How are the most important things in your ideal self picture similar to your current most important things list?

Feel the contentment of knowing you do whatever it takes to take good care of yourself, because you know that without good self-care, there won't be anything to share with others. Deeply relax and allow these positive feelings to soak in.

In a moment I will ask you to write out a plan for reaching this state within the next five years. Picture what steps are needed. Break your plan into easy-to-achieve chunks. Set a time to begin one small part. Don't overload—trying too much at once is a key to discouragement. (pause 2–3 minutes)

In just a moment I will ask you to open your eyes. (pause 10–15 seconds)

Now slowly open your eyes and slowly move around and stretch in your chair. Take a moment to write yourself some notes on your plan. In groups of three, share your plans (allow enough time for everyone to share.) Now complete your plan write-up. Be specific, clear, and realistic.

Session 7
Topic: Birth order

Resources
- Chart paper and pens

Beginning
1. Ask participants to rate how they are feeling on a scale of 1–10, and to share one thing they have done to nurture themselves lately.
2. Review last meeting.

Middle
1. Participants get into groups according to birth order—oldest children, middle children, youngest children, and only children. Each group lists the characteristics of that position and how it felt to grow up in that position.
2. Each group has a recorder, who reports the characteristics to the whole group. One way to accomplish this reporting is to have each group list their characteristics on a poster or blackboard. After all groups have reported, post the lists side by side for easy comparison. The discussion can evolve into how these positions carry over into adult life and how these characteristics are seen in participants' own children.
3. Sometimes participants may not feel that they fit neatly into a profile of only, youngest, oldest, or middle child. Refer to your readings of Adlerian psychology, which explains that it may be your perception of your position in the family, rather than the actual birth order, that influences behavior. *Example:* Ask a sibling or parent how they saw you, and you may get a different perception from yours. The psychological birth order may be more significant than the physical birth order. For instance, the second child may exhibit characteristics of the oldest child.

End
Ask participants to complete one of the following:
"One thing I learned was . . ."
"One thing I relearned was . . ."
"One thing that surprised me was . . ."
The idea that birth order affects our personality development is an Adlerian concept. For additional information, you may want to read:

Parenting Young Children: Systematic Training for Effective Parenting (STEP) of Children Under Six by Don Dinkmeyer

Parenting Teenagers: Systematic Training for Effective Parenting (STEP) of Teens by Don Dinkmeyer

Adlerian Family Counseling by Oscar Christenson

Session 8
Topic: Strength bombardment

Resources

- My Strengths handout
- Group Evaluation form (page 10)

Beginning

1. Ask participants to complete the following sentence stem in a go-round: "One thing I'm looking forward to is . . .".

2. Review the last seven sessions. Ask teachers to recall some of the activities that were meaningful to them and share. After sharing the activities that were most meaningful, ask: "What changes can you start right away?" Ask participants to write these changes down and then share them with the group. Ask them to identify longer-range changes and what they need to do. After listing these changes, have them share in the group.

Middle

1. Pass out strength circles (My Strengths handout). Ask each teacher to sign his/her name on a strength circle and pass it to the next teacher. Each teacher writes positive qualities about every other teacher as the strength circles are passed around.

These positive comments are written in the outer circle, leaving the inner circle blank. After everyone finishes the strength circles, give them back to their owners.

2. We call this next part "Spotlighting" or "Strength Bombardment." One by one the group focuses on a teacher. Each participant tells the focus teacher one or more things that they appreciate about him or her. After everyone has spoken, the next person is spotlighted.

Instructions for giving and receiving compliments: Direct eye contact, say "[person's name], one thing I really like about you is . . ." or "One thing I appreciate about you is . . .". The receiver simply smiles and says "thank-you."

3. To conclude this activity, ask teachers to write in the center of the circle the three most important strengths or positive qualities they see in themselves.

End

1. Have participants fill out a group evaluation.

2. Ask for volunteers to share closing comments with the group.

My Strengths

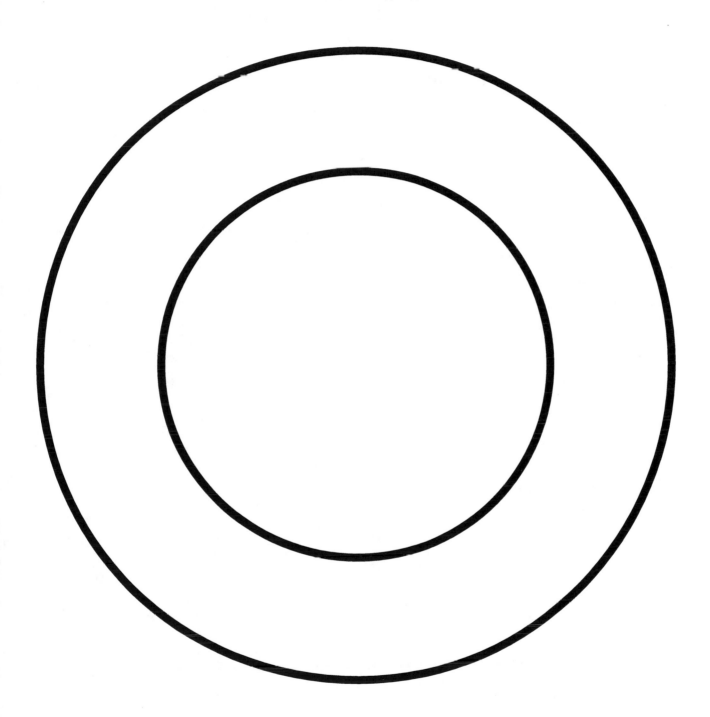

Bibliography

Admunson-Beckman, K., and A. R. Lucas. 1989. Gaining a foothold in the aftermath of divorce. *Social Work in Education,* 12, 5–15.

Albert, L. 1989. *A Teacher's Guide to Cooperative Discipline: How to Manage Your Classroom and Promote Self-Esteem.* Circle Pines, MN: American Guidance Service.

Albert, L. 1996. *Cooperative Discipline.* Circle Pines, MN: American Guidance Service.

Allard, H., and J. Marshall. 1977. *Miss Nelson Is Missing.* Boston, MA: Houghton Mifflin.

Alpert-Gillis, L. J., J. L. Pedro-Carroll, and E. L. Cowen. 1989. The Children of Divorce Intervention Program: Development, implementation, and evaluation of a program for young urban children. *Journal of Counseling and Clinical Psychology,* 57, 583–589.

Apodaca, B., and L. V. Nightingale. 1997. *My Parents Still Love Me Even Though They're Getting Divorced.* Yorba Linda, CA: Nightingale Rose Publishing.

Arem, C. 1993. *Conquering Math Anxiety.* Pacific Grove, CA: Brooks/Cole.

Asch, F. 1986. *Goodbye House.* Englewood Cliffs, NJ: Prentice-Hall.

Auch, M. J. 1993. *Bird Dogs Can't Fly.* New York: Holiday House.

Begun, R. 1996. *Ready to Use Social Skills Lessons and Activities.* West Nyack, NY: The Center for Applied Research in Education.

Begun, R. W., and F. J. Huml, eds. 1999. *Violence Prevention Skills: Lessons and Activities.* West Nyack, NY: The Center for Applied Research in Education.

Bernstein, J. E., and S. V. Gullo. 1977: *When People Die.* New York: Dutton.

Bete, C. L. 1997. *When Anger Heats Up.* South Deerfield, MA: Channing L. Bete Co., Inc.

Bienfeld, Florence. 1987. *Helping Your Child Succeed After Divorce.* Clairmont, CA: Hunter House.

Blitzer, M., and H. Shore. 1994. *My Life Turned Upside Down but I Turned It Right Side Up.* King of Prussia, PA: The Center for Applied Psychology.

Bloom, G. 1984. *Community Mental Health.* Belmont, CA: Brooks/Cole.

Borders, L., and S. Drury. 1992. Comprehensive school counseling programs: A review for policy makers and practitioners. *Journal of Counseling and Development,* 70, 487–489.

Boulden, J., and J. Boulden. 1991. *Let's Talk!* Santa Rosa, CA: Boulden Publishing.

Boulden, J., and J. Boulden. 1992. *All Together.* Santa Rosa, CA: Boulden Publishing.

Bourgeois, P. 1997. *Franklin's Bad Day.* New York: Scholastic, Inc.

Bowman, R., et al. 1998. *Aggressive and Violent Students.* Columbia, SC: Youthlight Inc.

Brigman, G., and B. Earley. 1990. *Peer Helping: A Training Guide.* Portland, ME: J. Weston Walch, Publisher.

Brigman, G., and B. Earley. 1991. *Group Counseling for School Counselors: A Practical Guide.* Portland, ME: J. Weston Walch, Publisher.

Brigman, G., D. Lane, and D. E. Lane. 1994. *Ready to Learn.* Minneapolis, MN: Educational Media.

Brown, D. 1999a. Improving academic achievement: What school counselors can do. Greensboro, NC: ERIC Clearinghouse on Counseling and Student Services.

Brown, D. 1999b. *Proven Strategies for Improving Learning and Academic Achievement.* Greensboro, NC: CAPS Publications.

Brown, L, and M. Brown. 1986. *The Dinosaurs Divorce.* Washington, MO: Paperbacks for educators.

Brown, M. T. 1988. *Dinosaurs Divorce.* Boston: Atlantic Monthly Press.

Brown, M. 1988. *When Dinosaurs Die.* Boston: Atlantic Monthly Press.

Buscaglia, Leo. 1982. *The Fall of Freddie the Leaf.* Washington, MO: Charles Slack and Paperbacks for Educators.

Campbell, C. A. 1991. Group guidance for academically under-motivated children. *Elementary School Guidance and Counseling,* 25, 302–307.

Campbell, C., and C. Dahir. 1997. *Sharing the Vision: The National Standards for School Counseling Programs.* Alexandria, VA. American School Counseling Association.

Carlson, N. L. 1992. *Arnie and the New Kid.* New York: Puffin Books.

Carruthers W., et al. 1996. Conflict resolution as curriculum: A definition, description, and process for integration in core curriculum. *The School Counselor,* 43, 326–344.

Casey, R., and J. Berman. 1985. The outcome of psychotherapy with children. *Psychological Bulletin,* 98, 388–400.

Christenson, Oscar, ed. 1993. *Adlerian Family Counseling: A Manual for Counselor, Educator, and Psychotherapist.* Minneapolis: Educational Media Corp.

Clark, B. 1998. *When Your Parents Divorce.* Minneapolis, MN: Educational Media.

Cohen, J. 1987. *I Had a Friend Named Peter.* New York: Morrow Junior Books.

Combs, H. 1993. A middle school transition program: Addressing the social side of schooling. *ERS Spectrum,* Winter, 12–21.

Cordell, A. S., and B. Bergman-Meador. 1991. The use of drawings in group intervention for children of divorce. *Journal of Divorce and Remarriage,* 17, 139–155.

Crosbie-Burnett, M., and L. L. Newcomer. 1990. Group counseling children of divorce: The

effects of a multimodal intervention. *Journal of Divorce,* 13, 69–78.

Cross, S., and R. Rosenthal. 1999. Three models of conflict effects on intergroup expectations and attitudes. *Journal of Social Issues,* 55 (3), 561–580.

Curran, D., 1983. *Traits of a Healthy Family.* New York: Ballantine Books.

Dahir, C., C. Sheldon, and M. Valiga. 1998. *Vision into Action: Implementing the National Standards for School Counseling Programs.* Alexandria, VA: American School Counseling Association.

Davidson, R., and E. Levitov, 2000. *Overcoming Math Anxiety.* New York: Addison Wesley Longman.

Delton, J. 1986. *Two Good Friends.* New York: Crown.

DePaolo, P. 1992. *Rosie and the Yellow Ribbon.* Boston: Little, Brown.

DiClemente, R. J., Ed. 1992. *Adolescents and AIDS: A Generation in Jeopardy.* Thousand Oaks, CA: Sage Publications.

Dinkmeyer, D., and D. Dinkmeyer Jr. 1982. *Developing Understanding of Self and Others* (rev. ed.). Circle Pines, MN: American Guidance Service.

Dinkmeyer, D.C., and L.E. Losoncy. 1980. *The Encouragement Book: Becoming a Positive Person.* Englewood Cliffs, NJ: Prentice Hall.

Dinkmeyer, D.C., and G.D. McKay. 1998. *Parenting Teenagers: Systematic Training for Effective Parenting (STEP) of Teens.* Circle Pines, MN: American Guidance Service.

Dinkmeyer, D.C., G.D. McKay, and J.S. Dinkmeyer. 1997. *Parenting Young Children: Systematic Training for Effective Parenting (STEP) of Children Under Six.* Circle Pines, MN: American Guidance Service.

Dolbrin, A. 1971. *Scat!* New York: Four Winds Press.

Duke, K. 1992. *Aunt Isabel Tells a Good One.* New York: Dutton Children's Books.

Eggert, L. L. 1994. *Anger Management for Youth: Stemming Aggression and Violence.* Bloomington, IN: National Educational Service.

Elkind, D., 1988. *The Hurried Child: Growing Up Too Fast Too Soon.* Reading, MA: Addison-Wesley.

Elliot, D., and S. Mihalic. 1997. *Blueprints for Violence Prevention and Reduction: The Identification and Documentation of Successful Programs.* Boulder, CO: Center for the Study and Prevention of Violence.

Engel, D. 1993. *Fishing.* New York: Macmillan.

Friedman, J., and L. W. Girard. 1991. *At Daddy's on Saturday.* Morton Grove, IL: Albert Whitman and Company.

Gardner, R. 1971. *The Boys and Girls Book About Divorce.* Washington, DC: Paperbacks for Educators.

Garvin, V., D. Leber, and N. Kalter. 1991. Children of divorce: Predictors of change following preventive intervention. *American Journal of Ortopsychiatry,* 61, 438–447.

Geisel, T. (Dr. Seuss). 1998. *My Many-Colored Days.* New York, NY: Knopf Publishing.

Gladding, S. 1999. *Group Work: A Counseling Specialty.* Upper Saddle River, NJ: Prentice Hall.

Goffin, J. 1991. *Oh!* New York: H.N. Abrams.

Goldstein, A. P., and J. C. Conoley, eds. 1997. *School Violence Intervention: A Practical Handbook.* New York: The Guilford Press.

Goldstein, A., and E. McGinnis. 1997. *Skillstreaming the Adolescent: New Strategies and Perspectives for Teaching Prosocial Skills.* Champaign, IL: Research Press.

Gootman, M. 1994. *When a Friend Dies: A Book for Teens About Grieving and Healing.* Minneapolis, MN: Free Spirit.

Gray, L. M. 1994. *Small Green Snake.* New York: Orchard Books.

Griswold, R. *Taking Control of Your Life* (audiocassette). Bonita Springs, FL: Effective Learning Systems, Inc.

Grollman, E. 1993. *Straight Talk About Death for Teenagers: How to Cope with Losing Someone You Love.* Boston, MA: Beacon Press.

Grollman, E. 1995. *Bereaved Children and Teens: A Support Guide for Parents and Professionals.* Boston, MA: Beacon Press.

Grych, J. H., and F. D. Fincham. 1992. Interventions for children of divorce: Toward greater integration of research and action. *Psychological Bulletin,* 111, 434–454.

Guidance Club for Teens. 1993. *Anger, Temper Tantrums and Violent Emotions* (videocassette). Santa Monica, CA: Ready Reference Press.

Gumaer, J. 1986. Group workers' perceptions of ethical and unethical behavior of group leaders. *Journal for Specialists in Group Work,* 11(3), 139–50.

Haley, G. E. 1988. *A Story, a Story: An African Tale.* New York: Aladdin Books.

Hall, K. 1995. *A Bad, Bad Day.* New York: Scholastic.

Hattie, J., J. Biggs, and N. Purdie. 1996. Effects of learning skills interventions on student learning: A meta analysis. *Review of Educational Research,* 66, 99–136.

Hawkins, W. E. 1986. *Circle of Friends Project.* Des Moines, IA: Iowa Department of Public Instruction.

Hebert, T. P., and J. M. Furner. 1997. Helping high-ability students overcome math anxiety through bibliotherapy. *The Journal of Secondary Gifted Education,* 4, 164–178.

Hechinger, F. M. 1992. *Fateful Choices.* New York: Carnegie Corporation of New York.

Heegaard, M. 1990. *When Mom and Dad Separate.* Minneapolis, MN: Woodland Press.

Heegaard, M. 1993. *When a Parent Marries Again.* Minneapolis, MN: Woodland Press.

Henkes, K. 1990. *Jessica.* New York: Puffin Books.

Hipp, E. 1995. *Help for the Hard Times: Getting Through Loss.* Center City, MN: Hazelden.

Hoctor, S. K. 1999. *Changes: My Family and Me.* Washington, DC: Child Welfare League.

Hood, S. 1999. *Bad Hair Day.* New York: Grosset & Dunlap.

Hutchins, P. 1993. *My Best Friend.* New York: Greenwillow Books.

Ives, S. B., D. Fassler, and M. Lash. 1985. *The Divorce Workbook.* Burlington, VT: Waterfront Books.

Ivey, A., P. Pedersen, and M. Ivey. 2001. *Intentional Group Counseling: A Microskills Approach.* Belmont, CA: Brooks/Cole.

Jackson, A. 1998. *When Your Parents Split Up.* Washington, MO: Stern Sloan and Paperbacks for Educators.

Jackson, T. 1993. *Activities That Teach.* Washington, MO: Red Rock Publishing, Paperbacks for Educators.

Jackson, T. 1995. *More Activities That Teach.* Washington, MO: Red Rock Publishing, Paperbacks for Educators.

Jacobs, E., 1992. *Creative Counseling Techniques: An Illustrated Guide.* Odessa, FL: Psychological Assessment Resources, Inc.

Jacobs, E., R. Masson, and R. Harvill. 1998. *Group Counseling Strategies and Skills.* Pacific Grove, CA: Brooks/Cole.

Jett, D., D. Pulling, and J. Ross. 1994. Preparing high schools for eighth grade students. *National Association of Secondary School Principals Bulletin,* December, 85–91.

Johnson, D., et al. 1997. The impact of conflict resolution training on middle school students. *The Journal of Social Psychology,* 137 (1), 11–21.

Johnson, J., and M. Johnson. 1998. *Children Who Grieve Too: A Book for Families Who Have Experienced a Death.* Omaha, NE: Centering Corp.

Kivel, P., et al. 1997. *Making the Peace.* Washington, MO: Paperbacks for Educators.

Komaiko, L. 1988. *Earl's Too Cool for Me.* New York: Harper & Row.

Korb-Khalsa, K., S. Azok, and E. Leutenberg. 1991. *Life Management Skills II.* Beachwood, OH: Wellness Reproductions Inc.

Kramer, P. 1994. *The Dynamics of Relationships.* Baltimore, MD: Equal Partners.

Kroen, W. 1996. *Helping Children Cope with the Loss of a Loved One.* Minneapolis, MN: Free Spirit.

Kübler-Ross, E. 1974. *On Death and Dying.* New York: MacMillan Publishing Co.

Lee, V. E., L. F. Winfield, and T. C. Wilson. 1991: Academic behaviors among high-achieving African-American students. *Education and Urban Society* 24, no. 1, 65–86.

Le Shan, E.J. 1976. *Learning to Say Good-Bye: When a Parent Dies.* New York: Simon and Schuster.

Long, C. 1978. *Albert's Story.* New York: Delacorte Press.

Loretta, J., and P. Keating. 1995. *After the Funeral.* New York, NY: Paulist Press.

McCully, E. A. 1984. *Picnic.* New York: Harper & Row.

McCully, E. A. 1988. *The Christmas Gift.* New York: Harper & Row.

McGinnis, E., and A. P. Goldstein. 1997. *Skillstreaming the Elementary School Child: New Strategies and Perspectives for Teaching Prosocial Skills.* (rev. ed.) Champaign, IL: Research Press.

McWhirter, J. J., et al. 1998. *At Risk Youth: A Comprehensive Response.* (2nd ed.) Pacific Grove, CA: Brooks/Cole.

Margolin, S. 1996. *Complete Group Counseling Program for Children of Divorce.* West Nyack, NY: Center for Applied Research in Education.

Mariotti, M. 1989. *Hanimations.* Brooklyn, NY: Kane/Miller Book Publishers.

Marks, A. 1995. *Good-bye, Daddy!* New York: North South Books.

Marta, S. Y., and M. Laz. 1997: *Rainbows: Facilitator Component Module.* Schaumburg, IL: Rainbows.

Masten, A., and J. Coatsworth. 1998. The development of competence in favorable and unfavorable environments: Lessons from research on successful children. *American Psychologist,* 53, (2), 205–220.

Mayer, G., and M. Mayer. 1995. *Just a Bad Day.* Westport, CT: Reader's Digest Kids.

Mellonie, B., and R. Ingpen. 1987. *Lifetimes, the Beautiful Way to Explain Death to Children.* Toronto, NY: Bantam Doubleday Dell.

Merrill, K. 1992. *School Social Behavior Scales.* Austin, TX: PRO-ED, Inc.

Michaels, B. 2000. *Bulbasaur's Bad Day.* Mahwah, NJ: Troll Associates.

Miller, B. C., et al. 1992. *Preventing Adolescent Pregnancy: Model Programs and Evaluations.* Newbury Park, CA: Sage Publications.

Monroe, R. P., and C. Ackelmire. 1998. *Why Don't We Live Together Any More?: Understanding Divorce.* St. Louis, MO: Concordia Publishing House.

Monroe, R. P., and N. Barnet. 1998. *I Have a New Family Now.* St. Louis, MO: Concordia Publishing House.

Moote, G. T., N. J. Smythe, and J. S. Wodarsky. 1999. *Social Skills Training with Youth in School Settings: A Review.* Thousand Oaks, CA: Sage Publications, Inc.

Morganette, R. 1990. *Skills for Living: Young Adolescents: Group Counseling Activities.* Champaign, IL: Research Press.

Morganette, R. S. 1994. *Skills for Living: Group Counseling Activities for Elementary Students.* Champaign, IL: Research Press.

Mosel, A. 1989. *Tikki Tikki Tembo.* New York: H. Holt and Co.

Mudy, M. 1998. *Sad Isn't Bad.* St. Meinrad, IN: Abbey Press.

Musick, J. S. 1993. *Young, Poor, and Pregnant.* New Haven, CT: Yale University Press.

Myrick, R. 1998. *Developmental Guidance and Counseling: A Practical Approach.* Minneapolis, MN: Educational Media.

National Peer Helpers Association, P.O. Box 32272, Kansas City, MO 64171, peerhelping.org.

Newcomb, A., W. Bukowski, and L. Patee. 1993. Children's peer relations: A meta-analytic review of popular, rejected, neglected, controversial, and average sociometric status. *Psychological Bulletin*, 113, 99–128.

Oates, M. 1993. *Death in the School Community: A Handbook for Counselors, Teachers, and Administrators.* Alexandria, VA: American Counseling Association.

O'Rourke, K., and J. C. Worzybt. 1996. *Support Groups for Children.* Philadelphia, PA: Accelerated Development.

Palmer, P., and D. Burke. 1994. *I Wish I Could Hold Your Hand.* Atascadero, CA: Impact Publishers Inc.

Parkinson, K., and C. Spelman. 1998. *Mama and Daddy Bears Divorce.* Morton Grove, IL: Albert Whitman and Company.

Pellowski, M. 1986. *Benny's Bad Day.* Mahwah, NJ: Troll Associates.

Peterson, J. S. 1995. *Talk With Teens About Feelings, Family, Relationships, and the Future.* Denver, CO: Free Spirit Publishing, Inc.

Pfister, M. 1992. *The Rainbow Fish.* Translated by J. Alison James. New York: North-South Books.

Poleski, T. 1983. *The Hurt.* Mahwah, NJ: Paulist Press.

Prout, S., and R. A. DeMartino. 1986. A meta-analysis of school-based studies of counseling and psychotherapy: An update. *Journal of School Psychology*, 24, 285–292.

Prout, S., and T. Prout. 1998. A meta-analysis of school-based studies of counseling and psychotherapy: An update. *Journal of School Psychology*, 36, 121–136.

Prout, T., and D. Brown. 1999. *Counseling and Psychotherapy with Children and Adolescents.* New York: John Wiley and Sons.

Rizzon-Toner, P. 1993. *Stress Management and Self-Esteem Activities* (Unit 5). New York: The Center for Applied Research in Education.

Robins, A., and P. Mayle. 1988. *Why Are We Getting a Divorce?* New York: Harmony Books.

Rogers, F., and J. Judkis. 1998. *Let's Talk About It: Divorce.* New York: Paper Star.

Rohmann, E. 1994. *Time Flies.* New York: Crown.

Rollenhagen, L. 1989. FOTP: A school transition program that works. *National Association of*

Secondary School Principals Bulletin, November, 130–132.

Romain, T. 1999. *What on Earth Do You Do When Someone Dies?* Minneapolis, MN: Free Spirit.

Rose, S. 1998. *Group Counseling with Children and Adolescents.* Thousand Oaks, CA: Sage Publications.

Rose, S. R. 1998. *Group Work with Children and Adolescents: Prevention and Intervention in School and Community Systems.* Thousand Oaks, CA: Sage Publications, Inc.

Roth, L. 1991. *Middle Level Transition: Policies, Programs, and Practices.* Reston, VA: National Association of Secondary School Principals.

Russo, M. 1992. *Alex Is My Friend.* New York: Greenwillow Books.

Schilling, D., and G. Dunne. 1992. *Understanding Me.* San Francisco, CA: Innerchoice Publishing.

Schneider, M., and J. Zuckerberg. 1996. *Difficult Questions Kids Ask and Are Too Afraid to Ask About Divorce.* Washington, MO: Fireside and Paperbacks for Educators.

Showers, P. 1991. *The Listening Walk.* New York: HarperCollins.

Shure, M. B. 1992. *I Can Problem-Solve: An Interpersonal Cognitive Problem-Solving Program.* Champaign, IL: Research Press.

Silverman, J. 1999. *Help Me Say Goodbye: Activities for Helping Kids Cope When a Special Person Dies.* Minneapolis, MN: Fairview Press.

Silverstein, S., 1964. *The Giving Tree.* New York: Harper & Row.

Simon, C. 1998. *The Good Bad Day.* Brookfield, CT: Millbrook Press.

Skivington, J., and A. Care. 1998. *Balloons for Trevor.* St. Louis, MO: Concordia Publishing House.

Slavin, R. E., N. L. Karweit, and N. A. Madden. 1989. What works for students at risk: A research synthesis. *Educational Leadership,* 46 (5), 4–13.

Smead, R. 1994. *Skills for Living: Group Counseling Activities for Elementary Students.* Champaign, IL: Research Press.

Smead, R. 1995. *Skills and Techniques for Group Work with Children and Adolescents.* Champaign, IL: Research Press.

Smead, R., 2000. *Skills for Living, Volume Two: Group Counseling Activities for Young Adolescents.* Champaign, IL: Research Press.

Stern, Z., and E. Stern. 1997. *Divorce Is Not the End of the World.* Berkeley, CA: Tricycle Press.

St. Germain, S. 1990. *The Terrible Fight.* Boston, MA: Houghton Mifflin.

Steinberg, D. 1999. *Grief Group.* Ft. Lauderdale, FL: Unpublished manuscript.

Stinson, K. 1988. *Mom and Dad Don't Live Together Anymore.* Toronto, Canada: Firefly Books.

Sunburst Communications. 1991. *If Your Parents Break Up.* (videocassette): Pleasantville, NY: Sunburst Communications.

Sunburst Communications. 1993. *When You're Mad! Mad! Mad!* (videocassette) Pleasantville, NY: Sunburst Communications.

Sunburst Communications. 1995. *Anger: You Can Handle It.* (videocassette, teacher's guide) Pleasantville, NY: Sunburst Communications.

Sunburst Communications. 1995. *When Anger Turns to Rage.* (videocassette): Pleasantville, NY: Sunburst Communications.

Sunburst Communications. 1997. *Handling Your Anger.* (videocassette, teacher's guide, handouts) Pleasantville, NY: Sunburst Communications.

Sunburst Communications. 1998. *Anger Management Skills.* (videocassette) Pleasantville, NY: Sunburst Communications.

Taylor, J. F. 1994. *Anger Control Training for Children and Teens.* Warminster, PA: Mar-Co Products, Inc.

Tindall, J. 1995. *Peer Counseling.* Muncie, IN: Accelerated Development.

Tobias, S. 1995. *Overcoming Math Anxiety.* New York: Norton.

Traisman, E. S. 1992. *Fire in My Heart Ice in My Veins: A Journal for Teenagers Experiencing a Loss.* Omaha, NE: Centering Corporation.

Turkle, B. 1976. *Deep in the Forest.* New York: Dutton.

Ueno, N. 1973. *Elephant Buttons.* New York: Harper & Row.

Varley, S. 1992. *Badger's Parting Gifts.* New York: Mulberry Books.

Vernon, A. 1998. *The Passport Program: A Journey Through Emotional, Social, Cognitive, and Self-Development.* Champaign, IL: Research Press.

Vernon, A. 1989. *Thinking, Feeling, Behaving: An Emotional Education Curriculum for Children.* Champaign, IL: Research Press.

Viorst, J. 1972. *Alexander and the Terrible, Horrible, No Good, Very Bad Day.* New York: Atheneum.

Viorst, J. 1988. *The Tenth Good Thing About Barney.* New York: Aladdin.

Vollmer, D. 1988. *Joshua Disobeys.* Kansas City, MO: Landmark Editions.

Waber, B. 1972. *Ira Sleeps Over.* Boston: Houghton Mifflin.

Waber, B. 1988. *Ira Says Goodbye.* Boston: Houghton Mifflin.

Wang, M. C., G. D. Haertel, and H. J. Walberg. 1994. *Educational Resilience in Inner City America: Challenges and Prospects.* Hillsdale, NJ: Lawrence Erlbaum Associates.

Wang, M. C., G. D. Haertel, and H. J. Walberg, 1994. What helps students learn? *Educational Leadership,* 51 (4), 74–79.

Ward, L. 1973. *The Silver Pony: A Story in Pictures.* Boston: Houghton Mifflin.

Watson, J. W., R. E. Switzer, and J. C. Hirschberg. 1988. *Sometimes a Family Has to Split Up.* New York: Crown Publishers.

Weisz, J. R., et al. 1987. Effectiveness of psychotherapy with children and adolescents: A meta-analysis for clinicians. *Journal of Consulting and Clinical Psychology* 55, 542–549. EMBASE

Weisz, J. R., B. Weiss, and G. R. Donenberg. 1992. The lab versus the clinic: Effects of child and adolescent psychotherapy. *American Psychologist* 47, 1578–1585.

Weisz, J. R., et al. 1995. Effects of psychotherapy with children and adolescents revisited: A meta-analysis of treatment outcome studies. *Psychological Bulletin* 177, 450–468.

Whitehouse, E., et al. 1996. *A Volcano in My Tummy: Helping Children to Handle Anger.* Gabriola Island, BC, Canada: New Society Publishers.

Wiesner, D. 1991. *Tuesday.* New York: Clarion Books.

Wilde, J. 1994. *Hot Stuff to Help Kids Chill Out.* Washington, MO: Paperbacks for Educators.

Wilde, J. 1995. *Anger Management in Schools.* Lancaster, PA: Technomic Publishing Co.

Wilson, J. 1982. School counselor interventions with low-achieving and underachieving elementary, middle, and high school students: A review of the research literature. *The School Counselor,* 30(2), 113–120.

Wittmer, J. 1993. *Managing Your School Counseling Program.* Minneapolis, MN: Educational Media, Inc.

Wolkstein, D. 1994. *Step by Step.* New York: Morrow Junior Books.

Zimmerman, M., and R. Arunkumar. 1994. Resiliency research: Implications for schools and policy. *Social Policy Report: Society for Research in Child Development,* 8 (4), 1–17.

Ziegler, J. 1993. *Mr. Knocky.* New York: Macmillan.

Share Your Bright Ideas with Us!

We want to hear from you! Your valuable comments and suggestions will help us meet your current and future classroom needs.

Your name_____Date_____

School name_____Phone_____

School address_____

Grade level taught_____Subject area(s) taught_____Average class size_____

Where did you purchase this publication?_____

Was your salesperson knowledgeable about this product?   Yes_____   No_____

What monies were used to purchase this product?

____School supplemental budget   ____Federal/state funding   ____Personal

Please "grade" this Walch publication according to the following criteria:

Quality of service you received when purchasing .... A   B   C   D   F

Ease of use... A   B   C   D   F

Quality of content... A   B   C   D   F

Page layout .... A   B   C   D   F

Organization of material .... A   B   C   D   F

Suitability for grade level .... A   B   C   D   F

Instructional value.. A   B   C   D   F

COMMENTS:_____

_____

What specific supplemental materials would help you meet your current—or future—instructional needs?

_____

Have you used other Walch publications? If so, which ones?_____

May we use your comments in upcoming communications?   ____Yes   ____No

Please **FAX** this completed form to **207-772-3105**, or mail it to:

Product Development, J. Weston Walch, Publisher, P.O. Box 658, Portland, ME 04104-0658

We will send you a **FREE GIFT** as our way of thanking you for your feedback. **THANK YOU!**